Dedicated to my dearest parents

PORTRAITS OF SUCCESSFUL ENTREP
AND HIGH-FLYERS

Portraits of Successful Entrepreneurs and High-Flyers

A psychological perspective

SYRINE KIT SUM LAM
B.Soc., M.Ed., Ph.D

Ashgate

Aldershot • Brookfield USA • Singapore • Sydney

Published by
Ashgate Publishing Limited
Gower House
Croft Road
Aldershot
Hampshire GU11 3HR
England

Ashgate Publishing Company
Old Post Road
Brookfield
Vermont 05036
USA

Ashgate website: http://www.ashgate.com

British Library Cataloguing in Publication Data
Lam, Syrine Kit Sum
  Portraits of successful entrepreneurs and high-flyers : a
  psychological perspective
  1.Entrepreneurship - China - Hong Kong - Psychological
  aspects 2.Success in business - China - Hong Kong -
  Psychological aspects 3.Businesspeople - China - Hong Kong
  - Psychology 4.Businesspeople - China - Hong Kong -
  Attitudes 5.Successful people - China - Hong Kong -
  Psychology 6.Successful people - China - Hong Kong -
  Attitudes
  I.Title
  338'.04'095125

Library of Congress Catalog Card Number: 99-73696

ISBN 1 84014 791 1

Printed and bound by Athenaeum Press, Ltd.,
Gateshead, Tyne & Wear.

Contents

List of figures and tables

Figures

Tables

Acknowledgements

I would like to take this opportunity to express my sincere gratitude to those people who have made the publication of this book possible.

Firstly, I wish to thank all the entrepreneurs and high-flyers who had kindly spared their precious time in sharing their stories of success. These stories are virtually stories of their lives, with joys and tears. I was indeed greatly inspired by their attitudes towards life and living. Their words of wisdom have always been a rejuvenating incentive to me in times of hardships.

My gratitude also goes to Mr Charles Cox who was my Ph D supervisor. He is a gentleman who gives his support in a subtle yet unreserved way. Without this patience, I could not have completed my Ph D thesis on which this book is based.

I am greatly indebted to my husband, Alain, and my children, Long Ching, Ho Ching and Yui Ching, for their unfailing love and encouragement. My family has always been my strongest motivator, particularly for completing my Ph D study and this book.

Finally I wish to thank the editorial staff at Ashgate, particularly Claire Annals, Sonia Hubbard and Anne Keirby, for their valuable support and help in enabling this book to be published.

1 Hong Kong Success and Entrepreneurship

Hong Kong is a city which never ceases to amaze people in its vibrance, its diversity and its extraordinary economic performance. An English visitor to Hong Kong once stated,

> I was so thrilled by what I saw when I first walked on the street: the vitality of everything in the surroundings. It was amazing to find even an old woman was selling things on the street, she had her own business.

This statement aroused mixed feelings in the author. It could have been a sad story in which the old woman who was selling things on the street might be doing so for survival, that she was being neglected by her relatives and the government. But one thing is true. The old woman was revealing a very positive attitude to life that she did not wait for fate to come onto her. Instead, she was making use of an opportunity, however small, that could be found in the environment to help herself. The hardworking and self-reliant attitudes shown by the old woman are typical of the majority of the local people. It is also common experience that newcomers to Hong Kong absorb its frenetic atmosphere and learn how to take opportunities.

Success is not guaranteed but earned. And in Hong Kong this applies more than in most places, given its limited natural resources and its dependence on trade in goods and services with the outside world. The only way to compete with the rest of the world is through its people whose entrepreneurial dynamism, innovative skills and sheer hard work have made success possible.

Hong Kong is one of the original four dragons in Asia,[1] so called for its extraordinary economic performance and its potential for further economic growth. Hong Kong has enjoyed a period of economic affluence since the economic take-off in the 1970s when most of the

1

western world was undergoing economic stagnation, if not recession, and increasing unemployment rates.   When the government of People's Republic of China negotiated with the British government concerning the future status of Hong Kong, the colony's continual prosperity was taken as the principal consideration.   The Chinese government assured preservation of conditions which have encouraged economic affluence and social stability, with a view to continually attracting overseas investment and deterring the vast emigration of competent individuals who have contributed to Hong Kong's achievements.   With a commitment to sustaining the success achieved by Hong Kong, communist China, however reluctant, introduced the concept of 'One Country, Two Systems' as the guiding principle for administering the future Hong Kong after 1997.   There has been no precedence in history that a sovereign state, particularly a communist one, would allow part of its polity to operate under a different system.

If success can be indicated in economic terms, the followings are but a few examples[2] illustrating the success of Hong Kong.   On a collective level, the Hong Kong people have generated and accumulated extensive wealth.   Hong Kong has risen to the third ranking banking centre in the world league in 1994, after New York, London and Tokyo.   Over the past two decades, the Hong Kong economy has more than quadrupled in size.   With its GDP growing at an average annual rate of about seven per cent in real terms, Hong Kong has significantly out-performed the Organization for Economic Co-operation and Development (OECD) countries and has been growing more than twice as fast as the world economy.   Hong Kong per capita GDP now exceeds that of UK.   The local workforce has been able to enjoy a continuous rise in income, as well as full employment since 1986.   The Hong Kong government reported annual budget surplus for a continuous period from 1985 to 1994.   There are few other countries in the world which are able to sustain a budget surplus over a decade.

At an individual level, *Fortune* magazine in 1994 named two Hong Kong businessmen among the ten top ranking persons in the world based on the individual's total asset value.   On a regional basis, Chinese businessmen are leading entrepreneurs throughout Asia, particularly in Singapore, Indonesia and Malaysia.

These economic achievements stem from a number of Hong Kong's strengths: a good administration, advanced technology, stable socio-political conditions, and above all, an unbeatable geographical location on the southern coast of China, at the trading crossroads of Asia, with a deep natural harbour. However, these traditional explanations are not the whole story. These assets alone are not enough to explain the economic success. They need the right kind of people to allow them to flourish. Sato (Cheng, 1995, p.154), a Japanese sociologist, draws from the experiences of Taiwan, Thailand and Malaysia in the 1970s to explain the differences in these countries' economies is making analysis of individual economic endeavours, particularly those undertaken by the entrepreneurs, rather than structural analysis of the economy. Thailand and Malaysia adopted economic policies similar to those in Taiwan but their economic growth was much weaker than that achieved by Taiwan. Hong Kong's economic success stem fundamentally from its people, whose entrepreneurial dynamism, innovative skills and sheer hard work have made it all possible.

Among the people of Hong Kong, successful entrepreneurs and managers (high-flyers) in the commercial and industrial sectors play a particularly important role. They generate wealth and lead the workforce to make Hong Kong a success story.

This book is based on a study of 60 successful entrepreneurs and high-flyers in Hong Kong. The study was motivated by a desire to understand the personal characteristics of successful career people in the business sector in Hong Kong. The interest originated from an observation in the latter half of the 1980s, that there was an increasing number of publications in Hong Kong centred around the theme of success. Success stories of entrepreneurs and managers in business became popular topics for academic discussion as well as social conversation. The idea to study particularly the personal characteristics of successful entrepreneurs and high-flyers was inspired by the work of Hingley and Cooper (1985) and that of Cox and Cooper (1988). It was felt that to carry out a similar study in Hong Kong would provide understanding beyond what is said in these individual success stories. This systematic study of successful entrepreneurs and high-flyers aims to conceptualize what is in them which make them successful in their careers.

In addition, this book is an attempt to apply western theoretical perspectives in understanding Chinese personality and behaviours, in general and in management. In doing so, one needs to recognize what western theories can offer in understanding an ethnic group with quite different conceptions of man/woman and his/her relationship with the environment. Until the presence, most psychological studies of Chinese personality, both theoretical and substantive, have employed western theories due to their much more well-developed and systematic conceptualizing and empirical procedures.[3] However, it is important to note that all theories of human behaviours convey a notion of man/woman and hence assumptions of human nature, and that western theories are built on a notion of man/woman that is rooted in individualism (Yuen, 1995). On the contrary, Chinese define man/woman in collective terms by his/her relationships in a network. These differences in the conception of man/woman implies that western theories cannot simply be transplanted[4] hard and fast on studies of Chinese personality. Instead, western psychological theories can be seen as providing alternative frameworks for understanding Chinese personality and behaviours. They can also contribute to indigenous theorizing[5] by helping to identify the gaps between western theories and Chinese social reality, such as phenomena in Chinese society which western theories cannot or are found inadequate to explain, hence a direction for indigenous theorizing.[6] Insofar as the present study is concerned, western theories are used to guide the initial theoretical and empirical structuring of the research problem, with a goal to uncover interesting and important ideas for developing indigenous theories on Chinese personality and organizational behaviours. Every care is taken when using western theories to examine and draw conclusions about the personal characteristics of the Hong Kong Chinese entrepreneurs and high-flyers.

In terms of scope, the study was concerned with success in career. Successful entrepreneurs and high-flyers are those who achieve success in their career. They may not necessarily be successful as a person. Similarly, being successful in their career does not necessarily mean they are 'good' bosses or managers. The scope is therefore confined to understanding personal characteristics that are related to career success.

Entrepreneurs and high-flyers, however, are different because they make different career choices. Successful entrepreneurs choose to achieve career success in their own business whereas high-flyers choose to prosper as salaried employees. The high-flyers are so called because they are relatively younger in age than their counterparts, suggesting a rapid career advancement and hence career success at a relatively young age.

In almost all studies of success-related behaviours, there is the primary difficulty in defining success. A useful definition is offered by Derr (1986) who views success as both being able to live out the subjective and personal values one really believes in and make a contribution to the world of work. This definition combines both the personal value element and the more objective aspects. In addition it implies that people on both high and low level jobs can be successful. However, the present study can only take into account the objective aspects of success when defining and identifying successful entrepreneurs and successful managers (high-flyers). Success is stipulated in terms of the individual's contributions to his/her profession and the world of work.

This book contains ten chapters. This Introduction chapter outlines the objectives of the study, the background to the study and its significance. Chapter Two defines the theoretical framework of the study by identifying the theoretical perspectives to be adopted and the personal variables to be studied, leading to the construction of a conceptual model to guide the collection and analysis of data. Chapter Three gives a detailed account of the method chosen for this research. The subsequent six chapters discuss each of the personal variables studied, namely, childhood, education, career history, personality, motivation and management approach. The final chapter portraits the Hong Kong successful entrepreneurs and high-flyers. The element of culture in career success is also discussed to throw light on the theoretical framework.

Notes

1   The original four dragons in Asia are Hong Kong, Singapore, Taiwan, and South Korea, representing the first group of Asian countries to develop economically. The term dragon now covers other recently emerging economy such as Malaysia, Thailand and Indonesia.

2   Source of data: Hong Kong Government. *Hong Kong 1995: A Review of 1994.*

3   Personal characteristics in this text refers to patterns shown in a particular aspect of the person, such as family, education, work, personality, relationship, values, and beliefs. Such aspects of the person are termed personal variables.

4   Psychology as a scientific discipline originated in the West. To the Chinese, human behaviours was more of a topic concerning religion and morality. The interest of the Chinese in empirical and systematic studies of human behaviours as they are only came with economic and societal modernization in the last four decades, which is influenced by western scientific values.

5   Cheng (1995) contends that there are two types of research on Chinese organizational behaviours: transplant studies and cultural studies. Transplant studies refers to using foreign theories in an exclusive way for studying local organizational behaviours as if principles of behaviours are universally true. Cultural studies however take into consideration cultural uniqueness in examining local organizational behaviours, hence require a theoretical framework amenable to unique cultural factors. For details, see Cheng, B. F. (1995) Differential order and Chinese organizational behaviours, *Indigenous Psychological Research, 3*, 142-291. (In Chinese)

6   By 'indigenous' the investigator refers to the fact that the authors of the theories are Chinese and the intent of their theorizing is to develop concepts responsive to Chinese social 'reality'. Bond (1986, p.217) notes that there has been a self-conscious and deliberate movement among Chinese social scientists to avoid being intellectually colonized, so that they can more sensitively portray the nature of Chinese behaviours. See Bond, M. H. (1986) The Social Psychology of Chinese People, *The Psychology of the Chinese People*. Hong Kong: Oxford University Press.

2   Theoretical Framework

This chapter aims at constructing the theoretical framework of the present study, following the context and objectives set out in Chapter One. The framework specifies the overall psychological perspective chosen to examine and explain personal characteristics of successful entrepreneurs and high-flyers, and the personal variables[1] which are to be studied in detail. Subsequently a conceptual model will be developed to provide the basis for the research design and interpretation of findings.

In developing the theoretical framework, previous studies on the topic personal characteristics of entrepreneurs and high-flyers will firstly be examined. The personal variables to be studied for the present research are identified through this review. Subsequently, the current psychological perspectives of understanding personal characteristics of successful business people will be deliberated, leading to a discussion on how the cognitive perspectives can be useful in explaining the topic in question.

Personal Characteristics of Entrepreneurs and High-Flyers

The study of entrepreneurship and managerial activities is not confined to psychologists. Sociologists, economists, and political scientists are all equally interested in the topic, and have made significant contributions to the subject.

Underlying all the studies of successful entrepreneurs and managers is one common unresolved difficulty, namely that of defining success. A useful definition is offered by Derr (1986) who views success as 'both being able to live out the subjective and personal values one really believes in and make a contribution to the world of work'. This definition combines both the personal value element and the more objective aspects. In addition it implies that people in both high and low level jobs can be successful. Success is a conception about an individual, and it is a

7

conception which constitutes the ideals prescribed by a particular culture, a profession, and the standards of an individual.

Then comes the question: how should the successful entrepreneur and the successful manager be conceived? Entrepreneurs have long been conceived as distinct from managers. Sociologists hold different conceptions of the entrepreneur and the manager primarily because of the difference in their role in the organization. It is argued that as modern organizations grow larger and more complex, the need for professionalization and bureaucratization of administration rises. Ownership is split from management. Economists also view them as two distinct groups because they show varied economic behaviours. In business there is an increasing use of resources other than the entrepreneur's personal capital. This trend has implication for the bearing of risks associated with business operation. The entrepreneur is considered more of a creator of risk whereas the manager, employed by the organization to operate the business, becomes a taker of risk.

The literature of organizational behaviour has highlighted the dualism concerning the extent to which individual behaviour is externally controlled versus proactively constructed by the individual manager (Pfeffer, 1981). Belief that organizational behaviour is externally controlled has resulted in studies which focus on the organization as the unit of study. Whereas belief in the theory that behaviour is proactively constructed by the individual manager has led to studies on the person. In the current research it is recognized that the two approaches should not be dichotomized, since the organization and the individual interact and influence each other in a mutual way. The current research, though putting the emphasis on personal characteristics, also takes into consideration the impact organizations have on the evolution of the entrepreneur or high-flyer.

To the psychologists, the entrepreneur exhibits behaviours and experiences psychological processes different from those of the manager. The decision to produce and market products independently reflects how the entrepreneur perceives and predicts himself in relation to a new business environment. By contrast, the manager is more concerned with routine administration along established lines, functioning in a known environment in which there is a set of expected behaviours. Porter and Lawler (1968) argue that, prior to the 1950s, entrepreneurs were imaged as self-made men of single-minded dedication, known for their forcefulness and imagination. They were inner-directed, independent, those who generated their own values in life. Beginning from the 1950s, coupled with the trend towards increasing bureaucratization of modern organizations mentioned above, success in organizations was likely to be achieved by the other-directed person, the one who is sensitive to the thinking and desires of others, who complies with the norms of a situation and adheres to the values of the organization. Other-directedness becomes the typical characteristic of the young generation of successful managers, the high-flyers.

Apart from inner- and other-directedness, organizational psychologists have looked at a number of variables in their studies of entrepreneurs and managers. Carsrud, Olm and Eddy (1986) summarized that some of the current psychological variables under investigation are: multidimensional achievement motivation, type A/B stress proneness, gender-predominate personality characteristics, intelligence, risk-taking, self-esteem, and personal responsibility. Personal variables appearing in contemporary studies are the role of mentors, age, gender, education, family support system, personal constraints (children, family), birth order and previous experience. Future focus is expected to be on the nature of previous business experience of family and the role of formal education in business. Taylor (1985) produced a similar list of personal variables from an extensive review of literature on the subject of entrepreneurial success.

In view of the many personal variables that worth studying, it is essential to provide some kind of integrative framework to study these variables, so that understanding of success-related personal characteristics can move beyond the anecdotal state, which tends to be the case at present. The present work concentrates on a manageable range of aspects of the individual, namely, childhood, education, career history, personality, work motivation, and management approach. There are three important considerations in choosing these variables as themes of the present research:

1. There is sufficient evidence from previous research that successful entrepreneurs and managers show distinctive characteristics in these variables (Hingley and Cooper, 1985; Cox and Cooper, 1988; White, Cox and Cooper, 1992; Jennings, Cox and Cooper, 1994).

2.   From a pilot study[2] conducted prior to the present research, it was found that experiences in childhood, education and career development had significant influences on entrepreneurial/managerial performance such as work motivation, management philosophy and skills.

3.   The influences identified in the pilot study present themselves by shaping the way of thinking of the entrepreneur and high-flyer. The conception that an individual's way of thinking has important bearing on successful entrepreneurial and managerial behaviours leads to the adoption of the cognitive perspective as the explanatory framework for the present research. In order to understand one's way of thinking, it is necessary to examine the possible forces affecting cognition.

The personal variables that are being studied can be divided into two categories: past personal experiences, such as childhood, education and career history; and current experiences, such as personality, motivation and goals, and leadership styles. Past experiences and current experiences are related in that past experiences shape current thinking and behaviours and current perceptions determine how past experiences are interpreted and have meaning in the present.

In the present study, childhood, education and career history are conceived to be developmental variables examining the personal experiences that have significant impact on later career success. Personality, work motivation and management approach are current behavioural variables that are associated with success-related personal characteristics. However, the researcher does not intend to treat the current behavioural variables as dependent variables as it is not the objective to establish a direct one-way cause-effect relationship between developmental experiences and current behaviours. The researcher holds the view that developmental experiences have significant impact on current behaviours, but the nature and extent of this significance is influenced by current perceptions, hence developmental variables and current behavioural variables are seen as inter-related rather than as direct causes and effects.

Current Psychological Perspectives for Explaining Personal Characteristics of Entrepreneurs and High-Flyers

Taylor (1985) comments that the extensive research carried out on the question of what makes an entrepreneur has merely discovered a list of variables and the impacts on entrepreneurs' success, but the question remains unanswered. Most of the work on entrepreneurial and managerial success tend to be descriptive rather than explanatory. It is thought that studies on the subject of success have reached a stage that an integrative model of some kind is needed to synthesize the many variables discovered so far, to offer a holistic view of the successful entrepreneur and manager. This section examines the current psychological models in explaining the personal characteristics of successful entrepreneurs and high-flyers. It should be noted that the models discussed hereafter are not exhaustive.

Humanistic Perspectives

The work of two humanistic psychologists, Carl Rogers (1961, 1977) and Abraham Maslow (1968) has been widely used to explain the underlying motivation of successful entrepreneurs and managers. Both psychologists assume that all people are motivated by the self-actualization tendency.

Rogers postulates that all human behaviours originate from one master motive: the actualizing tendency. In the course of human development, if an individual experiences unconditional positive regard from significant others, a sense of unconditional positive self-regard will result and the tendency towards actualization strengthened. Hence he paid particular attention to studying an individual's parental relationship in childhood to illustrate the notion of unconditional positive regard. Rogers argued that creativity,[3] a trait commonly desired by individuals and society, can be fostered in positive environments. There are two kinds of environment which will encourage the development of creativity. One is that provides safety (the feeling that one has unconditional personal worth) and the other offers psychological freedom to engage in unrestrained expression of ideas and thoughts. Creativity is claimed by Rogers to be a salient characteristic of self-actualizers. Successful entrepreneurs and managers are supposed to be actualizers. According to Derr's definition of success discussed earlier in Section I, success partly reflects the ability to live out one's personal goals. Hence understanding the successful entrepreneurs and managers can be achieved through reviewing the quality of their relationship with significant others, particularly the parents, so as to identify whether unconditional positive regard is experienced.

Much of the research into what motivates entrepreneurs and managers has been based on the work of Maslow, particularly his model of hierarchy of needs.[4] Successful entrepreneurs and managers indicated that they were motivated by the desire to achieve higher level needs such as self-actualization.

The contribution of the humanistic perspectives lies in its view of the individual as an integrated whole. It reminds investigators that the study of successful people should not merely aim at describing patterns in aspects of the individuals, instead, these successful people should be understood through their total functioning. However, the humanistic theories generally remain philosophical and vague. Their tenets are not well defined and well linked enough to provide a framework for understanding the individual as an integrated whole. Explaining through the notion of self-actualization appears all-encompassing, to the extent that it creates self-serving conclusions. Almost all success-related behaviours can be conceived as a pursuit of self-actualization. There is inadequate consideration of the mediating psychological processes between an individual being motivated by the self-actualizing tendency and the emergence of particular patterns of attitudes and behaviours which are related to career success.

Neoanalytic Perspectives

While humanistic perspectives tend to be vague, the theory structure of neoanalytic perspectives is much more coherent and their concepts more specific. Neoanalytic perspectives, following the traditions of Freudian psychoanalysis, focus on individual psychodynamics as their subject of study. Despite possible divergence from Freudian principles, neoanalytic theorists generally agree that individuals are motivated by powerful, often conflicting, innate forces, and assume early childhood experiences as deterministic of personality development.

Two theoretical frameworks with psychoanalytic origins are found to have offered useful explanations to entrepreneurial and managerial success, one is Transactional Analysis which was used by Cox and Cooper (1988) and Jansen (1986) in explaining the personal characteristics of their subjects.

Cox and Cooper employed in particular the model of the three ego states[5] in explaining what they called the anatomy of managerial success. They argued that a well-developed Parent, Adult and Child are essential. These will be influenced by experiences in childhood, education and career. Experiences in early childhood will have a particularly strong influence on the Parent value system and the Child intuition, while the Adult reasoning will be most influenced by education and school experience. The three factors which actually determine managerial performance - management philosophy, skills and motivation - are in turn determined by aspects of the individual. Management philosophy will be partly a product of Parent values and Adult reasoning. Skills will be determined by all three ego stages. Motivation will be primarily a function of Parent values and Child needs. This conceptualization of success through the ego states is creative and substantive, and is able to integrate the many aspects of the individual to form a general picture of successful managers.

Jansen, however, favoured the notion of life script[6] in his explanation. He claimed that successful business people were scripted to win, and such scripts were developed early in childhood. A common pattern of their childhood experiences is a lack of warmth at home and compensating for this by becoming winners, substituting admiration and respect for love. These successful business people learn from very early in life to delay gratification and take the long view. The idea of compensation and how it operates to influence human behaviour has been thoroughly discussed by Kohut (1971).

Heinz Kohut, a self-psychologist, employs the concept of compensation in understanding the self as a unifying agent of psychological forces, often conflicting and competing in nature.[7] The motive for all behaviours follows the principle of self-preservation, and compensation is viewed with favour as it helps to preserve the integrity of the self, hence the total functioning of the individual. His concept of compensation is borrowed to interpret success-related behaviours as a form of rectification of deficiencies in childhood. A striking finding derived from the study by Hingley and Cooper (1985) was that the childhood of their successful British entrepreneurs was characterized by a kind of deprivation due to prolonged absence of father. The motivation to achieve success is conceived as an attempt to overcome adversities in early life.

While offering powerful explanations for the behaviours of successful entrepreneurs and managers through understanding their psychodynamics, there exists a possibility that such explanations are an exclusively subjective interpretation of the investigator and that it leads to self-fulfilling conclusions. The neoanalytic explanations hold the assumption that unconscious is present in influencing behaviours, and that personality and behaviours are the result of the interaction of a set of intrapsychic forces. The complicated and intertwined nature of the relationship between these forces makes it difficult for the psychodynamic relationships to be well articulated and made clear. The quality of the explanation relies on the analytical ability and criticality of the investigator rather than the attributes of the model itself.

Cognitive Perspectives[8]

The cognitive paradigm assumes individuals are conscious and capable of being aware of their internal events. This belief is in contrast to that inherent in neoanalytic perspectives that individuals are involved in unconscious processes.

The work of George Kelly, Raymond B Cattell,[9] Julian Rotter and Albert Bandura, are the more popular cognitive perspectives which have been employed in the study of the motivation, beliefs and values of entrepreneurs and managers. Kelly's personal construct theory is regarded as a 'pure' cognitive theory of personality, whereas the latter two theorists have a social-cognition orientation. This section begins with a review of the contributions of Kelly, Cattell, Rotter, and Bandura to the understanding of successful entrepreneurial and managerial behaviours. It is followed by a discussion of the notion cognition as an aspect of culture, arguing that culture should be considered in understanding occupational behaviours. It is thought that general cognitive perspectives do not suffice for a study on Hong Kong entrepreneurs and managers. Such a study should, in addition to understanding how cognitive learning is acquired, reinforced and modified, consider the influence of culture on individual cognitions because the Hong Kong successful career people live and work in a unique cultural context which is different from other parts of the world.

Cognition as Construction - George Kelly

Kelly (1991) assumes an individual to be like a scientist whose ultimate aim is to predict and control. He/she has the creative capacity to represent the environment, not merely to respond to it. Since he/she can represent the environment, he/she can place alternative constructions upon it and, indeed, do something about it if it does not suit him/her. An individual can freely choose what construction to represent the world. Constructs are used in the process of construing. Constructs are precisely the patterns or templets through which an individual creates to look at the world and attempts to fit over the realities of which the world is composed. Some constructs are more central than the others. In general an individual seeks to improve his/her constructs by increasing his/her repertory, by altering them to provide better fits and predictive efficiency, and by subsuming them with superordinate constructs, forming a hierarchy of constructs (the construct system).

Entrepreneurial and managerial behaviours related to success can be conceived to be reflecting their personal constructs about life in general and work in particular, such as work values, motivation, and management philosophy. Though the personal construct theory is criticized as too simplistic and having little explanatory power, it offers an organizing framework to show that there is a hierarchical system of constructs. The superordinate constructs are more resistant to change. Besides, the notion of permeability of constructs suggests that constructs are open to new ways of construing new events. These concepts are important for understanding success because they tell how success-related behaviours are sustained even when rewards are absent, and behavioral repertoire modified to increase the probability of success in new environments. Critics of Kelly's theory claim that while the commonality and sociality corollaries[10] in the theory suggest that it might be possible to extend the theory to account for experiences in evolving, dyadic, interpersonal relationships, such an elaboration has not yet occurred (Jahoda, 1988, p.10).

Cognition and Trait - Raymond Cattell

Constructs of traits are always employed in conceiving what successful entrepreneurs and managers are like, and how they differ from others. According to Cattell (1970), traits are relatively permanent and broad reaction tendencies and serve as the building blocks of personality. He distinguishes between constitutional and environment-mold traits; ability, temperament, and dynamic traits; and surface and source traits. He claims that traits are genetically based but subject to modification by learning experiences, and that it is important to consider the ways and the extents to which the culture and various groups within it influence individuals and are, in turn, influenced by them.

From his process of theory building, Cattell has identified, using factor analysis, sixteen major source traits. Some of these are constitutional in nature and remain rather stable, some are more prone to environmental influences such as organization. The psychometric instrument developed by Cattell, the 16 Personality Factors (16 PF) is used as a tool in selection and recruitment, in vocational guidance, and as a predictive tool for later career achievement when promotion decisions are made, because it can tell something about the person as to whether he/she fits the organization or job, and vice versa. The major limitation of Cattell's trait approach relates to the language of his theory which is rather difficult to understand.[11] His use of neologisms and highly complicated specification equations is aversive to many people. In addition, Cattell (1984) himself recognized that the ability and personality tests he has developed have not yet achieved maximum usefulness. Nevertheless, credit should be given to Cattell due to his respect for the integrity of the many parts that constitute the individual. Besides, his attempt to explain the role played by situations in bringing about behaviours is thought relevant for understanding success in a rapidly changing society such as Hong Kong.

Social Cognition - Julian Rotter and Albert Bandura

While the personal construct theory is criticized as too simplistic, and the trait approach entails a language that is too difficult to understand, the work of Rotter and Bandura represents an attempt to establish a framework with clear and precise terminology and hypotheses that are capable of being tested. They also set out to construct a theory that would emphasize the role of motivational and cognitive factors in learning. Furthermore, both of them stressed the understanding of behaviours in the context of social situations. Hence their theories were built on a social-cognition orientation.

Rotter (1966) claims that most human behaviours are determined by the capacity to think and to anticipate. To anticipate what individuals will do in a certain situation must take into account such cognitive variables as perception, expectancies, and values. Behaviours are determined by expectations that a given action will bring about future rewards. The integration of expectancy and reinforcement concepts within the same theory is thus a unique feature of Rotter's theoretical framework. In deliberating his notion of expectancy and rewards, Rotter developed the construct of locus of control orientation. Rotter (1966) suggested that there are two dispositions to perceive the control of events and rewards: internal and external locus of control. Individuals who believe that they exercise some control over their destiny are described as having an internal locus of control. These individuals are termed internals. In contrast, individuals with an external locus of control (externals) believe that their rewards are controlled by luck, chance, fate or powerful others. An individual's locus of control orientation provides a direction for his/her behaviours. Hence underneath an individual's motivation is his/her belief, a belief about control. The idea that beliefs provide the basis for behaviours offers a useful construct which explains in a clearer way, compared with the humanistic and neo-psychoanalytic constructs, the psychological processes leading to the emergence of particular behaviours.

Rotter believed that need for achievement is related to the belief in internal locus of control. He hypothesized that individuals with internal beliefs would more likely strive for achievement than would individuals with external beliefs. Since successful entrepreneurs and high-flyers are often seen as achievers, Rotter was able to suggest a specific direction to study the psychology of entrepreneurs and high-flyers through the notion of locus of control.

Bandura (1971) believes that behaviours, cognitions and environment are reciprocally determined, and that behaviour occurs as a result of a complex interplay between inner processes and environmental influences. He started his explanation of behaviours with the concept of observational learning through which, he argued, most of the human behaviour are acquired. Attitudes and behaviours are learned simply by observing how others behave and are rewarded. The motivation to perform these observed behaviours lies in the expectation of reward. Through reinforcement experiences, an individual becomes able to self-respond, self-reinforce (and self-punish), hence self-regulate. So far Bandura's line of thinking is very similar to that of Rotter who equally stresses on cognitive processes such as expectancy and value, and learning through social experiences. However, Bandura later moved onto the notion of self-efficacy expectancy to explain behaviours. Self-efficacy is the perceived ability to cope with specific situations. It can enhance or reduce the probability of an individual performing a particular behaviour, influences how much effort they will expend in the face of frustrations and how long they will persist in the face of difficult circumstances. In short, self-efficacy influences behavioral patterns, motivation, and performance.

Rotter and Bandura have developed a precise and plausible approach of understanding the cognition-behaviour relation. The notions of expectancy, reinforcement, self-efficacy are useful in articulating the mechanisms through which an individual acquires and performs behaviours as a result of cognitive learning experiences in social situations. Their work are seen relevant to explaining the behaviours of entrepreneurs and high-flyers because they often need to assess and respond to situations of which they have no prior knowledge. The successful outcomes they achieved implies there is something special about the ways they assess and respond to these situations.

Cognition as an Aspect of Culture[12]

The above review illustrates that cognitive perspectives are useful in explaining the personal characteristics of successful business people due to their precise and well-linked framework. They offer a series of 'middle-range' concepts to help understand the mediating processes between cognition and behaviours. The view of human individuals as being capable of conscious thinking avoids the difficulty of dealing with unconscious experiences. However, there is still a loophole in all these cognitive perspectives when they are used to explain individual characteristics.

While the cognitive perspectives discussed above convey a general agreement that individual cognition and environment influence each other in a mutual way, the problem of cultural modification of the individual cognitive processes has not been adequately dealt with.

Culture is a body of customary beliefs, social forms, and material traits constituting a distinct complex of tradition of a racial, religious, social or professional group. Culture informs individuals of what is desirable and what is not, including the ultimate goals and the means to achieve them, termed respectively as nominal values and instrumental values (Rokeach, 1973) Obviously the general beliefs and norms about success in general and career success in particular, and the ways to attain success will influence work-related behaviours. Models used in the cross-cultural study of organizations, and of managerial styles and processes, have tended to ignore the aspect of culture. Schollhammer's (1969) survey of approaches to comparative management indicates a tendency for research to have concentrated on socio-economic variables, or on managerial attitudes.

Redding (1980) and Hofstede (1980) address the lack of consideration of culture in organizational studies by confining the concept of culture within the cognitive domain, hence allowing more focusing of research.

Redding (1980) claims that culture can be studied under the term 'cognition'. He argues the connections between the way in which people perceive society's rules and the way in which they behave in organizations should not simply be left as a series of black boxes. He suggests an approach that puts cognition as the base layer, as it were the foundation for other aspects, namely the interpersonal and societal. All three are seen as interacting mutually with organizational behaviours.

Hofstede (1980) defines culture as collective programming of the mind. He argues that the more we know a person's mental programming, the more accurate our predictions about his/her behaviours will be, on the assumption that each person carries a certain amount of mental programming which is stable over time and leads to the same person showing more or less the same behaviour in similar situation. Hofstede identifies three levels of mental programming: universal, collective and individual. The universal level is most likely entirely inherited whereas the individual level must at least be partly inherited. It is the collective level that is mostly learned. It represents mental programming that is common to people belonging to a certain group or category, but different among people belonging to other groups or categories. It is transferred from generation to generation and the learning of collective mental programmes mainly occurs at an early age when the mind is relatively empty.

Redding and Hofstede have made a theoretical progress on defining culture which helps to link culture and individual behaviours. The culture-individual interplay can be examined by studying the learning through which the individual acquires collective mental programmes, and the individual's cognitions or constructs that reflect the collective mental programmes. As Hofstede argues that cognitive learning goes on during the entire life but most occurs at the early years, and Redding emphasizes the reciprocal influence of cognition, interpersonal and societal contexts, a life-span development approach which takes into account interpersonal and societal environment is considered most appropriate to examine the individual's learning of collective mental programmes.

With this logic of thinking, it is proposed that such aspects of the person as his/her childhood, education, career history, personality, work motivation and management approach are the personal variables to be studied. Childhood, education and career brings experiences in an individual's life when significant learning takes place. Personality, work motivation and management approach reveal an individual's collective mental programmes or constructs that are learnt as a result of experiences of childhood, education and career history. The conceptual framework which guides the study of these six personal aspects must be one which recognizes the importance of cultural influences in shaping individual cognitions, because the present research focuses on a specific ethnic group, namely the Hong Kong Chinese entrepreneurs and high-flyers.

In proposing connections between culture and organizational behaviour, care must of course be taken to acknowledge other parallel influences such as historic, economic, technological, and political,[13] all of which are essential parts of any full understanding of career success.

Summary

Organizational psychologists are interested in a wide range of personal variables of entrepreneurs and managers. In view of the practical limitations on the scope of this study, six of the personal variables which are thought to be more central to the successful entrepreneurial and managerial behaviours are selected. These six personal variables are: childhood, education, career experiences, personality, work motivation, and management approach. The six personal variables in fact cover many of the variables Carsrud, Olm and Eddy (1986) mentioned that are popular topics currently being studied. Childhood includes parent-child relationship, watershed events, deprivation. Education includes subject and level of education, the role of formal education and management education. Career history includes early and wide responsibility, mentoring and career paths. Personality involves traits, the impact of stress and family support. Work motivation examines values and sources of motivation. Management approach investigates leadership styles, managerial skills and attributes. Hence the six chosen personal variables indeed include most of the personal experiences that have been found significantly related to career success.

In an examination of the current psychological perspectives in understanding success-related behaviours, the cognitive perspectives are thought to be precise and strong in explanatory power, hence chosen to be the guiding framework for the present research. The cognitive perspectives view that individual cognition evolve through experiences during his/her course of development. Hence a chronological dimension can be adopted in linking up the six personal variables, starting from childhood, education, career history, to the present situation reflected by personality, work motivation and management approach.

The literature on the six personal variables is presented and discussed from Chapters Four onto Nine following a chronological order of life-span development. It is noted that literature on high-flyers is relatively light when compared with the literature on entrepreneurs. Studies on managerial success do not usually focus on the young, fast-rising managers (high-flyers). Also, there are few direct comparisons between successful entrepreneurs and managers. Jennings, Cox and Cooper (1994) for example is one of the few of this sort. However, the intrapreneurs studied by these authors are far from the same as the high-flyers studied in the present research. As a result, the literature reviewed and discussed here is related to entrepreneurial and managerial success in general, and at some points, it is inevitable that there is disparity, in terms of the amount of literature reviewed, with regard to entrepreneurs and managers respectively.

The Conceptual Model

The relationship of the six personal variables are presented in the conceptual model shown in Figure 2.1. The conceptual model serves to guide the data collection and analysis.

Figure 2.1 The Conceptual Model for the Present Study

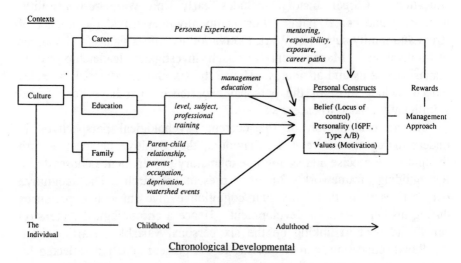

Note: The italics indicate the personal experiences in the course of life development

The review of literature shows that there have been few studies which directly compare entrepreneurs and high-flyers. The most direct claim, which makes reference to the difference between entrepreneurs and successful managers, is that of McClelland who suggests that entrepreneurs possess high nAch while successful managers do not need to possess the achievement need but they should exhibit the leadership motive pattern. Although there are other studies (Porter and Lawler, 1968; Jennings, Cox and Cooper, 1994) which do mention differences such as inner-directedness and outer-directedness, social origins and educational level of entrepreneurs and managers, the current literature does not provide clear evidence on the similarities and differences of entrepreneurs and successful managers. Hence the conceptual model used in this study, based on the review and discussion of the literature does not establish precise hypotheses on entrepreneurs-managers differences. The present study is an exploratory study aimed at generating data on both groups of successful people from which further conceptualization and theorizing can be developed, representing the approach of grounded theory in knowledge building (Glaser and Strauss, 1967).

The traditional approach of building knowledge is verifying original theories by testing hypotheses through evidence. The theories may be modified as a result of the tests. Grounded theory is an alternative approach of knowledge building which puts the emphasis on generating theory through what is emerged from the data. Glaser and Strauss (1967, p.29) contend that generating theory carries the same benefit as testing theory, plus an additional one:

> Verifying a logico-deductive theory generally leaves us with at best a reformulated hypothesis or two and an unconfirmed set of speculations; and, at worst, a theory that does not seem to fit or work. A grounded theory can be used as a fuller test of a logico-deductive theory pertaining to the same area by comparison of both the speculative theory and the newly generated theory than an accurate description used to verify a few propositions would provide. Whether or not there is a previous speculative theory, discovery gives a theory that 'fits or works' in a substantive or formal area (though further testing, clarification, or reformulation is still necessary), since the theory has been derived from data, not deduced from logical assumptions.

In view that not much is known, at the present stage, concerning the similarities and differences between Hong Kong successful entrepreneurs and high-flyers, and the validity of applying western theories in examining Chinese organizational behaviours, a grounded theory approach was adopted to generate data from which a sound theory that fits the local context can be developed.

Referring to Figure 2.1, the individual, be he/she a successful entrepreneur or a high-flyer, in the course of life development acquires a system of cognitions, named as personal constructs, through a series of personal experiences in childhood, education and career. These experiences bring the individual into contact with the influences of family, schools and work organizations, all of which convey the influences of the larger culture. Hence individual cognitions are connected with culture.

Personal constructs are conceived to be a result of both individual learning and collective programming, forming the individual's unique set of knowledge of the world. Personal constructs guide the individual's ways of behaving, leading to the emerged personality, work motivation and management approach.

From the review of literature, the substantive personal experiences that are found to be important in shaping an individual's personal constructs at different stages of life include parental influence in childhood, watershed events, subject and level of education, professional and management training, career history including career path, mentoring, training and exposures in work. Aspects of an individual which can reflect his/her constructs are type A/B behaviour and 16 personality factors patterns, locus of beliefs, motivational characteristics, management and leadership approach.

Cognitive learning occurs throughout an individual's life span, hence existing personal constructs are, in principle, modifiable. Feedback to an individual's behaviours in the form of reinforcement provides the basis of modifications to specific constructs and the overall construct system. Being reinforced in a specific construct leads to increased self-efficacy and expectancy of reward in that construct, further consolidating attitudes and behaviours amenable to that construct. On the contrary, if a construct is low in predictive efficiency and therefore not reinforced, the likelihood of that construct being modified or replaced is increased.

Notes

1   Personal variables in this text refer to the six aspects of the person chosen to be studied, namely childhood, education, career history, personality, work motivation and management approach.

2   A pilot study was carried out on 10 British high-flyers and 14 British entrepreneurs. The high-flyers are all director of subsidiary companies of a large British corporation. The entrepreneurs vary somewhat in terms of the size of their business. Some are small business owners, while the majority are big names in the British business world.

3   Creativity is viewed by Rogers as the ability to generate new and useful ideas, often by combining existing information in novel or unusual ways.

4   Maslow's model of hierarchy of needs has levelling implications. He regards physiological needs, material needs such as monetary rewards as low level needs. These needs are basic, but not sufficient to explain most human behaviours. He conceives people as striving towards high-level needs, and ultimately self-actualization.

5   One of the central tenets in transactional analysis. The structure of individual personality is composed of three ego stages which are separate and distinct sources of behaviour: the Parent ego state, the Adult ego state, and the Child ego state. For definitions of these three ego states and discussion on how they constitute behaviours, see Muriel James and Dorothy Jongeward (1978) *Born to Win*. Signet.

6   A psychological script, resembling much of a theatrical script, is a person's ongoing program for a life drama which dictates where the person is going with his/her life and the path that will lead there. See Muriel James and Dorothy Jongeward (1978) *Born to Win* for how scripts are developed and the different kinds of script.

7   For more of Kohut's self-psychology, see Kohut, H (1971). *The Analysis of Self*, New York: International University Press.

8   Cognitive psychology, in the broadest sense, is about events that occur inside people that help them make sense of the world. Technically, cognitive theories are concerned with how people gain information about events and how they process this information in order to act on the environment. Cognitive perspectives with different approaches to studying information processing have evolved. See Lynda Malm (1993) The eclipse of meaning in cognitive psychology, *Journal of Humanistic Psychology*, 33:1, 67-87 for a review of cognitive psychology in historical perspective.

9   In psychological literature, Cattell is classified as a trait theorist. However, a deeper examination of his assumptions reveals his strong belief in individual cognitive activity. His focus is on the complicated kinds of cognitive and motivational learning that guide people's action. In view of this recognition of cognition, Cattell's trait approach is discussed under the cognitive perspectives.

10   For definitions of the commonality corollary and sociality corollary, and other corollaries, see Kelly, G (1991). *Personal Construct Theory*.

11   For a critique of Cattell's trait approach, see Wiggins, J S (1984). Cattell's system from the perspective of mainstream personality theory. *Multivariate Behavioral Research, 19*, 176-190.

12   The thought of including a cultural perspective in forming the theoretical framework for the present research was first inspired by an article, S Gordon Redding (1980). Cognition as an aspect of culture and its relation to management processes: an exploratory view of the Chinese case. *Journal of Management Studies, May*, 127-148.

13   These parallel influences, and that of culture, on organizational behaviours are treated in Redding, G. and Hicks, G. (1983) Culture, causation and Chinese management, Mong Kwok Ping Management Data Bank Working Paper, School of Management, University of Hong Kong.

3   Research Methodology

This chapter gives a detailed account of the research methods used for the study. Section I describes the research approach adopted and gives the rationale for adopting such an approach. The strengths and weaknesses of the quantitative and qualitative methods are examined. Section II begins with a review of the considerations taken in choosing appropriate research methods for this. This is followed by an account of the data collection and data analysis methods used.

The Research Approach - Combining Quantitative and Qualitative Methods

Webb et al. (1966) have suggested that social scientists are likely to exhibit greater confidence in their findings when these are derived from more than one method of investigation. The present study had employed a research approach that combines qualitative methods and quantitative methods.

Rationale

The present approach of combining quantitative and qualitative methods is based on the perceived need for more than one method of investigation to be used in understanding the variables, hence more than one type of data. This is a strategy in which multiple theoretical perspectives, sources of data and methodologies are combined.

There is a general view that the quantitative approach and the qualitative approach are in direct opposition since they are built on paradigms[1] with quite contrasting epistemological assumptions about the nature of social reality and how it should be represented. Bryman 1995, p.94) summarizes finely some of the major differences between the quantitative and the qualitative research approaches. Conceiving the quantitative and the qualitative research methods as antagonistic views implies a rather partisan, either/or tenor of the two traditions in studying the social sciences. However, it is the intention of the investigator to undermine the assumption that these two paradigms are incommensurable or, indeed, that they offer any worthwhile alternative directions of psychological research. It is proposed the two paradigms be viewed as offering different and not mutually exclusive approaches to understanding social reality. The choice between them should be made in terms of their appropriateness in answering particular research questions.

Within this context, quantitative and qualitative research are perceived as different ways of examining the same research problem. The strategy of combining methods is to deal with the research problem with different methods that have non-overlapping weaknesses and complementary strengths. The main advantage is that it ensures that the variance observed is due to the trait being observed rather than the method of observation. Besides, the researcher's claims for the validity of the conclusions are enhanced if they can be shown to provide mutual confirmation, whereas if different methods yield dissimilar results they demand that the research reconcile the differences. Such divergence of results is often an opportunity to enrich the explanation. The convergence of the methods may enhance the belief that the results are valid and not a methodological artifact (Bryman, 1995).

In the present study, the methods were combined in a way that the qualitative methods were used to facilitate the quantitative methods and not the reverse. Whilst not attempting to go into the philosophical debate concerning the two paradigms, the researcher did not lose sight of the distinction between quantitative and qualitative data.

Strengths and Weaknesses of Quantitative and Qualitative Methods

Taking a technical view to treat the differences of the qualitative approach and the quantitative approach and to argue that the choice between them is to do with their suitability in answering particular research questions must involve an understanding of the relative strengths and weaknesses of the two research traditions.

The distinction of the qualitative approach and the quantitative approach which has tended to emphasize social actions and facts has at times revolved around the type of scientific procedures employed in testing and developing knowledge (Pfeffer, 1981). The qualitative researchers have, for the most part, been essayistic, conceptual, and not concerned with developing testable empirical predictions.   When data have been employed, it has been frequently in a case-study style of argument.   By contrast, the quantitative approach to organizational research has employed more comparative, quantitative data and more statistically rigorous analytical procedures.

McCracken (1988) sees the most striking difference between the methods as the way in which each tradition treats its analytic categories. The quantitative goal is to isolate and define categories as precisely as possible before the study is undertaken, and then to determine, again with great precision, the relationship between them. The qualitative goal, on the other hand, is often to isolate and define categories during the process of research. The qualitative researcher expects the nature and definition of analytic categories to change in the course of the inquiry. For one field, well defined categories are the means of research, for another they are the object of research.   Qualitative methods and quantitative methods can be complementary in the way that unique aspects may be discovered which would be neglected by other methods.

With regard to the present study, a descriptive profile of the personal characteristics of successful entrepreneurs and high-flyers is important and considered basic. The quantitative data precisely and clearly illustrate in what ways and to what extent successful business elites concur and differ from other groups of people.   They identify unique and distinctive characteristics that may have implications for success in careers. Statistical analyses can also point out directions for explaining success-related behaviours by establishing correlations between variables.

On the other hand, qualitative methods allow an in-depth description showing the complexities of variables and interactions.

Warwick and Lininger (1975, pp.9-10) contend that in making the technical decision as to whether a method fits a research problem, the critical issue is not a matter of the area of social life being investigated but the nature of the issues or factors being involved in relation to it, which is related to the type of information to be sought.

Zelditch (1962) provides some guidelines in matching methods of obtaining information with information types being sought. In the present research, the use of a particular research method is based on the assessment of the nature and the objectives of the research.

The central objective of the present study is to identify patterns of success-related personal characteristics and to understand these personal characteristics from a cognitive perspective. Such investigation would best be conducted by collecting detailed information on successful people's personal experiences showing how their ways of thinking are developed and how they affect their behaviours. The present study employed an in-depth interviews, structured questionnaire and published psychometric instruments to collect detailed information on personal experiences for the following reasons:-

• Published psychometric instruments yield clear and precise data on personality. The information obtained is also in a standardized form, thus facilitating cross-group comparisons. However, there are three important issues in using psychometric tests in the present study. First, statistical analyses of psychometric data was constrained by the relatively small sample size, hence the instruments were only used to provide descriptive personality profiles. Second, there is a limit on the number of psychometric instruments which the successful entrepreneurs and high-flyers can be expected to complete. Busy managers do not take kindly to filling in questionnaires. Third, most psychometric tests are developed from western theories, affecting their validity in measuring Chinese personality and behaviours.

• An individual's way of thinking can best be seen in how he/she describes himself/herself in relation to events in the self-reporting of personal experiences. Self-reporting in a face-to-face interview allows the investigator to make clarifications when required. More importantly, self-reporting in an interview permits in-depth examination of value bases of attitudes and behaviours, hence enabling the understanding of the cultural and social dimensions of personal experiences.

• A structured questionnaire was used to test consistency and hence validity of data obtained from interviews, in the belief that convergence of data from different methods enhances accuracy of results and that divergence in data provides an opportunity to enrich explanations.

The use of these three research methods in the present study will be further elaborated under Data Collection section in this chapter.

The Research Methods

Before going to the data collection and data analysis methods, it is important to define the subjects and how they were identified.

The Subjects

Hong Kong successful entrepreneurs and high-flyers are the subjects of the study.

Defining the entrepreneur and the high-flyer   Entrepreneurs are taken as those who started their own business. High-flyers are those who are rising fast on the career ladder. They reach senior management positions (not director's level) at a relatively younger age than their counterparts at the same level in the organization. In order to operationalize the definition of high-flyer in terms of his/her relatively young age in reaching senior management, a simple survey was carried out in five companies from which five of the high-flyers interviewed in the present study came. A list of all the managers, who have reached one level below chief executive officer or director, totalling 38, was obtained. The ages of these managers was identified and hence their mean age was derived, which was 46. After taking into account the standard deviation which was 5.18, it was decided that 40 was a reasonable indicator of young age for that level, which differentiates the high-flyers from the average senior managers.

Defining the Hong Kong entrepreneurs and high-flyers   Hong Kong Entrepreneurs refers to those Chinese entrepreneurs who started their business in Hong Kong. Hong Kong high-flyers are those Chinese managers who moved their way up in an organization located in Hong Kong.

Chinese entrepreneurs who started own business elsewhere to Hong Kong before relocating to Hong Kong are excluded. Similarly, Chinese managers recruited from elsewhere to a senior management post in a local organization are excluded since their previous career advancement did not take place in the Hong Kong context.

Defining success   As suggested earlier, Derr's definition that success is 'both being able to live out the subjective and personal values one really believes in and make a contribution to the world of work' is found to be a useful conception of success because it combines both the personal value of the individual and the more objective measures of success. However in identifying successful people, it is difficult to ascertain whether one feels he/she is able to live out the subjective and personal values he/she believes in. In the present research, success was ascertained more by external measures such as social and peer judgement.

Identifying the subjects Bearing in mind the above definitions, the successful entrepreneurs and high-flyers were identified from one of the three following sources:

a) Departmental Advisory Board Membership lists of the Hong Kong Polytechnic University. Members serving on the advisory boards of various departments at the Hong Kong Polytechnic University are appointed on a basis that they make significant contributions to the professions and industries concerned, hence they are considered successful people in their respective professions and industries. Ten successful entrepreneurs and twelve high-flyers are such advisory board members.

b) Various financial and industrial journals and magazines such as *Capital, Fortune, Industrialists.* Twelve successful entrepreneurs and seven high-flyers appeared in the focus articles of these publications. Among them, two high-flyers were awarded for their performance and two successful entrepreneurs were selected as the Ten Most Outstanding Young Industrialists of the Year.

c) Peer recommendation. The successful entrepreneurs and high-flyers who were identified from the above two sources and interviewed were asked to recommend successful career people who could be approached for interviews for the study. It was thought that being successful career people, they should be able to judge whether another individual has achieved success in career or business. Eight successful entrepreneurs and eleven high-flyers were identified this way and agreed to being interviewed.

It can be seen that success in the present research is mainly determined by social and peer perception. It is obvious that the entrepreneurs and high-flyers selected in this manner by no means warrant a claim to be a statistically representative sample of the Hong Kong entrepreneurs and high-flyers in general, and those in a specific profession or trade in particular. There is no solid ground to argue for generalization. However stating the limitations of the data set obtained is not to undermine the value and the relevance of the current study.

Demographic characteristics   The present research studied thirty entrepreneurs and thirty high-flyers. Their sex distribution, age distribution, and the type of business/trade in which they are involved are shown in Table 3.1, Table 3.2, and Table 3.3 respectively.   These demographic characteristics inform us about the specific time period and the socioeconomic environment in which the successful entrepreneurs and high-flyers were brought up, which have important implications for moulding their personal characteristics.

Table 3.1   Sex Distribution

	Male	Female	Total
Entrepreneur	28	2	30
High-Flyer	21	9	30
Total subjects	49	11	60

The majority of the successful entrepreneurs and high-flyers are male, with only a few female subjects. Since it is not the aim for this research to focus on gender as an aspect of study, the entrepreneurs and high-flyers were not selected in a way to ensure an equal number of male and female respondents. The small number of female entrepreneurs and high-flyers indicates, first, that there is actually fewer women entrepreneurs and women managers who have reached senior management level. Secondly, the business environment has traditionally been a male-dominant arena, which may have encouraged the advancement of men more than women.

Table 3.2 Age Distribution

Age range	Entrepreneurs	High-Flyer
26 – 30	1	2
31 – 35	2	9
36 – 40	6	19
41 – 45	12	-
46 – 50	5	-
51 – 60	3	-
Over 60	1	-
Total subjects	30	30

On average, the high-flyers are younger in age than the entrepreneurs. This is because high-flyers is operationally defined as those who have reached senior management at a relatively younger age than their peers.

From a simple survey in five companies, it was found that the average age of managers who are one level below chief executive officer is forty-six. Hence high-flyers are expected to be under the age of forty.

Most of the successful entrepreneurs (60 percent) are in their late thirties and early forties. With the exception of one very young and four old entrepreneurs, and two young high-flyers, the majority of the successful entrepreneurs (83 percent) and high-flyers (97 percent) were born shortly after the Second World War or during the 1950s and began their careers in the late 1960s and early 1970s.

All of the Hong Kong entrepreneurs and high-flyers are Chinese in terms of ethnic origin. Seven entrepreneurs and one high-flyer were born in China but moved to Hong Kong at an early age. Twenty-three entrepreneurs and twenty-nine high-flyers were born in Hong Kong. All grew up in Hong Kong since childhood.

Besides, the entrepreneurs are at different stages of their business development. The entrepreneur who is oldest in age is a long-established entrepreneur who has been very successful for a long time, whereas the rest have prospered in a more recent time, in the 1980s. The entrepreneurs and high-flyers are engaged in a wide array of industries, which can be seen in Table 3.3.

Table 3.3 Distribution of Companies by Industry

	Entrepreneurs	High-Flyers
Engineering	2	8
Electronics/Computer Technology	3	2
Trading	3	4
Public Utility	-	3
Construction	1	1
Manufacturing	6	-
Courier/Forwarding	1	1
Shipping	3	-
Estates and Surveying	3	1
Steel	1	-
Food/Catering Services	2	1
Insurance	-	1
Bank	-	4
Motor Car	-	1
Stationery	-	1
Printing and Publishing	2	-
Footwear	1	2
Environmental Technology	2	-
Total Subjects	30	30

All the successful entrepreneurs own and manage their companies. Twelve of the high-flyers are the chief executive officers of their organizations but they do not have shares in the business. The rest (18) of the high-flyers are posted one level below the chief executive officer.

Table 3.4 indicates that the size of their organization, in terms of annual turnover, vary widely. This is more so in the case of the successful entrepreneurs. Three are small business owners whose entrepreneurial history are comparatively short but business is growing.

Table 3.4 Company Annual Turnover

Annual Turnover (in HK Dollars)	Entrepreneurs	High-Flyers
10 – 50 million	6	-
50 – 100 million	5	4
1 - 5 billion	13	17
5 – 10 billion	4	9
Over 10 billion	2	-
Total subjects	30	30

Table 3.5 Size of Workplace in Terms of Number of Employees

Number of employees	Entrepreneurs	High-Flyers
Less than 50	10	3
50 – 100	3	3
101 – 300	7	11
301 – 600	5	7
601 - 1,000	3	3
Over 1,000	2	3
Total subjects	30	30

Table 3.5 shows the size of their organizations in terms of the number of employees. It is noted that some high-flyers work in the local office of multinational corporations and that only the employees in the local office are counted.

Seven successful entrepreneurs own and manage a relatively smaller organization because their business is service-oriented such as trading and technology consultancy.

After identifying potential subjects, they were approached in two ways. First a standard letter was sent to each of the potential subjects explaining the background of the present study and to ask whether he/she would participate in the study. It was followed up by a telephone contact to clarify any queries about the purpose and logistics of the research. The telephone contact was also useful in that it conveyed a personal touch which allayed the psychological mistrust of the researcher by the subjects. More often than not, the subjects' agreement to being interviewed were obtained through the telephone contact.

Data Collection

In the present study, information were gathered through:

1.   An individual face-to-face interview, and
2.   A self-administered Personal Characteristics Questionnaire, and
3.   Three psychometric questionnaires consisting of Borland's Type A/B Behaviour Questionnaire, Levenson's IPC Scale, and Cattell's sixteen Personality Factors Questionnaire.

These methods of obtaining information for the present study are addressed below.

The interview   As the present study is interested in how successful entrepreneurs and high-flyers see themselves in relation to various personal aspects, interview is considered the most valuable and practical among the various qualitative methods because it least violates the privacy of respondents. No individuals or organizations would welcome the presence of an observer for an extended period of time, due to the concern of privacy and time commitment, hence impeding the use of observation, whether participant or non-participant. Interview can take us into the mental world of the individual, to glimpse the categories and logic by which the entrepreneur/high-flyer sees the world.

The kind of interview conducted in the present study was a semi-structured interview. The interview was carried out following an interview schedule. The interview schedule was constructed on the basis of the conceptual model outlined in Chapter Two. It consists largely of open-ended questions focused on the six personal variables and their relationship: childhood, education, career history, personality, work motivation and management approach. Though the interview schedule was aimed at standardizing the sequence of questions and the way in which they were asked, the standardization was compromised to a certain extent when interviewing a group of independent thinking adults reporting their life experiences. Hence the questions were asked in an order that tuned with the flow of the ongoing conversation. The interview was started with easy, factual questions such as those related to career history. More sensitive questions such as those related to relationship with parents were asked at a later stage of the interview. Every effort was taken to lessen if not to eliminate both researcher and subject bias.

In understanding the developmental experiences of the successful entrepreneurs and high-flyers, the present study relied on data collected from the respondents' retrospective reports, though longitudinal studies are considered best for obtaining developmental data and understanding changes during the development.

The interview was designed to be semi-structured because it makes sure the researcher collects both abundant and manageable data. McCracken (1988) notes that every qualitative interview potentially generates endless, various and abundant data. The aim is to control the kind and amount of these data without also artificially constraining or forcing their character. Most important the interview permits probing into the context of, and reasons for answers to questions. The open-ended questions which comprise the interview schedule provide a frame of reference for the respondents answers but, put a minimum of restraint on the answers and their expression.

The interviews were carried out at a place suggested by the interviewees which was considered to be providing privacy and minimum disturbance, in all cases, this was the office of the interviewee. The dialogues between the interviewer and the interviewees were tape-recorded with the latter's agreement. All of the interviewees consented to the tape-recording. It was understood that potential audience effects[2] were present in the present research using interviews as one of the methods of data collection. One of the major considerations involved in the analysis of interview data is that, whatever its form, it is not to be taken at face value. The respondent in the interview has expectations regarding who might hear what they are disclosing. These thoughts shape the nature of the interview by determining what is socially relevant, what should and should not be said to maintain the image. Jennings et al (1994) cautions that what are tapped from interviews may be highly developed and sophisticated rationales.

The single interviewer was not blind to the research problem meant that precautions were taken during the interview to monitor potential interviewer bias. This requires constant self-reminding and -monitoring on the part of the interviewer to make sure that leading questions were not asked, and that the interviewees were encouraged to give their genuine views instead of what they thought were right answers.

Many scholars (Derrida, 1972; Denzin, 1989; Bruner, 1986) have contributed to the understanding that there is no clear window to the inner life of a person, for any window is always filtered through the glaze of language, signs and the process of signification. Language, in both its spoken and written form, is always inherently unstable. Hence there can never be a clear, unambiguous statement of anything, including an intention or a meaning.

The successful careers questionnaire   In response to the above issues that may arise from using interview as a data collection method, a structured questionnaire (with some open-ended questions) was used to collect specific data on defined aspects of personal characteristics. The data collected from the questionnaires serve to cross-check the interview data, ensuring the results are valid and variance observed is due to the trait being observed rather than a methodological artifact. The Questionnaire design was based on the pilot study on a group of British entrepreneurs and high-flyers (Lam, 1988) and the conceptual model developed for the present research. The questions are similar to those contained in the interview schedule, which were aimed at collecting data on the substantive personal experiences with regard to childhood, education, career history, work motivation and management approach. The questionnaire does not collect data on personality characteristics which would be precisely obtained from psychometric instruments. However, there are questions on stress and family support which are considered relevant to understanding type A/B personality.

Psychometric instruments   The three psychometric instruments were left to the entrepreneurs and high-flyers to complete in their free time. They were briefed of the purpose of using psychometric instruments and were told to give their immediate responses to questions and items in the tests rather than giving what they thought were 'good' answers. A stamped self-addressed envelope was provided for them to return the completed instruments to the researcher. A reminder (refer to Appendix E) was sent to them if the questionnaire was not yet received one month after the interview. It was followed up by telephone contact. Twenty-five entrepreneurs (83 percent) and twenty-eight high-flyers (93 percent) returned all three instruments. The response rates are considered satisfactory.

Data Analysis

There are two sets of data collected, the qualitative data obtained from the interviews (verbally self-reported data) and the questionnaires, and the quantitative data obtained from the psychometric instruments as well as the questionnaires. The qualitative data were content analysed with respect to the developed conceptual model. Content analysis is a method of studying and analyzing qualitative data, whether newly or previously collected, in a systematic manner to measure variables (Kerlinger, 1986), and one of the first steps of content analysis is categorization. Kerlinger suggests that categorization is perhaps the most important part of the analysis because it is a reflection of the theory being used. It spells out, in effect, variables of the research question.

In the present study, the conceptual model provides an organizing framework to categorize the massive amount of information obtained from the in-depth interviews. The interview contents were sorted into statements which were categorized and coded to establish patterns in relation to the six personal variables. For example, nature of parent-child relationships were categorized into close, normal and hostile. The categories were mostly generated from the data, which is a significant feature of developing grounded theory. Subsequent to categorization and coding, the number of respondents giving the same category of response was counted. Counting, or nominal measurement, is one of the ways of converting qualitative data into crudely quantifiable form ready for comparison and hypothesis testing found in quantitative research (Strauss and Glaser, 1967). After the patterns and their quantitative properties had been established, analysis proceeded by referring to existing theories with an aim to develop new theoretical notions.

Similarly, the data obtained from the Successful Careers Questionnaires were categorized and counted. In addition, the Questionnaire data were also quantified using ranking, or ordinal measurement. For example, the respondents were asked to rank from a list of choices, such as need for achievement, monetary rewards and social recogniztion, their three most important motivators. These listed choices were adopted for their proven validity with regard to the research question. Other choices given by the respondents themselves, other than those listed provided additional categories for analysis. The motivator selected by most respondents as their first choice was also identified.

Concerning the treatment of data obtained from the psychometric instruments, each completed instrument was first scored, based on the specified procedures stated for that particular instrument. The scores were then categorized to indicate various patterns of personality characteristics, these were then counted to indicate the number of respondents having the same pattern. The Locus of Control data were statistically analysed using correlation coefficients in order to test what kind of relationship exist between internal control orientation and the powerful others and chance orientations. A strong negative correlation will suggest a true internal control orientation. The use of statistical tests was to some extent inhibited and constrained by the relatively small sample size in the present study, hence only simple quantitative methods were used.

Notes

1   Very often quantitative research is said to have built on the positivist paradigm, and qualitative research built on a paradigm which is generally termed the alternative paradigm. The positivist paradigm represents an epistemological position implying that only research which conforms to the doctrines of scientific method can be treated as contributing to the stock of knowledge. Similarly, the alternative paradigm including such epistemological stances as phenomenology and naturalism rejects the imitation of the natural scientist's procedures and advocates that greater attention be paid to actors' interpretations. For a detailed discussion of the debate on quantitative and qualitative research, see Bryman, A. (1995) *Quantity and Quality in Social Research.* London: Routledge.

2   What is meant by audience effect in field research is well discussed in Becker, H S (1958). Problems of inference and proof in participant observation, *American Sociological Review*, 23, December: 652-60.

4 Childhood

Super (1957) suggests that the adequacy of a career decision will partially depend upon the similarity between the individual's self-concept and the vocational concept of the career that he/she chooses.

An individual's self-concept reveals itself through the constructs of values, beliefs and trait used to describe oneself. Each individual has a unique personal history which originates out of a familial context with its own characteristics such as genetic, economic, educational and cultural. At a group level, individuals compare themselves with others, using constructs of values, traits, and beliefs, etc. Values are desirable end states or desirable modes of behaviour for achieving those end states (Rokeach, 1973). Traits refer to consistent and stable modes of adapting to the environment. Beliefs are taken as assumptions about how the world works, such as the degree of personal control possible over events (Rotter, 1966). Bond (1993) states that one's self-concept then becomes one's perceived location in this geography of values or traits or beliefs relative to the location of other persons or other groups.

Self-concept is developed since early childhood. The people who are most significant to an individual in his/her childhood are assumed to be his/her parents. Parents influence their children in different ways to different extents with different outcomes, but one common function all parents play in influencing their children is early socialization. Through socialization, the child acquires constructs of beliefs, constructs of values and constructs of traits, shaping the individual self-concept or identity. In particular, the individual's propensity in career choices and orientation to work is developed. Parents influence their children both in direct and indirect ways, and the quality of the parent-child relationship will determine the extent of parental influence.

Parental Influence

Parents are the primary carers of a child. Due to their direct and frequent contacts with the child, and the natural parent-child bonding, parents have great influence on the child in terms of shaping personality and transferring values. The following examines parental influence in relation to career and managerial success.

Parent-Child Relationship

Quality of relationship with parents affects the nature and extent of parental influence upon the individual.

A variety of parent-child relationships were reported in a study of successful women in industry and career (White, Cox and Cooper, 1992). In most cases the parent-child relationship facilitated the development of an early sense of independence and self-sufficiency.

Children are supposed to be dependent, but as they mature, independence striving will increase. Early independence exploration requires a secure affective base. Baumrind (1971) points out that a secure base is necessary but not sufficient for the development for independence behaviour. The child also requires opportunities for independence behaviour and parental encouragement. The entrepreneurs and intrapreneurs (successful managers) studied by Jennings, Cox and Cooper (1994) were found to have extremely supportive parents, mainly the mother. However, they were not overprotected as children. Parental support becomes disenabling for independence if it becomes overprotectiveness. An overprotective parent may offer too much help too quickly, with the result that the child lacks the opportunities for independence behaviour, hence cannot develop the ability to tolerate frustration.

Similar findings to that of the study by Jennings were obtained by Firth (1987) and Cox and Cooper (1988). High-flyers in the study by Firth were found to have enjoyed a happy childhood. The CEOs in the study by Cox and Cooper reported a normal and happy childhood. However, one-fifth of the high-flyers mentioned a feeling of separation which was mainly due to the death of the father or being sent away from home for some reason. Cox and Cooper suggest that this separation may have produced an early feeling of independence and self-reliance.

In contrast, 44 percent of the successful women in White's study experienced a problematic relationship with their mothers or had a remote relationship with both parents. White argued that this lack of bonding in the parent-child relationship could have encouraged the development of a separate sense of identity. Hoffman (1972) claims that this increases the probability of early experiences of coping with the environment independently, which is thought to be essential in the development of competence and self-confidence.

It is observed from these studies that although there is no one single kind of parent-child relationship which contributes to the development of independence and self-reliance, parents who are supportive but not overprotective and with some degree of detachment have most likely encouraged independence and self-reliance behaviours in the childhood of the successful managers.

In the case of the entrepreneurs, most literature has portrayed their childhood as disturbing and turbulent (Kets de Vries, 1977).

Familial Origins of Locus of Control

Findings have been quite consistent in indicating that successful people have internal locus of control (White et. al., 1992). Levenson (1973) studies locus of control in the light of perceived parental antecedents of the internal, powerful others, and chance control orientations. Her findings suggest that those who reported that their parents used more punishing- and controlling-type behaviours were found to have greater expectations of control by powerful others, while those who viewed their parents as using unpredictable standards had stronger chance control orientations. Regarding internality, there was some controversy in the type of childrearing experienced by male and female subjects respectively.

It is claimed by Rotter (1966) that consistent and nurturant child-rearing practices should be related to the development of an internal locus of control orientation. His hypothesis was supported by Katkovsky, Crandall and Good (1967) who conducted a study with families participating in a longitudinal study of human development in which the results suggested that, in general, a child's beliefs in internal control of reinforcements are related to the degree to which parents are protective, nurturant and non-rejecting. Subsequently a group of researchers discovered there was sex difference in the relationship between nurturing type of parenting and the degree of internality. Both MacDonald (1971) and Reimanis (1971) found that for males there is a relationship between consistent home environments and internality; however, there was no such findings for females. MacDonald (1971) discovered that maternal protectiveness was related significantly to externality. Whereas Reimanis (1971) found that girls who felt that their mothers did not care about them had significantly higher internal scores.

Levenson (1973), in addressing the inconsistent findings regarding sex difference in control-home environment relationship, extended Rotter's IE scale to differentiate two classes of externals: to measure belief in chance expectancies as separate from a powerful others orientation, the rationale being that people who believe the world is unordered (chance) behave and think differently from people who believe the world is ordered but that powerful others are in control. In the latter case, a potential for control exists.

In examining the inconsistency arising from these various studies, it is important to note that nurturance and protectiveness (overprotectiveness) should be conceptually and empirically distinct. Indiscriminate reinforcement in the case of protectiveness can lead to feelings of helplessness or a very external locus of control. Protectiveness can arrest the child's move to independence as he/she grows and is exposed to environments other than the home, thereby preventing the child from developing his/her coping behaviours, suffocating the child's natural curiosity and intrinsic motivation.

Values

One of the principal functions parents play in socialization is the imparting of values in their descendants. Rokeach (1973) has the following definition of values:

> A value is an enduring belief that a specific mode of conduct or end-state of existence is personally or socially preferable to an opposite or converse mode of conduct or end-state of existence. A value system is an enduring organization of beliefs concerning preferable modes of conduct or end-states of existence along a continuum of relative importance.

Rokeach distinguishes values into nominal values and instrumental values, and developed the Rokeach Value Survey in identifying individuals' values systems. His instrument was also employed in researching the personal values of managers (Clare and Sanford, 1979). England and Lee (1974) conducted a cross-cultural study to examine the link of values to managerial success and the possibility of using values as a recruitment tool. They derived from their study the following assertions which are relevant in establishing the importance of considering values when investigating managerial success:

1. Personal value systems influence a manager's perception of situations and problems he faces.
2. Personal value systems influence a manager's decisions and solutions to problems.
3. Personal value systems influence the way in which a manager looks at other individuals and groups of individuals; thus they influence interpersonal relationships.
4. Personal value systems influence the perception of individual and organizational success as well as their achievement.
5. Personal value systems set the limits for the determination of what is and what is not ethical behaviour by a manager.
6. Personal value systems influence the extent to which a manager accepts or resists organization pressures and goals.
7. Some personal value systems may contribute to managerial success, some may be irrelevant, and some may be antithetical to achievement efforts.

England and Lee conducted their survey in four countries: USA, Australia, India and Japan. They developed 'tailor-made value keys' for each of these countries so that cultural influence in value systems are considered in measuring values. The values which are related to success are similar across the four countries: high productivity, profit maximisation, labour unions, ability, aggressiveness, prejudice, achievement, creativity, success, change, competition and liberalism. The values related to less successful managers are social welfare, obedience, trust, conformity, leisure, dignity, security, conservatism, equality and religion. In general, England and Lee conclude that successful managers emphasise 'pragmatic, dynamic, achievement-oriented values' whereas less successful managers tend to emphasise 'static and passive values'.

The Chinese work ethics   Confucian traditions emphasize the duty of officers to serve with dispassionate loyalty, representing an extended form of filial piety in the family to work relationships.   Many folk stories glorify those who give up personal wealth and fame to maintain virtues such as loyalty to the master.   This ideology was congruent with the cultural system of traditional China which was basically an agrarian state. The agricultural economy tied the vast majority of the population to the land and its constraints, supporting the peasants at only a subsistence level.   Their livelihood became even more precarious in times of famine when a great portion of China's huge population faced starvation.   This kind of ecological backdrop predisposed the Chinese peasantry to accept Confucian philosophy, which encourages restraint over one's desires and equal distribution of the limited resources among members of a group (the family in most cases).   Group interest is placed above individual interest, thereby social stability and harmony is achieved.   Collective and cooperative behaviours are crucial for survival in a rural economy.

Career Orientation

Astin (1984) argues that the work motivation is the same for men and women by pointing out that they share a common human condition and live together in the same world of personal obligations and social conditions.   They make different occupational choices, however, due to early socialization.   Astin's model incorporates four major constructs: motivation, expectations, sex-role socialization and the structure of opportunity.

Figure 4.1 Astin's Need-Based Sociopsychological Model of Career Choice and Work Behaviour

A. Work Motivation	B. Sex-Role Socialization	C. Structure of Opportunity
Three Basic Drives	- Play	- Distribution of Jobs
- Survival	- Family	- Sex-Typing of Jobs
- Pleasure	- School	- Discrimination
- Contribution	- Work	- Job Requirements
		- Economy
		- Family Structure
		- Reproductive Technology

D. Expectations
↓
Career Choice and Work Behaviour

Source: Astin, (1984) *The Counselling Psychologist, 12:4*, 121.

The model outlined in Figure 4.1 entails four major tenets. First, work behaviour is described as a motivated activity to satisfy three basic needs: survival, pleasure and contribution. Second, career choices are based on expectations of accessibility of alternative forms of work and their capacity to satisfy needs. Third, expectations are shaped by early socialization and in part by the perceived structure of opportunity. Finally, expectations can be modified by changes in the structure of opportunity and this change in expectations can lead to changes in career choice and in work behaviour.

Parents play an important role in the child's early socialization and have a guiding influence upon the child's vocational choices. The influence may be directly or indirectly exerted. What the parent does as an occupation has direct effect on the child because he/she is exposed to a real life model.

Many studies (see Table 4.1 and Table 4.2) report similar findings that the majority of entrepreneurs, male and female, have parent(s), usually the father, who was self-employed in one form or another (Bowen and Hisrich, 1986). The vicissitudes of self-employment, its ups and downs, its turmoil and other psychosocial uncertainties have a profound effect upon the family atmosphere under which the entrepreneur was being brought up. The independent nature and flexibility of self-employment exemplified by the father or mother is ingrained at an early age, influencing the entrepreneur's career orientation at a later stage.

Table 4.1 Studies of Entrepreneurs in General or Male Entrepreneurs Only

Brockhaus (1982) cited four studies suggesting that entrepreneurs tend to have entrepreneurial fathers.

Brockhaus and Nord (1979) found that 31 St. Louis male entrepreneurs were no more likely than male managers to have entrepreneurial fathers.

Cooper and Dunkelberg (1984) reported that 47.5 percent of 1,394 entrepreneurs had parents who owned a business.

Jacobowitz and Vidler (1983) found that 72 percent of mid-Atlantic state entrepreneurs had parents or close relatives who were self- employed.

Shapero and Sokol (1982) reported that 50 percent to 58 percent of company founders in the United States had self-employed fathers (at a time when self-employed persons were only 12 percent of the work force). They cited data on the same pattern in nine other cultures.

Source: Bowen, D. D. and Histrich, R. D. (1986) The female entrepreneurs: a career development perspective, *Academy of Management Review, 11*, 397.

Table 4.2 Studies of Female Entrepreneurs

Hisrich and Brush (1983) reported a nationwide sample of 468 female entrepreneurs; 36 percent had entrepreneurial fathers; 11 percent had entrepreneurial mothers.

Sexton and Kent (1981) found that 40 percent of 48 Texas female entrepreneurs had entrepreneurial fathers and 13 percent entrepreneurial mothers (vs 13 percent and 11percent for 45 female executives).

Watkins and Watkins (1983) found that 37 percent of 58 British female entrepreneurs had self-employed fathers (self-employment in the male United Kingdom labour force is 9 percent). 16percent of mothers were whole or part owners of businesses (female self-employment was 4 percent).

Source: Bowen, D. D. and Histrich, R. D. (1986) The female entrepreneurs: a career development perspective, *Academy of Management Review, 11*, 399.

Separation from Parent(s) as Childhood Deprivation

The review of the parent-child relationship of successful entrepreneurs and high-flyers unfolds a theme of overcoming early adversities as leading to success in later life. Among various forms of adversities, having suffered some sort of separation in childhood is discovered to be the major feature in the childhood of successful people.

Illingworth and Illingworth (1966) claim that a surprisingly large number of children destined for fame lost one or both parents during childhood. They gave a list of 70 famous persons who lost their parents under the age of 10. Silver (1986) found from an extensive survey that most of the highly successful people in America were driven by conscious feelings of deprivation and guilt stemming from broken families and connections. Many had lost their fathers in childhood through death or divorce.

Such kind of separation from parents was also reported by the change-makers (Hingley and Cooper, 1985), the British CEOs (Cox and Cooper, 1988), and the business elites (Jennings, Cox and Cooper, 1994).

In the case of the change-makers, separation was due to prolonged absence of parents especially the father. They mentioned experiencing a strong sense of loneliness, and they saw the separation a kind of deprivation. In contrast, Cox and Cooper's CEOs did not see themselves as loners. Among them, eight had suffered the death of their fathers under the age of 16. Ten others were separated from parents at an early age, either through being sent away to boarding school at a very young age, or through being evacuated during the Second World War. Separation occurred at a critical formative stage of their life. However, they reported they were gregarious children and had many friends. At this point, it becomes rather apparent that separation from parents itself does not necessarily lead to feeling deprived if favourable conditions exist to compensate for the absence of parent(s).

It also cautions in examining the deprivation-success relationship. Those successful people studied by Illingworth and Illingworth, Cooper and Hingley, Cooper and Cox, grew up in the war years when most other people faced similar kind of separation with their fathers away in the army. Therefore, separation itself does not suffice to explain success. Instead it is, as Cox and Cooper suggest, how the successful people respond to these adversities.

Watershed Events in Childhood or Later Life

Watershed events are significant life events which calls for readjustment on the part of the individual.

Most people will agree that during the course of human development, an individual will experience some events which have important impact upon his/her way of thinking and behaving. Rahe and Gunderson (1974) called these important life events significant life events (SLE). They are events which call for transitions, hence readjustment, in an individual's life style. Significant life events (SLE) include death of spouse, divorce, personal injury, loss of job, moving to a different line of work, retirement, etc, all of which can create some kind of stress in the individual.

Studies of entrepreneurs and managers reflect the same belief that life events play an important role in career success. Taylor (1985) remarks that life experiences, particularly those concerned with business experiences, is the variable most frequently mentioned.

Birth Order

The impact of birth order has had conflicting research results. Being first born or an only child is postulated to result in the child's receiving special attention and thereby developing more self-confidence. In a national sample of 468 female entrepreneurs, Hisrich and Brush (1984) found 50 percent to be first born, whereas in many studies of male and female entrepreneurs the first born effect has not been present (Bowen and Hisrich, 1986).

Growing up in a Chinese Family

Traditional Chinese culture place great emphasis on the family in the life of an individual. Almost all kinds of interpersonal relationship are symbolized as replications of familial relationships. An individual's close friends are taken as one's brothers and sisters. A group of people who share similar interests or goals are paralled as belonging to a family.

Lau (1982) introduced the concept of 'utilitarian familism' as one of the two key social fabrics of the Hong Kong society. He found that the families remain the basic survival units, that they are largely self-sufficient, that they do not fuse naturally into a general community, that they are fundamentally competitive, and that their members are largely motivated by the pragmatic exigencies of protecting and enhancing the family resources on which they in turn are highly dependent. These characteristics of the modern Chinese families in Hong Kong are in many ways remnants of the traditional role and functions of families in the Chinese society. The existence of the individual has been very much defined in terms of his/her immediate family network. Yang (1945, p.45) suggests the notion of what a family is extends beyond its members to encompass its property, its reputation, its internal traditions, its ancestors' spirits, and even its future unborn generations. Inside the family, male domination is normal. The father is the head of the family and makes major decisions for its members.

Recognizing the centrality of the family for its members, it is expected that the impact of the family on its members' thinking and behaviour through socialization is particularly strong in the Chinese case. Ho (1986), in his review of empirical studies on the Chinese patterns of socialization, identified several plausible generalizations which have received relatively strong and consistent empirical studies on the Chinese patterns of socialization, identified several plausible generalizations which have received relatively strong and consistent empirical support or on which there is overall agreement among observers. These are:

1. Traditionally, great emphasis was placed on obedience, proper conduct, moral training, and the acceptance of social obligations, in contrast to the lack of emphasis placed on independence, assertiveness, and creativity.

2. Chinese parents tend to be highly concerned with impulse control. Chinese children tend to be physically non-aggressive; in particular, aggression directed toward authority figures is rarely expressed.

3. Traditionally, the father has been perceived to be a harsher disciplinarian than the mother, and is the parent of who the child is more afraid. Father-child affectional distance is greater than that between the mother and the child. However, contemporary mothers appear to be assuming a more important role as disciplinarians.

4. Achievement motivation is more firmly rooted in the collectivist than in the individualistic orientation. Cooperative efforts by members of a group individualistic orientation. Cooperative efforts by members of a group toward achieving collective goals are emphasized more than individual competitiveness.

5. Most results conform to the expectation that positive parental attitudes are conducive to desirable effects (higher achievement motivation, superior cognitive development and academic performance, and better personal and social adjustment) and that negative parental attitudes have the opposite effects in Chinese children. A number of studies, however, suggest that boys and girls may be influenced differently by patterns of parenting (for example, the relationship with the father and that with mother and the quality

of these relationships). These differing patterns are far from simple and the evidence in support of them is far from unequivocal.

Childhood Experiences of Hong Kong Successful Entrepreneurs and High-Flyers

The present study examined such aspects of the successful career people's childhood experiences as relationship with parents, parental values, childhood deprivation, and watershed events in development. The major findings are presented below.

Relationship with Parents

Most of the entrepreneurs and high-flyers were very enthusiastic in talking about their relationship with parents though not everyone described the relationship as positive and pleasant. A few even got very emotional implying something concerning the relationship had not been worked through. It is noted that the Chinese are rather reserved when discussing emotional matters, especially with strangers. Personal matters concerning one's family background, parents and childhood can be a sensitive area. However, the entrepreneurs and high-flyers in general were more open than expected.

Parents were the principal childcarers of the successful entrepreneurs and high-flyers. Only two entrepreneurs (E21 and E26) were looked after by their grandparents. It was not a common practice to hire childminders in their time. They lived with their parents under the same roof. This physical closeness, in addition to the assumed natural bonding between parents and child, helped make relationship with parents a significant aspect of childhood experiences.

Two entrepreneurs and four high-flyers described their parental relationship as cold or hostile. The remaining entrepreneurs (28) and high-flyers (26) recalled enjoying a normal and satisfactory relationship with parents. It was normal in the sense that there were no particular highs and lows and the relationship had been satisfactory to both parties. Among these, four entrepreneurs and seven high-flyers described their relationship with parents as very close.

The closeness in relationship helped to magnify the extent of parental influence on the entrepreneurs and high-flyers. Twenty-five of the entrepreneurs and twenty-three of the high-flyers claimed one or both of their parents had influenced them in some ways.

Table 4.3 Parental Influence

Influence from Parent(s)	Entrepreneurs		High-Flyers	
	Male	Female	Male	Female
Both	5	1	7	1
Father	13	1	6	2
Mother.	5	-	2	5
None	5	-	6	1
Total subjects	28	2	21	9

Table 4.3 shows the parental influence on the successful entrepreneurs and high-flyers. The entrepreneurs as a group showed a stronger identification with father. Almost half of the entrepreneurs (46 percent) claimed they were influenced more by their fathers while six of them (20 percent) were influenced by both of their parents. Only five (17 percent) of them identified with their mothers and five (17 percent) did not identify with any of the parents.

The high-flyers exhibited quite a different pattern which is generally more evenly distributed. When compared to the entrepreneurs, less of the high-flyers were influenced by their fathers (27 percent) but more of them were influenced by their mothers (23 percent). This contrasting difference in influence from father and mother between the successful entrepreneurs and high-flyers is due to the greater number of female high-flyers. However, it is worth noting that both the two female entrepreneurs indicated greater influence from their father, which may suggest that identification with a male figure will lead to greater tendency to participate and compete in a male-dominant business world. However, this apparent relationship remains a speculation due to the very small sample size of female entrepreneurs.

The following interview transcripts help to show the kind and extent of parental influence on the successful entrepreneurs and high-flyers.

Influence from father The fathers of the entrepreneurs and high-flyers were found to have exerted their influence on their children particularly with relation to such important life issues as education and career.

One entrepreneur described his relationship with his father:

> I am fortunate that I have a good father. He is very liberal. I learned a lot from him. He had his business but he never expected any one of us to inherit the business. He thought every person should create things for himself/herself. I was very close to him. I was attracted by his attitudes and the ways he treated us. (E20)

This entrepreneur is not the only one who viewed his father almost as an idol, in fact, five other entrepreneurs and two high-flyers had expressed such kind of admiration for their fathers.

> My interest in business came from my father. He ran his business with his own money and efforts. We respect him and adore him. In a Chinese family, the father is the head. I adore his success. Because of the political change (the Communist takeover of China in 1949), he was forced to come to Hong Kong. His business declined afterwards due to the change in environment. I wanted to be successful one day so as to make him happy. I try hard partly because of my father. He is our model. (E5)

> If you ask me who is the key person in my life, I must mention my father. I have been very much influenced by him since early childhood, including education and choice of career. (E13)

> We respect our father. He was a gentleman. He was intelligent and he tried his best in everything he did. He was such a kind person that we really respect him a lot. (E17)

> I admire my father very much. He was a successful businessman when I was a child and he brought me along to meet his friends. I was glad that I got to know a lot of people and things about the world. He showed me the wisdom in life. (E22)

I am like my father in a lot of aspects. He is a man of determination. I picked this (trait) up from my father. He always told me his ideas and feelings. I know him very well. (E24)

My father worked very hard to provide us with a decent living. He worked more than 12 hours a day, seven days a week. He insisted that we received good education. Without my father, I could not have been able to achieve what I have now. (HF28)

I respect my father a lot. I can remember many of the things he taught me when I was a child. (HF17)

As one of the entrepreneurs suggested, father is the head in a Chinese family, hence the fathers are in a strong position to exert their influence on their offsprings. Apart from influencing the entrepreneurs and high-flyers through making decisions and giving advice on matters of education and career, they also showed their children the kind of attitudes and behaviours which they thought were important, incalcating a particular personality orientation which is related to their children' career success in later life.

Influence from mother In contrast to the fathers, the mothers of the entrepreneurs and high-flyers were described as exerting their influence in a subconscious way. One entrepreneur had labelled her mother as the power behind the scene.

My mother is very feminine and yet the power behind the scene. She is very caring. We all have this gentle temperament. (HF20)

Three other entrepreneurs recalled their mothers as below:

My mother showed me how to relate to people. She taught me to be generous. She is very active, outgoing, likes to meet people. She likes to share what she has with others. She took care of my cousins when they first came to Hong Kong from Mainland China. When I was young, there were always a lot of children in the house, more than ten. We played together. Later we, my brother and one cousin and I went to university in UK together. Because of her generosity, many people respect her. (E14)

I respect my mother. She has a strong character. She is a model to me for how to persevere. (E18)

I learnt a lot of things about relating to people during the time I helped my mother in her store. She is a nice and kind woman but yet she does not let others take advantage of her. She showed me how to protect myself, to negotiate with people, so that we can come up with a win-win situation. (E29)

One high-flyer suggested his domineering personality was picked up from his mother:

My mother is very domineering. I think I am domineering too. I expect things to be done my way. I try not to be too domineering in work, because I think any management theory will say a domineering boss does not encourage participation. (HF13)

One entrepreneur and one high-flyer were very impressed and hence influenced by the way their mothers took care of them in the absence of their fathers:

My mother is a strong woman. After my father had died, she took up the roles of both parents. She worked very hard and even did some domestic industry. But she is very liberal and never gives pressure onto us. (E19)

My mother has a strong character. I never saw her complain even though she had to look after us all by herself when we were young. I learn from her how to stand in the face of hardships. (HF7)

Apart from one entrepreneur whose mother had influenced him in the ways to relate to others, the rest of the entrepreneurs and high-flyers were impressed by their mothers' toughness which was particularly apparent in times of difficulties. Their mothers had exhibited contrasting characteristics from those of the traditional Chinese mothers who were expected to be passive, dependent and submissive. Observing and being impressed by their mothers' perseverance and strong will-power were important in developing similar qualities of self-reliance and hardworking personality in the entrepreneurs and high-flyers, which will be elaborated below.

Influence from both parents For those who indicated they were influenced by both parents (six entrepreneurs and eight high-flyers), the influence from each of the parents were of different nature.

> I came from a poor family. Both of my parents were teachers. Because of the Japanese occupation of Hong Kong during the War, we returned to China. We gave up everything we had in Hong Kong. My parents insisted they did not want to be slaves of the Japanese. I respect my parents very much. I admire the way they stick to their principles. (E6)

> I was affected by both of my parents in a subconscious way. They didn't tell me what to do, but the things they said affected me, even now. I am fair in doing things, so is my mother. I like doing things according to my principles which makes me difficult to be an employee. You have to make compromise to your boss if you are an employee. This was affected by my father. (E9)

> I picked up different things from my father and my mother. I got wisdom from mother. She is a intelligent, smart and flexible woman. She taught me how to deal with others and solve problems. My father influenced my personality. He likes philosophy, Marxist theories and reads a lot of books. We both like to find out the roots of things, we are not satisfied just with facts. Actually he taught me what is wisdom too. (E26)

> My parents do not have a happy marriage, because one of them is too tough and the other is too soft. They always quarrel. My father is a typical nice man, he is honest and straightforward. But my mother is very aggressive and she dislikes my father being too soft. I can't say who is right and who is wrong, but I learn to see things from both sides. (HF16)

> Both of my parents worked. I saw how they cooperated to run the family. I was quite good at school and they gave me a lot of opportunities to develop myself and to achieve. I became rather reliant on them. Even when I got to university I ended up studying something which I had not planned. I was being over-influenced by them. (HF29)

Whether their parents worked in harmonious partnership or had frequent conflicts, the entrepreneurs and high-flyers were able to learn lessons and benefit from their parents' experience.

Independence and self-reliance   Among the various influences the parent(s) had on the entrepreneurs and high-flyers, cultivating a sense of independence and self-reliance was regarded by eleven entrepreneurs and ten high-flyers as the most significant influence.

One high-flyer acknowledged her independent character was developed by the way she was brought up:

> It (family background) actually helps a lot. I'm the oldest, and I have a few younger siblings. My father had a store and my mother helped him. We as a family were very close and supported one another. Since I was young, I had to do the housework and I was quite independent. When I studied in primary school, my father helped me in homework. However, when I was promoted to a more advanced level, my father didn't have the knowledge to teach me. I had to find ways to help myself. We weren't able to afford a family tutor. We didn't have many contacts with relatives, so I relied on myself in study. That made me very independent. I'm forced to complete the work by myself. Apart from this, my parents' policy towards our study was that if you are able to study (in terms of ability and money), go ahead. If not, then don't study at all. As soon as I was allowed to do summer job, I earned money for my school fees. That's how I completed my study at the Polytechnic. I made my own decision on study. My parents didn't bother me at all. I think the greatest influence from my family is that it cultivated my independent character. You know that you can't rely on others to help you. (HF1)

One entrepreneur recalled:

> My father has three wives and fifteen children, which was very socially acceptable at that time. I guess he did not remember the names of all his children. I was very independent since I was a child because my mother had too many things and people to look after. I always slept outside the home, went to far away places by myself and never got frightened. (E26)

This kind of laissez-faire attitude of parents towards child-rearing encourages the development of self-reliance and independence in the child.

One woman entrepreneur remarked she has a very intimate relationship with her parents who had great impact on her personality and outlook, in both positive and negative ways:

My parents are very liberal. I think my mother affected us a great deal subconsciously. But we respect our father because he was a very good scholar. He was not talkative but very stubborn, stubborn in his gentle way. (But) I know clearly that I don't want to be like my dad. Other people liked to take advantage of him. I realized this when I was very young. I once saw him in court for a case concerning professional malpractice. My father was not very articulate, he did not know how to argue with people. I saw him being bullied. I knew my father was such a gentleman that he would not fight back when he was confronted. Actually, we all carry this (temperament). Everyone thinks that we are bright and we are intelligent in everything. But we are the worst at arguing with others. My mother is the same. She never scolds us. Even when she is angry, she just takes a walk with us and slowly tells us what went wrong. Both of them are so gentle that we did not learn how to have temper and react to people who are aggressive. (E15)

My parents had opposite characters. They were on two extreme ends, so they often quarrelled. They did not have a happy marriage. I saw the two sides of the story and then I could tell myself "that's wrong", so as not to repeat the same mistake. (HF30)

It can be seen from these two cases parental influence may not be deliberate. The woman entrepreneur witnessed her father in many situations and came to perceive aspects of him as weaknesses and strengths. The high-flyer saw why their parents often got into conflicts. They learnt from their parents' experiences and made their own judgement as to which of their behaviours they would and would not emulate.

One entrepreneur, with the opportunities brought about by his father (though might not be deliberately), developed an independence in social situations.

My father often brought me along to his social functions. I was very excited to meet so many people, adults and their children. I got used to mixing with people with ease. (E23)

While fostering a sense of independence and self-reliance, the parent-child relationships of the above successful individuals are indicative of two other common familial characteristics shared by most entrepreneurs and high-flyers. First, they were able to have a lot of interaction with their parents. While it is far from conclusive that the parental relationships experienced by the Hong Kong entrepreneurs and high-flyers were intimate, they can at least be described as close. Second, their parents involved them in a wide range of situations including their own personal activities. Parents took them to their workplace, brought them along to their social functions and engaged them in gatherings with relatives fairly frequently. The entrepreneurs and high-flyers came to know many aspects of the larger society at an early age, and they learnt how to cope with these aspects of life from their parents' experiences.

Hardworking Another success-related characteristic developed through parental influence in the entrepreneurs (15) and high-flyers (10) is their hardworking attribute.

> I remember the days when I sat beside my father watching him seeing his patients. We understood very well the money was earned with his blood and sweat. (HF28)

> I had my first paid job when I was thirteen. I worked in a restaurant as a labourer. It was my father's idea that I should go out and feel what it takes to earn each and every cent. I did find it a precious experience (E22)

> I spent a lot of time on studying since primary school. My parents insisted that if I wanted to achieve something, I must put efforts, more than others do. (HF26)

> I felt lots of love from my parents. They were very happy when I first got the best results in class. From then on, I always worked hard so that I didn't let them down. (HF29)

> My father closed his business when I was studying primary school, so I had to change to another school that cost cheaper but the quality was not so well. I realized then that every family member had to share responsibility for reducing their burden to the family. When I finished secondary school, I decided to find a job because my examination results were not good, and I did not want to repeat which would cause extra spending. I knew working hard could make my parents more comfortable. (E25)

In those days (when he was a small child) I think life was hard for everybody. We worked hard and we could tolerate hard work. So I think our generation came to learn to persevere. The young people I meet nowadays are so well-protected that they do not know how to handle crises. They just collapse in difficult times. (E26)

From these experiences, it can be seen that the entrepreneurs and high-flyers were not only hardworking literally, they were also willing to be hardworking, that is, they see it as a desirable attribute.

Parental Values

Apart from being influenced by their parents in aspects mentioned in the above section, the successful entrepreneurs and high-flyers reported they were influenced by their parents in value orientations.

The entrepreneurs and high-flyers were asked to identify what values they had inherited from their parents. Table 4.4 shows the values the entrepreneurs and high-flyers perceived they had inherited from their parents, and the figures shown in the Table represent the total counts for each of the values obtained from the Questionnaires. It is noted that 4 entrepreneurs and high-flyers did not think they had inherited any values from their parents.

The values identified in Table 4.4 are broad categories of goals that are important to the entrepreneurs and high-flyers. They are supposed to provide guiding principles for daily life behaviours.

Table 4.4   Parental Values

Values Acquired from Parents	Entrepreneurs	High-Flyers
Self-Respect	8	6
Integrity	10	9
Freedom	3	-
Wisdom	3	-
Accomplishment	6	9
Comfortable Life	5	7
Social recognition	2	6
Honesty	-	1
Mutual Trust	-	1
Contentment	2	1
Total subjects	26*	25*

* Four entrepreneurs and five high-flyers did not think they had inherited any values from their parents

As indicated in Table 4.4, the values emphasized by parents of the entrepreneurs and those of high-flyers are similar in most aspects. Parents of both groups stress behavioural virtues such as self-respect and integrity. The major differences between the two groups concern the values of freedom and wisdom which more entrepreneurs' parents emphasized and the values of accomplishment and comfortable life which more high-flyers' parents emphasized.

> My parents hold strongly to their principles. They refused to be slaves of the Japanese, so we gave up all we had here and returned to China. When we moved to Macau, none of the schools would take me because I was not born there and had no religious background and could not pay the expensive school fees in private school. So our parents, themselves as teachers, decided to teach me at home and I managed to get up to form three standard. They showed me freedom is important and we create freedom for ourselves. (E5)

> My father was very liberal in outlook. He thought that no one single way is the best way to succeed, and that we can learn from each and every experience we have. Experience builds wisdom. (HF26)

When contemplating the nature of all the values identified in Table 4.7, these values are basically of two types, one emphasizing an individual's behavioral virtues and obligations to society such as integrity and self-respect, and the other emphasizing an individual's pursuit of personal needs and rights such as comfortable life and social recognition.

The former type of values represent the Confucian ideals upheld in the traditional Chinese society. Proper individual conduct is seen as the foundation for a stable social and political entity. It seems natural that the parents of the entrepreneurs and high-flyers, being Chinese, emphasized such values.

> He taught me honesty and being accountable to society. We never cheated nor took advantage of others. We always pay our creditors on time, whereas we allow others to delay their payment to us. We learn to be contented, easily satisfied, because we can't take all the world has to give. (E13)

On the other hand, values such as achievement, comfortable life, freedom, social recognition are more related to personal enjoyment. All the parents of the successful entrepreneurs and the high-flyers are immigrants from Mainland China at different periods of time, mostly during the Japanese occupation of China and the subsequent civil war in the Mainland. Since it was not among the objectives of the present study to explore the social origins of their parents, the entrepreneurs and high-flyers were not asked to give details of the background and experiences of their parents. However some entrepreneurs and high-flyers, in describing their parents, gave a strong impression that their parents had experienced quite drastic changes as a result of the War and then the civil war. Moving to Hong Kong had posed a need for adjustment to a new social, economic and work environment. Some of the parents felt contented with having a place to settle down. However, a few of the parents were still haunted by memories of the hardships they had suffered. It is possible that surviving in a new environment engendered greater effort and determination to succeed, and greater aspiration for achievement and social recognition.

> We were very well off when I was young. There were many servants at home. My elder brother and sister were university graduates. The family moved to Hong Kong when the communists took over China. My father continued his business here and it began to decline. He was not familiar with the environment. He got very upset and retired. I and my younger siblings started to go through a difficult time. I went to work so as not to become a burden for the family. I studied and worked at the same time until I completed secondary school. (E5)

> Life was very hard in China. I always dreamt of going to Hong Kong which I thought was a land full of gold and opportunities. That was the impression I got from my father who had moved to Hong Kong. I decided to go there as well and so I swam all the way across Mirs Bay (the water between China and Hong Kong) and luckily I didn't get drowned. Life was not as good as I had imagined. My father and I had to work very hard but we still believed that one day we would get rich with our own hands. (E28)

These entrepreneurs clearly witnessed how their families had lost what they used to have which very much upset their fathers. Together with the strong attachment they had with their fathers, they were determined to recover the lost fortune and status.

Parents' Influence on Career Aspirations

Parental influence on the individual's career decisions can be explicit or subtle. In the former case, the parents of the entrepreneurs and high-flyers expressed clearly their expectations about what jobs they wanted their children to have and not to have, which is found to be very much related to their own occupation. Table 4.5 shows the occupation of the parents of the entrepreneurs and high-flyers.

Table 4.5   Parents' Occupation

Occupation	Entrepreneurs		High-Flyers	
	Father	Mother	Father	Mother
Self-employed	18	3	8	1
Professional	5	5	10	3
Clerical	2	-	5	1
Manual Labourer	3	1	3	5
Service	1	-	3	-
Fishing	1	-	-	-
Housewife	-	21	-	20
Unemployed	-	-	1	-
Total subjects	30	30	30	30

It is seen that more of the fathers of the entrepreneurs (60 percent) were self-employed whereas the majority of the high-flyers' fathers were professionals or self-employed (33 percent and 27 percent respectively). The mothers of most of the entrepreneurs and the high-flyers were housewives (70 percent and 67 percent respectively) with three of them as a whole helping their husbands in the family business. In their parents' time (around 1950s), the wives usually stayed at home and carried out the domestic functions whereas the husbands were the sole or principal breadwinners of the family.

The following interview transcripts demonstrate that directly observing what their parents did as a job had great impact on the career orientations of the entrepreneurs and high-flyers.

> I am very much influenced by my father since early childhood, including my choice of career and education. I accepted the need of my family. My father had established the business but he had not received much education, hence he wanted his children, someone he could trust, to help the family business. All my brothers and sisters are working in the company. About key persons in my life, I must mention my father. He put me in this company. (E13)

From my early childhood, I already knew my parents expected me to take over the family business and be successful. (E3)

I had worked in my father's mini-bank since 7 or 8. The thing I learnt from that is never invest in current assets. They can turn to nothing overnight. I was convinced that the most secured investment is fixed premises. (E30)

One entrepreneur had the opposite experience. His father expressed that he did not want him to follow his footsteps.

My father had his own business. But strangely enough he made it clear from the very beginning that he did not want any of us to inherit the business from him. The business was actually declining. He and his partners always argued. My father was very upset (about the conflicts with partners). He did not want us to experience what he had experienced before. (E20)

These expectations to a great extent reflect the parents' own unfinished business and that they considered their children an extension of themselves who could fulfil their own goals.

The two cases show how parents directly influenced their children's occupational choices. Parental influence can operate in other ways and still be powerful:

I think my motivation that I wanted to do a job which others couldn't look down on me was affected by my family. My mother is very concerned with face-saving. You know people residing in public estates live so close together that they like to compare with one another and like to be better off than their neighbours. This kind of face-saving made us not wanting to be looked down upon. I think this is the influence on my work concept. (HF18)

This experience of the high-flyer illustrates that the influence of parents was present at the psychological level, which can be true for other entrepreneurs and high-flyers. The influence simply came from everyday life interaction. They internalized what they observed and heard from their parents, and then became steered towards a certain orientation.

Childhood Deprivation

Most of the entrepreneurs and high-flyers reported having a happy childhood and not feeling themselves deprived in any way. Only seven entrepreneurs and four high-flyers reported experiences of deprivation in childhood, due to one of the following:-

1. Separation from father/both parents (2 entrepreneurs and 1 high-flyer)
2. Interrupted schooling/unsatisfactory education (3 entrepreneurs)
3. Cold family atmosphere/lack of support (3 high-flyers)
4. Poverty (2 entrepreneurs)

Separation from father/both parents   Five entrepreneurs and one high-flyer experienced separation from one or both parents in their childhood. However, only two of the entrepreneurs and the one high-flyer felt the separation, as a result of prolonged absence of father, a kind of deprivation. They described their deprivation as follows:-

The father of one entrepreneur died when he was around ten:

> My mother became the breadwinner. She was illiterate but she was very liberal. She worked very hard to make ends meet. The elder children, I am the second eldest, were made to look after the younger ones. I do wish my father could have lived to see my achievements. That's the only thing I feel deprived. (E19)

The other entrepreneur and the high-flyer reported their fathers were away from home working:

> I had a very lonely childhood. I was born in a wealthy family, my father was a very successful businessman who was always absent from home. My mother was a housewife who was very submissive to my father and emotionally reserved. I did not have someone close that I could talk to. All they cared was that I behaved well and follow his footsteps in my career. When I graduated from university, I decided to break away, to prove to him that I could do equally well without his blessings. (E16)

Prolonged absence of father has quite a different impact on one woman high-flyer:

> My mother and I emigrated to Canada when I was twelve, and I studied high school there. My father stayed in Hong Kong to earn money. I knew why he made such a decision but I did not like it to happen. My mother and I worked very hard in a foreign environment. Being the eldest I had to take care of my sisters. I seemed to have taken up my father's role. My mother was strong in character. I learned to be like her. I began to make decisions independently for myself and the family. (HF7)

This woman high-flyer, though expressing negative feeling about being separated from her father at a formative stage of her development, did not report feeling of loneliness. She had a mother to whom she was attached and on whom she could model. In addition, her siblings could also give her company.

Three other entrepreneurs did not feel any impact as a result of separation from one or both of their parents:

> I was brought up by my grandparents. My parents had to look after the family business which was going through a difficult time. I was very attached to my grandparents. My parents often came to see me so we could still maintain a close relationship. (E21)

> My father died when I was young. My elder siblings had already started working and I had been rather independent. His death did not affect us a lot. (E12)

> When I was three, my parents sent me back to Shanghai (his place of birth) to be looked after by my grandfather after my twin sisters were born. My parents could not afford to look after three children at the same time because they had to work for a living. That was a period in which I learnt to be independent and I quite enjoyed the freedom and the time I had with my grandpa. (E26)

It can be seen from the above accounts of the entrepreneurs and the high-flyer that separation from father had encouraged a sense of responsibility and a hard-driving attitude. However separation itself does not necessarily instill a feeling of deprivation. In the absence of one parent or both, the other parent and the family network become decisive. The child can count on the staying parent as well as other family members for coping with the separation.

Interrupted schooling/unsatisfactory education   Three entrepreneurs expressed sorrow for being deprived of proper education in their childhood.   One of them were interrupted in their schooling due to the Second World War:

> Due to the War, our family had to move around.   I did not experience formal education though my parents were teachers and they taught me at home.   However I felt I had missed something in life. (E11)

The second entrepreneur felt angry with his father who had sent him to a mediocre primary school:

> I am somewhat angry that my father sent me to this primary school and not to a better one.   I think I had the ability to study in a more prestigious school so that I might receive better education and peer influence, and that my ability could be maximized. (E24)

The third entrepreneur was changed to a school lower in standard because of worsening family financial situation, and thought his learning was much affected:

> When I got there (the new school), I easily became the top in the class because I had learnt most of the things before in the old school.   When there was no one to compete with, I lost the momentum to push myself to do better.   In the end I got very poor   secondary school entrance examination results, I could not enter a proper secondary school nor the university of course.   The chained effects were there, so I realized it is important to have good education from the beginning. (E25)

Cold family atmosphere/lack of support   Three high-flyers claimed their families had little communication and were not supportive.   They had an intense feeling of loneliness.

> We lived under the same roof but it looked like we didn't know one another.   I became very independent that way. (HF25)

Poverty   Two entrepreneurs talked of the bitterness of experiencing poverty in his childhood.

I think of what I didn't get when I was young. I think of this everyday. I didn't have a rich material life. So now I have to take revenge. Because I have the need, I have an urge. I always need new things. I need new challenge. I need a new level of satisfaction. It maybe the driving force. (E9)

We were extremely poor when I was young especially after my father's death. We had no shoes to wear. We went to everywhere with bare feet. I can still remember how hard it felt, the physical pain and also the discrimination of others on us. I had always wanted to have a lot of money so that I did not have to suffer this anymore. (E29)

However, others who mentioned they had a poor childhood did not feel poverty had affected their enjoyment of a contented childhood.

I am not anxious about money, because I had been poor before. I had experienced the worst and I could still survive. I am willing to be patient and allow time for the business to grow. (E7)

The entrepreneurs and high-flyers indicated that though they were poor, they were able to enjoy what other children had when they compared themselves with their relatives, their neighbours, their schoolmates, in terms of living conditions, education, toys, attention from parents, etc. Hence they felt they had a normal childhood without any major deprivation and regret. However it seems the entrepreneurs and high-flyers are suggesting a kind of perceived deprivation rather than real deprivation. They did not have what they wanted, but when everyone around had the same situation, that is when poverty or deprivation was normalized, they would not regard and feel themselves as particularly deprived.

Many of them complain life is not satisfactory. But look back to when we were children, the people that we knew mostly lived in poor conditions. This made us feel poverty was more acceptable. And what could we do so that life could be better? It urged ourselves to seek improvement. (HF7)

I lived my early days in poverty. My friends were also poor so I didn't feel I was under-privileged. It's hard but I don't feel we are worse off than others. (E5)

Watershed Events

Not every successful entrepreneur and high-flyer has experienced such an event in childhood. Two entrepreneurs and four high-flyers mentioned experiencing a watershed event in childhood:

- broke leg when six years old, received six operations and was hospitalized for one and a half years, came to recognize death and that nothing is forever (E15)
- being caught lying, felt greatly embarrassed and shameful, became very concerned with face-saving (E27)
- emigrated to Canada, had to start all over again (HF7)
- very poor results in public examination, ending up in a bad secondary school which he feels to be a great failure as a person. His subsequent life has been characterized by a theme of wanting to prove himself through attaining academic qualifications. (HF18)
- entered a technical secondary school laying a good foundation for a career in engineering (HF24)
- obtained a scholarship to enter a good secondary school, without which the high-flyer would not have been able to further his study because of the stringent family finance (HF25)

Apart from these individuals, six entrepreneurs and six high-flyers reported watershed events occurring at a later stage of their life. Among all the events mentioned, having the opportunity for further study is regarded by one entrepreneur and five high-flyers as their watershed event.

> I had to give up study after Form 3 and started working. I continued my study in evening school and finally completed O-level. It was very difficult to both study and work at the same time, but I never thought of giving up the study. When I was better off, I always went to short courses. Now I am doing a MBA, which I find very stimulating. (E28)

> I left for Japan at 17, still very young. But I was forced to learn to be independent, self-reliant and self-disciplined. (HF15)

After I had graduated from secondary school, my father asked me to work but my mother insisted that I went to university. I therefore very much treasure every opportunity to have further study. (HF26)

Other watershed events include experiences in school/boarding school learning a lot about people (4 entrepreneurs), the opportunity to get into an elite boarding school receiving good education and an excellent set of values (1 entrepreneur), participation in social services such as girl guides (1 high-flyer).

It is evident that educational experiences constitute the watershed events for the majority of the successful entrepreneurs and high-flyers. These educational experiences offer opportunities for not only formal education but also social exposures.

There is one common point in all the reported watershed events. They offered exposures bringing new insight to the individual, allowing him/her to build up strengths which were not there previously, to see the world from new perspectives, to handle things in different manners and to rechart one's course of life.

Summary

The findings on the childhood of the successful entrepreneurs and the high-flyers indicate there are similarities as well as differences between the two groups.

Both the successful entrepreneurs and the high-flyers had experienced a close relationship with their parents all of whom were immigrants from Mainland China after the Second World War or during or after the civil rivalry in China around 1949. Their parents had to build up the families with rather weak financial and social bases in a new environment. Though living in poor conditions, the entrepreneurs and high-flyers recalled having a happy and contented childhood. It was because they realized the people they knew were also poor. The entrepreneurs and high-flyers had developed a high sensitivity to their environment and the people therein through being exposed to different social situations by their parents. In addition, they were able to observe and learn from their parents' experiences in these situations. These vicarious experiences, coupled with the direct experiences with their parents, had helped to foster a strong sense of independence, self-reliance and hardworking in the growing entrepreneurs and high-flyers.

There are three major differences between the entrepreneurs and the high-flyers.

1. More of the entrepreneurs were influenced by their fathers and less by their mothers
2. More of the entrepreneurs' fathers were self-employed
3. More of the entrepreneurs' parents stressed values such as wisdom and freedom while more of the high-flyers' parents held values such as accomplishment and social recognition

It seems that the fathers of the entrepreneurs who were self-employed had played a key role in providing the antecedents for their children, such as their self-employment experiences and values, to set onto an entrepreneurial course.

Childhood Experiences and Career Success

With reference to the findings on the childhood experiences of the successful entrepreneurs and high-flyers, an attempt was made to conceptualize their childhood experiences and their impact on the individuals, which is shown in Figure 4.2 below.

Figure 4.2 A Conceptualization of the Childhood Experiences and Their Impact on the Successful Entrepreneurs and High-Flyers

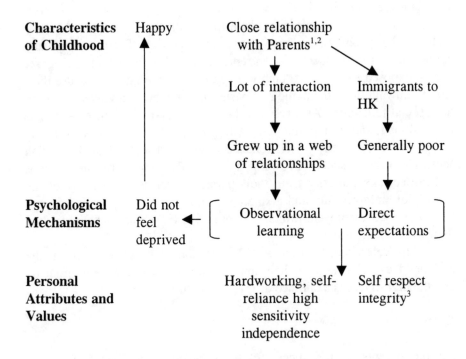

Note: The numbers in superscript indicate the major differences found between the entrepreneurs and the high-flyers

1   More of the entrepreneurs were influenced more by their fathers and less by their mothers
2   More of the entrepreneurs' fathers were self-employed
3   More of the entrepreneurs' parents stressed values such as wisdom and freedom while more of the high-flyers, parents held values such as accomplishment and social recognition

As shown in Figure 4.2, the parents of the successful entrepreneurs and the high-flyers were immigrants from Mainland China. Most of them had to bring up their children with rather weak financial and social bases in a new environment. Though living in poor conditions, the entrepreneurs and high-flyers recalled having a normal, happy and contented childhood, because they enjoyed close relationship with their parents and they realized the people they knew were also poor. There were many opportunities for the successful entrepreneurs and high-flyers to recognize and be exposed to the social environment outside the family because their parents always told them their experiences and even involved them in their social functions. As a result of both direct and vicarious experiences in childhood, the entrepreneurs and high-flyers had developed a strong sense of independence, self-reliance and hardworking and a high sensitivity to their social environment. They also acquired values such as self-respect and integrity from their parents. Furthermore many of the successful entrepreneurs and a smaller number of high-flyers had fathers who were self-employed, which is thought to have important impact on their own career orientations.

With reference to Figure 4.2, the intricate relationship of the childhood experiences and their impact on the successful entrepreneurs and the high-flyers is examined at greater depth.

Parents' Social Origins

All the parents of the successful entrepreneurs and high-flyers were immigrants from China, and four of the successful entrepreneurs were born in China and migrated to Hong Kong at an early age.

The need to survive in a new environment could generate powerful motivation for achievement and success, particularly for those who refused to accept the fact that they had become worse off than before. The parents of the successful entrepreneurs and high-flyers resembled the first generation of Chinese immigrants in many Asian countries such as Thailand, Vietnam, Indonesia, Singapore and Malaysia who had worked hard to settle down, and eventually the Chinese dominate the economies of these countries. Indeed, the histories of many economically developed and developing countries, with the United States being the classic example, illustrate that their immigrant population have contributed much to their prosperity. Immigrants are particularly hardworking and innovative because they will have to succeed by means apart from the established conventional paths to which they have more difficult access.

Parental Influence

Parents influence their children in a variety of ways. The way they bring up and relate to their children has long-lasting impact on the latter's self-concept, including their personality, motivation, values and beliefs, and behaviours in daily situations. Chinese parents are particularly significant in shaping their children's course of development because families are the basic unit around which the life of their members is organized. In addition, Chinese parents in tradition are accorded special authority over their descendants as a means to maintain social order and its associated structuring of relationships. Without exceptions, the successful entrepreneurs and high-flyers were greatly influenced by their parents. The following examines the parental influences which are found common in their childhood and are significantly related to their career success: the nature of the relationship with their parents and achievement orientation; the way they were brought up in a web of relationships and a high sensitivity; familial origins of their locus of control orientation; familial origins of high tolerance of stress; parents' social origins and their career orientation; and parents' work values and their own work ethics.

Nature of the parent-child relationship and its impact on achievement-related personality and orientation A normal or happy childhood was reported by 90 percent of the successful entrepreneurs and high-flyers. They described having close relationship with parents, and enjoying pleasurable peer and siblings activities. Only 10 percent of the entrepreneurs and high-flyers described their relationship with parents as cold and hostile, whereas 18 percent of them claim they had a particularly intimate relationship with parents.

Achievement-striving personality - independence and self-reliance, hardworking The quality of parent-child relationship is highly related to personality development particularly achievement striving orientation.[1] A common remark made by the successful entrepreneurs and high-flyers was their parents had helped cultivate a strong sense of self-reliance and independence. Most claimed they had parents who were liberal and did not exert too many expectations on them.   Such liberal attitude was conceived to be a result of pragmatic considerations rather than an intentional parenting style.   One of the conclusions made by Ho (1986, p.35) in his review of studies on Chinese patterns of socialization is that traditionally, great emphasis was placed on obedience, proper conduct, moral training, and the acceptance of social obligations, in contrast to the lack of emphasis placed on independence, assertiveness, and creativity. The sense of independence and self-reliance developed in the successful entrepreneurs and high-flyers was due to their parents' attention being shifted to other areas of life.   It is found that none of the successful entrepreneurs and high-flyers are the only child.   They all have sibling(s). They were not given exclusive care and concern from parents, reducing the possibility of their being overprotected.   It has been shown that parental overprotection deters the child's ability to tolerate frustration and to explore on his/her own initiative (Hoffman, 1972, Collard, 1964, Ho, 1986).   Besides, many of the successful entrepreneurs and high-flyers had an financially poor childhood when their fathers were usually busy working outside the home for long hours, leaving the responsibility of child-care to their mothers.   Although most of their mothers were housewives and were supposed to have more attention on the entrepreneurs and high-flyers, this attention was shared by their siblings, therefore very often they were left to look after themselves in daily life matters, even in studying.   As a result, the successful entrepreneurs and the high-flyers were trained to be independent and self-reliant since childhood.

Although it appears that the liberal attitude in parenting was developed out of pragmatic considerations, it does not mean the entrepreneurs' and the high-flyers' parents did not truly care about them. The majority of the successful entrepreneurs and the high-flyers (90 percent) enjoyed close parental relationship.   Many recalled, in an affectional way, very detailed episodes of experiences with their parents.

Achievement motivation   The need for achievement is found to be the most important motivational force for the majority of the successful entrepreneurs (60 percent) and one-third of the high-flyers (37 percent).

Higher achievement motivation is related to positive parental attitudes towards their children (Ho, 1986).   The close parental relationship enjoyed by the successful entrepreneurs and high-flyers had provided a safe psychological environment for the emergence of the achievement motivation in them.

In addition, six entrepreneurs and nine high-flyers claimed they directly picked up the value of accomplishment and achievement from their parents. It is mentioned above that not many of the successful entrepreneurs and high-flyers were expected to accomplish anything specific, however, they were constantly observing what their parents (especially the fathers) did in their work and took it as a reference for setting their personal goals. One entrepreneur remembered clearly what his father said to him and his father's ambition became his own ambition:

> He told me this, The houses there were so beautiful. They sure cost a fortune. I must have one for myself one day. He did not get one (house) in that district but he did manage to own a big house twenty years later. I was very impressed by his determination to achieve his goal and I learnt to be determined in whatever I do knowing that I will succeed in the end. (E24)

The achievement motivation is not only confined to material needs, it generally represents the drive to be successful in attaining one's goals, whatever these goals may be. It is also important to note that having goals is only a necessary but not a sufficient condition for success. The individual must also have the determination and the ability to realize the goals, hence success can be measured by the outcome of action. Indeed, determination and hard work are among the most important personal qualities leading to career success.

Growing up in a web of relationships and high sensitivity From the childhood experiences they described, the successful entrepreneurs and high-flyers did not just associate with the parents in the home, but their parents brought them along to their work and social environments, and even to unusual occasions such as the law court on matters relating to the parents. They grew up amid continuing or frequent contacts with a number of related individuals besides his own parents and siblings, thereby nurturing a collectivistic orientation. Being collectivistic means preferring a tightly knit social framework in which individuals can expect their relatives, clan, or other in-group to look after them in exchange for unquestioning loyalty (Hofstede, 1980). Very early in life they were conditioned to getting along with a wide circle of relatives and to appreciate the importance of differing circumstances. This is especially true for those successful entrepreneurs and high-flyers who were brought up in an extended family environment where they lived with grandparents and/or kinsmen under the same roof. Hsu (1981) remarks that the point of departure in the early experiences of Chinese and American children is that the Chinese child learns to see the world in terms of a network of relationships, but his/her American counterpart grows up in much greater physical isolation and is not used to associating with a set of relationships. As a result, the Chinese child learns to be *sensitive to his/her environment* and becomes situation-oriented.

On the other hand, the successful entrepreneurs and high-flyers came to understand their parents from different perspectives. Many of them were able to describe their parents with reference to a variety of aspects, for instance, how they related to others, how they approached work, and what they did was being reinforced. They learned the rules of the game through their parents' experiences of success and failure. This learning was very much a social learning process in which the child, through modelling on the parents, acquired attitudes and behaviours that were reinforced, forming a favourable basis on which success-related qualities were developed.

Since the successful entrepreneurs and high-flyers grew up in constant, close contact with the adult world, they were well-prepared to deal with the complicated interpersonal dynamics in a competitive business world. Hsu (1981, pp.89) remarks that Chinese youngsters enter into the adult world unobtrusively in the course of their mental and physical growth. From the beginning they participate in real life, not in an artificially roped-off sector of it. One entrepreneur points out the key for his success is his sensitivity to the social environment which had been developed over the years since childhood. The high sensitivity to social environment leads to the development of the flexible personality and the contingent management approach that characterized many successful entrepreneurs and high-flyers.

That the successful entrepreneurs and high-flyers came to see themselves in a web of relationships and well understood the importance of these relationships for their personal survival suggests a networked self, a term used by Redding (1993, p.63). The self is embedded in relationships, inextricable from them, and not thought of as independent of such attachment. This networked self certainly affects the psychological composition of the successful entrepreneurs and the high-flyers, which is evidenced in their personality and management approach which shall be discussed in later sections of this Chapter.

Familial origins of locus of control   Rotter (1966) hypothesized that an internal locus of control orientation is more highly related to achievement and success than an external orientation. As measured by Levenson's IPC Inventory, the successful entrepreneurs and the high-flyers show a high tendency to believe in internal control. The childhood experiences of the successful entrepreneurs and high-flyers in relation to their parent-child relationship are found to favour the development of an internal locus of control orientation. Lefcourt (1982) in a review of studies investigating the relationship between parental child-rearing practices and the development of locus of control suggests that the research findings show impressive consistency, given the different age groups in the samples and the diversity of procedures and measures employed for ascertaining locus of control and familial relationships. The research findings he refers to indicate a supportive, positive relationship between a child and his/her parents fosters an internal locus of control, while a relationship characterized by punishment, rejection and control encourages an external orientation.

The nature of the parent-child relationship of the majority of the successful entrepreneurs and high-flyers which was shown to have fostered a sense of independence and self-reliance in them is also contributive to the development of an internal locus. Their parent-child relationship was close and positive. The parents were described as liberal, showing concern for their children in a way that was not imposing nor pampering, eager to share their own experiences which became useful advice to the successful entrepreneurs and the high-flyers. All these suggest parental support, warmth and encouragement that are likely to develop in the children an internal locus.

However, there is 10 percent of the successful entrepreneurs and high-flyers reporting cold or hostile relationship with their parents when they were children, but they were also found to show a high internality. Crandall (1973) found that coolness and criticality on the mother's part was positively associated with an internal locus of control. Crandall suggests that the internal individual has experienced a greater 'push from the nest' than the external individual. This push puts the individual into more active intercourse with his/her physical and social environment, giving more opportunity to observe the effects of this behaviour uninfluenced by maternal intervention.

In summarizing the impact of the parent-child relationship of the successful entrepreneurs and high-flyers on their internality, it is thought that warm, caring and supportive parental behaviours were necessary for the assumption of personal responsibility during childhood, but these behaviours were not excessive to discourage internality in the long run. Perhaps internality was best facilitated by some degree of parental non-intervention and criticality so that the successful entrepreneurs and high-flyers did not become overly dependent on their parents, but were made to learn and differentiate cause and effect contingencies, recognize their own instrumentality in causing those outcomes and set goals for themselves.

Apart from encouraging the development of internality, there are aspects of the successful entrepreneurs' and the high-flyers' childhood experiences which would foster a belief in the control by powerful others. The successful entrepreneurs and the high-flyers were said to have grown up in a web of relationships, hence developed a sense of interdependency within the network of relationships and a high sensitivity to the social environment suggesting a situational orientation. These experiences which result in an emphasis on relationships would make the successful entrepreneurs and high-flyers prone to the influence of powerful others.

It is found that there is a strong negative correlation between the high-flyers' internality and powerful others scores, whereas such correlation is weak for the successful entrepreneurs. It appears that childhood experiences have greater influence on the control orientations of the successful entrepreneurs, whereas the high-flyers' control orientations may have been shaped by later developmental experiences apart from familial origins. An overall examination of the locus of control orientation is given under the section on work motivation below.

Familial origins of high tolerance of stress Many successful entrepreneurs and high-flyers reckoned that life was hard since childhood, but the majority did not feel they were deprived of anything. They observed how their parents triumphed over difficulties, particularly the remaining parent in those cases of separation from father. In fact, twenty two successful entrepreneurs and high-flyers (37 percent) identified perseverance[2] and similar attributes such as hardworking, stubbornness and determination as their personal attribute for career success. In addition they enjoyed close relationship with parents and siblings, and through a sensitivity to the social environment, they understood their hardships were shared, thereby alleviating the bitterness. Difficulties were counteracted by positive attitudes and family support. Hsu (1981, p.13) remarks that the individual Chinese is tied closer to his/her social environment, hence his/her happiness and sorrow tend to be milder since they are shared.

At present, many successful entrepreneurs and high-flyers perceive stress and difficulties as part of life, as a driving force, as opportunities for growth. One may argue these perceptions are rationalizations serving as psychological defense. Nevertheless, when backed up by strong family support, these perceptions were turned into constructive action leading to an increased ability to deal with difficulties. In fact, perseverance, stubbornness and determination are identified by nine entrepreneurs and high-flyers as their key personal qualities for career success.

Parents' values and work ethic The values emphasized by parents of the entrepreneurs and those of high-flyers are quite similar. Parents of both groups stress behavioural virtues such as self-respect and integrity reflecting the traditional Confucian ideals. These ideals would make a composed individual, which will contribute to bringing about harmonious interpersonal relationships, and a stable social and political entity. These parental values emphasize a collectivistic orientation.

On the other hand, individual-oriented values like achievement, comfortable life, freedom were also advocated by a smaller number of parents. Being forced to move to Hong Kong as a result of the Second World War and the subsequent civil war in the Mainland, these parents had to survive in a new environment and start all over again. They had a strong desire to recover what they had lost, thereby inculcating in the young hearts values like comfortable life, achievement, and social recognition.

Due to their close ties with their parents, the entrepreneurs and high-flyers were very much inspired by their parents in their approach to life, including work and career.

Parents and career orientations   A significant finding in relation to parental influence on the career orientations of the successful entrepreneurs and high-flyers is that 60 percent and 27 percent respectively of their fathers were self-employed. These percentages are higher than that of self-employment in the British male labour force which is 9 percent. In a study of Shanghainese textile industrialists in Hong Kong, Wong (1988, p.58) found that half of the respondents came from families with industrial experience, at least 30 percent had been engaged in the spinning industry for two generations, and 15 percent had fathers operating other kinds of factories, showing a moderate degree of occupational inheritance and accumulation of occupation-related experience.

As suggested above, the fathers in Chinese families exert a more direct influence on their children on crucial matters such as education and career. The self-employed father certainly had a strong modelling effect on the successful entrepreneurs in their decisions to be their own boss. Four of the entrepreneurs took over the family business and transformed it into a more successful business. Eleven entrepreneurs started their own business.

However, having a self-employed father does not necessarily lead to the decision of starting one's own business. Eight high-flyers had self-employed fathers but they chose to work for someone else.

It can be suggested that having self-employed parent(s) is a strong correlational factor for success in career. However it is not a decisive factor for one's career decision of starting own business or working for someone else.

Link to Success - Childhood Experiences Laying a Solid Foundation for Achievement

Super (1957) suggests that the adequacy of a career decision will partially depend upon the similarity between the individual's self-concept and the vocational concept of the career that he/she chooses. Bond (1993) states that self-concept is constituted by constructs of values, traits and beliefs, and one's self-concept then becomes one's perceived location in this geography of values or traits or beliefs relative to the location of other persons or other groups. Bond goes on to point out that Hong Kong presents a psychological environment where one might well expect identity concerns to be salient to the local Chinese. They are children of a diverse group of migrants from China in daily contact with the trappings of a colonial power. However, for a child, his/her family remains the most important aspect of life and hence its influence the most decisive with regard to socialization and value identification.

The families of the successful entrepreneurs and high-flyers were found to have provided them with a happy childhood and close relationship, helping to nurture the qualities of independence and self-reliance, hardworking, high sensitivity to the social environment. Through encountering economic hardships, the successful entrepreneurs and high-flyers learnt to deal with and developed a positive attitude towards difficulties, increasing their tolerance of stress. They were also taught the value of proper conduct, and learnt the importance of mutual support. All of these qualities are perceived by the entrepreneurs and high-flyers to have paved the way to success in their career.

Notes

1   See White, B (1992). *Women's Career Development* for a comprehensive review on the link between the qualitative nature of parent-child relationship and achievement striving behaviours.

2   Perseverance is a hard to define but nevertheless significant trait found in the Chinese. The literal meaning is long-term endurance, but more than this, it infers the willingness to defer gratification, or even the willingness to endure suffering for a distant goal.

5 Education

A significant portion of an average individual's life is spent in schools engaging in some form of educational activities. This chapter examines the educational characteristics of successful entrepreneurs and high-flyers and whether they exhibit distinctive educational profiles from those of the general population.

Educational Level

Walsh and Osipow (1983) have stated that educational level is one of the most powerful predictors of career achievement in both men and women. This is especially true in large organizations where they have a clearly defined and structured career system in which there is minimum requirement for educational qualifications for each and every post.

In Firth's study of high-flyers (1987), 66 percent of them completed a degree, and 50 percent went on to do graduate work of some sort, which suggests the high flyers were highly educated. The *Wall Street Journal* study in 1978 found that 6percent of American managers had reached high school level, 40 percent university graduates, 35 percent masters and 13 percent doctorate. Whereas Margerison (1980) discovered that 65 percent of British managers had at least a first degree.

Cox and Cooper (1988) found that less than half of their CEOs had university degrees, four of whom had postgraduate qualifications. The remaining twenty-four CEOs had all left school between the ages of 14 and 16. Cox and Cooper suggest that the low level of qualifications achieved by their CEOs may be exaggerated by their age. Most of them were in their fifties, indicating that they grew up at a time when educational opportunities were not as easily accessible as they are at present. Besides, they might have experienced interrupted schooling due to the War. It is thought that the next generation of business leaders will show a higher proportion of graduates, as the trend into higher education increases. On the other hand, White (1992) contends that the rates obtained in both the *Wall Street Journal* and Margerison studies may be due to the postal survey method employed in data collection which tends to result in higher response rate by the more highly qualified managers.

In a study which compares entrepreneurs and intrapreneurs by Jennings, Cox and Cooper (1994), it was found that 68 percent of their intrapreneurs were university graduates compared with only 21 percent of entrepreneurs.

The successful women in White's study (1992) have attained a high level of education. Approximately 50 percent have a degree, compared to only 6 percent of British women in general.

Apart from formal education, professional training and qualification is equally important, perhaps more in some cases, for career success and advancement in the new technological society.

Professional Qualifications

The importance of professional qualifications can be analysed in a number of aspects. First, professional qualifications give a licence to practice and they have universal validity. These qualifications are transferable, hence enabling movement between employers and settings. Brown (1982) suggested three strategies underlying individual choices and actions in relation to employment:

1. The entrepreneurial strategy - resources are developed such that self-employment is possible.
2. The organizational strategy - advancement is sought within an employing organization.
3. The occupational strategy - skills are required to enable movement between employers.

Crompton and Sanderson (1986) claim that qualifications can be thought of as lying along a continuum relating to these employment strategies. Pure occupational qualifications (referred to as professional qualifications herein) lie on one end of the continuum. At the opposite end of the continuum are pure organizational qualifications which are seen as a necessary element of a linear career. They may include 'in-house training', which is used to identify individuals as promotion material. These qualifications, unlike professional qualifications, are not transferable. Crompton and Sanderson further state that occupational qualifications may be used to pursue both entrepreneurial and occupational career strategies. These qualifications are a universal guarantee of competence, which facilitate upward movement or movement between employers. It is argued that professional qualifications can also be used to pursue the organizational strategy. More and more organizations are using these qualifications in the same way as they are using educational attainment as one of the considerations for recruitment and/or promotion particularly to a professional post. It is because such qualifications represent standards of a professional discipline. They assure the professional capability of the holder of the qualifications, and in a way safeguarding the reputation of the organization.

Management Training and Qualifications

A study by the British Institute of Management (Firth, 1987) suggests that few of the 90,000 managers entering management each year have had any prior formal management training at all.

Kakabadse and Margerison (1985), when comparing their study of 711 American CEOs and the British chief executives surveyed by Margerison earlier, observe that becoming the head of a major company seems to be a very personal developmental process independent of the organization or educational system.

> The results seems to suggest that CEOs see themselves, first, as individuals who have worked hard, hold unique styles and approaches to managing, and are sincerely attempting to act on their responsibilities toward the organization and its employees. Their credibility and successful performance do not stem from the fact that they are corporate people who follow a corporate line. In fact the tension between personal views and 4 corporate ways of doing things causes frequent difficulties. Rather they are people who have achieved success by developing their skills - in dealing with people and organizational problems.

The picture that emerges from these reports is one of management development in reality continuing to be a matter of pragmatic experience. The academic endeavour of the last 20 years seems to have had little impact.

The women entrepreneurs in the study of Hisrich and Brush (1986) expressed educational needs in the areas of finance, strategic planning, marketing, and management. Entrepreneurs had indicated the importance of being able to deal with people and communicate clearly. Margerison (1980) opined that off-the-job training would likely be an influence in the years to come. Special long term programmes such as MBAs are attracting more and more of the rising generation of managers.

These studies indicate that managers, especially the more recent generation of managers, have generally attained higher qualifications. Apart from increasing educational opportunities being available, entrepreneurs and managers are likely to hold different views of the need for advanced training due to their different work situations. It is thought that managers will consider management knowledge and skills more imperative for their jobs. They are held accountable for the functions assigned to them. Their career prospect is linked with how well they can get the job done. Hence high-flyers are more in need for anything that can better equip themselves for the job, including professional qualifications and management training.

The Chinese Conception of Education

Chinese parents hold a serious attitude towards their children's education, hence the younger generation are influenced to go for more as well as higher level educational qualifications. These common people admitted their lowly status and deferred in speech and contact to members of the literati-bureaucracy. Hsu (1981) discussed the Chinese attitude towards a change in status which is revealed in two terms: 'newly rich', and 'recently prominent'. The former is self-explanatory, and the latter describes those who have recently climbed the bureaucratic ladder. The first kind of people were sometimes slighted and ridiculed, but the second kind of people were accepted at once.

Due to its respectable position in society, a place in the literati-bureaucracy was aspired to by the common people, and success in examinations became the key for upward social mobility. The top scholar of the capital city examination was given the honour to come before the emperor. If the emperor prized the scholar, the latter would even be arranged to marry a princess and became member of the royal family. Fame and wealth, not only for the scholar himself, but for his whole family, would definitely follow suit.

Such perception of education is still prevalent in the Hong Kong modern society. Parents pay every effort to secure, for their child, a place in a good kindergarten, primary school, and secondary school. Competition in schools is very keen. Academic achievement is a major indicator of a child's ability. If a teenager cannot enter a local university, some parents will use up the family's savings to support the teenager to study in an overseas university, in the belief that academic qualifications is a determinant for a decent job.

Educational Characteristics of Hong Kong Successful Entrepreneurs and High-Flyers

The study examined the successful career people's personal characteristics in relation to the educational level they had achieved, their professional qualifications, and the management training received. Their perception of education, professional qualifications and management training, and their respective importance was also examined.

Highest Educational Level

Table 5.1 shows the highest educational level of the entrepreneurs and high-flyers interviewed in the current study.

It is quite obvious from Table 5.1 that more high-flyers achieved higher level of educational qualifications than the successful entrepreneurs. All of the high-flyers received post-secondary education, 93 percent (27) have at least a bachelor degree, and one-third of them (9) even have a master's degree. With regard to entrepreneurs, successful careers appear to correlate less strongly with educational level. Only 19 of them (63 percent) received post-secondary education.

Table 5.1 Highest Educational Level of Entrepreneurs and High-Flyers

Educational Level	Entrepreneurs		High-Flyers	
Below O-level	2	(7%)	-	
O-Level	9	(30%)	-	
Diploma/Certificate	3 (1)	(10%)	2	(7%)
Bachelor	11 (9)	(36%)	19 (13)	(63%)
Master	2 (2)	(7%)	7 (1)	(23%)
Ph D	3 (1)	(10%)	2 (2)	(7%)
Total subjects	30		30	

Note: The figure shown in brackets indicates the qualification is obtained in an overseas institution.

Subject of education The subject distribution of the bachelor degree of the Hong Kong entrepreneurs and high-flyers is given in Table 5.2. The three entrepreneurs and the two high-flyers who hold a high diploma are also included because it is thought that the training is at a tertiary level and is related to their future career choices. More than half of the qualifications obtained are related to professional subjects such as engineering, banking, law, business administration, surveying.

Table 5.2   Subject of Education of Hong Kong Entrepreneurs and High-Flyers

Subject	Entrepreneurs	High-Flyers
Banking	-	2
Marketing	-	1
Business Studies	1	-
Arts	-	2
Science	2	2
Food Science	-	1
Social Sciences	-	3
Engineering	10	14
Law	2	-
Business Administration	1	4
Surveying	1	1
Fine Art	1	-
Others	1	-
Total subjects	19	30

The choice of subject of education itself reflects individual preference which may involve the influence from significant others and their perception of the current structure of opportunities. Such perception is vividly recited by one male entrepreneur:

> I studied industrial engineering. At the same time I went to fine arts courses. In fact I took more credits in fine arts than I did in industrial engineering. (You asked me why) Well I like fine arts, that's my lifetime interest, but you've got to eat, right? You've got to be realistic. So I chose a practical subject. I have never given up my interest in fine arts. I plan to go back to fine arts after my retirement at 50, when I can do anything I want. (E20)

The choice of subject is not only an educational decision, but also to a very large extent a career decision.

Professional qualifications

Twelve entrepreneurs (40 percent) and seventeen high-flyers (57 percent) indicate in the Questionnaire they possess professional qualifications. These qualifications are mainly of two kinds: degree in a professional discipline or membership of a professional body. Both represent a license to practice in a particular profession, often constituting the basic entry requirement to a professional post. Professional qualifications are very much closely related to the subject of undergraduate education. More than 50 percent of the entrepreneurs and high-flyers chose professional disciplines.

The successful entrepreneurs and high-flyers had suggested in the interviews that they liked to become members of a professional body and participate in its activities because all these could provide opportunities to meet people in the field and establish personal and organizational connections, which is important for career advancement and business development.

Management Training and Qualifications

The successful entrepreneurs and high-flyers were all heavily involved in some kind of management functions, such as personnel management, financial management. Their approach to management was developed partly from experience, and partly from taking management courses. Table 5.3 illustrates the patterns of management training received by the successful entrepreneurs and high-flyers.

Table 5.3 Management Training

Management training	Entrepreneurs	High-Flyers
Short course	3	4
Diploma in management	1	-
BBA or equivalent	1	4
Postgraduate diploma in management	3	2
MBA or equivalent	*4**	*7**
Total (percent of total subjects)	12 (40%)	17 (57%)

* One entrepreneur and two of the high-flyers are in the course of completing their MBA programmes.

It can be seen that more high-flyers (57 percent) than entrepreneurs (40 percent) have received some kind of management training, ranging from short courses to formal management degree education. There is no one exclusively popular form of management training for the entrepreneurs, whereas nearly half of the high-flyers had management training (7 out of 16) have taken or are taking MBA programmes.

The figures reflects another interesting phenomenon that most of the entrepreneurs and high-flyers received their management training in the course of their career development. Only one of the entrepreneurs and four of the high-flyers had a bachelor's degree in business administration, whilst the rest started off their careers with no specialized training in management. Instead they came to realize the need for management training when they gradually took up management responsibilities. Many of the Hong Kong entrepreneurs and high-flyers took self-initiated efforts to secure their management training by paying for their own training fees and using after-office hours and/or annual leave to attend courses and complete coursework.

Management training is seen as important but not absolutely essential. This is particularly so in the case of the successful entrepreneurs. It is due to the their role in the organization. The entrepreneurs are the boss. They have a better say about what they themselves like to do and what can be delegated to staff. One entrepreneur has stated this perception very clearly:

> I have attended conferences but not any (management) courses ... though I think it's necessary. (But) I'am a little bit dependent on others. Because if I need that (management knowledge), I can send others to attend the course ... I won't say in a cruel way that right people can be bought. however, you can search for them. It's a deal. Everything is a deal. If a post is suitable for him/her and he/she can do the job, that becomes a deal. That's business. (E12)

Importance of Education for Entrepreneurs and High-Flyers

According to the indications they gave in the Questionnaire, a majority of the successful entrepreneurs (19) and high-flyers (28) think the education they received is helpful in their work in one or more of the following ways:

1. Provide essential skills (9 entrepreneurs and 17 high-flyers)
2. Helped develop critical thinking (8 entrepreneurs and 11 high-flyers)
3. Provide conceptual background (11 entrepreneurs and 12 high-flyers)
4. Others, such as problem solving (1 entrepreneur)

The usefulness of education can be further illustrated by what the successful entrepreneurs and high-flyers mentioned in the interviews. The usefulness is threefold. Firstly, education and training provides a qualification for a post, especially a professional post such as in banking, financial management and technical consultancy.

> If you came here (the bank) with a Form 5 (O-level) or even matriculation (A-level) certificate, it's impossible for you to be promoted to my present position within 7 or 8 years (as I was). I think you may not even have the chance though you have worked for 10 or 20 years. So I think study is the most important, at least you don't have to start from the lowest level of the bank from the beginning. (HF1)

Secondly, education and training provides the knowledge and skills necessary for handling the sophisticated business world. The process of education grooms entrepreneurs and high-flyers for critical thinking which is required for making crucial decisions. Furthermore, the process of education and training exposes the individual to various perspectives of life, and that things can be done in a variety of ways. If one way is blocked, he/she does not have to give up, some other alternatives can be found. As discussed above, most of the Hong Kong entrepreneurs and high-flyers had their management training well after they had accumulated considerable experience in the workplace, the training renders space for reflection and consolidation of experiences from which they can gain new insight into doing business. To quote a Hong Kong branch director of a large British corporation:

> (The institute) chose a post-experience approach to organizing its MBA (programme) accepting students with three or up to five years' experience and from different sectors. The course organization was good with a lot of projects and seminars. My vision's changed with that group of friends. (HF29)

Thirdly, education and professional training can offer, according to one high-flyer, the confidence to manage.

> As I had no degree, it (MBA) brought great satisfaction to me. I got a degree which I had never thought I could get. That's a great satisfaction. Now I am qualified for my job (as the director and general manager). I have experiences and the qualification. I now feel very secure doing management work. I think I have enough experience and qualification for the job. (HF18)

Apart from its importance for career building, education is valued for its own right, which is an attitude acquired partly from parents and partly through personal experiences.

> I remembered clearly when I finished primary school, my father took a long trip, on foot, to go to a well-known secondary school to get an application form for me. He even paid a few dollars for the form, which at that time was very expensive. I was very touched by what he did. In the end I got into another school based on my examination results and I did not have to pay any school fees because of my good performance. (HF1)

I think it was the family philosophy that it was good to receive education. My family was actually very poor especially after my father's death, but my mother insisted that I continued education even under financial difficulties. I never thought of giving up my study. (HF7)

My father passed away when we were still very young. My mother did not receive much education, but she knew that it was good to let the children receive more education. Hence although life was hard, all the children finished at least secondary school. (E19)

I got very scared when my father started checking my homework. It was not because I was bothered that I did not finish the homework but I was afraid my father would get upset if he found out I was not studying hard. He thought studying was important but I thought that what was important was the pursuit of knowledge not fulfilling school requirements. (E26)

Looking back, I realize one cannot stop learning. If you stop, you lose all the stamina for improving yourself. I can say I possess the most shipping books among the shipping merchants in Hong Kong. (E25)

My parents had high expectations of my education. I worked very hard and I always got awards in schools. (HF29)

My father puts lots of emphasis on education. All my siblings and myself studied abroad which at the time meant very heavy expenses, but he still insisted on it. He thinks education helps a person depend on oneself. He agrees very much with the saying that the clever use the head, while the foolish use the hands. (HF17)

My parents wished that I could complete university education and then find a decent job. They did not expect me to be very successful. (HF25)

My father was a Chinese herbs physician (a medical doctor using herbs as medicine). He expected me to complete university education and be a medical doctor. (HF28)

All in all, the most predominant perception of the importance of education is that education is instrumental to achieving better career opportunities, hence social mobility. The pursuit of formal education, professional qualifications, and management training is very often originated with the perception that they are required instead of being essential in its own right. This perception of education has been fixed in the mind of the successful entrepreneurs and high-flyers, by their parents, since very early in life.

Summary

The data reported clearly indicates that the Hong Kong entrepreneurs and high-flyers did achieve high level of education. Sixty-three percent of the entrepreneurs and 100 percent of the high-flyers had post-secondary qualifications. Nearly half of the individuals in both cases possess professional qualifications. Forty percent of the entrepreneurs and 53 percent of the high-flyers had undergone some kind of management training. Though it remains premature to conclude that education, qualification and management training are prerequisites for success, they do provide valuable exposure and experience for the entrepreneurs and high-flyers and enhance their probabilities of being successful in career.

While it emerges from the figures that more high-flyers have higher educational level, obtained professional and management training, it is proposed entrepreneurs and high-flyers go through different educational paths, and that high-flyers may have a greater need for more educational and professional qualifications in order to climb their career ladder and to satisfy organizational requirements.

Education and Career Success

Having a happy childhood and close relationship with parents is seen to have laid a foundation for the successful entrepreneurs and high-flyers to pursue achievement in careers. However, childhood experiences is not the sole determinant of career success. It was found that 75 percent of the watershed events identified by the successful entrepreneurs and high-flyers were educational experiences. The importance of education for the successful entrepreneurs and high-flyers is also evident in the high levels of education they achieved. Hence the link of education with success in careers is established and is discussed in this section.

Zest for Education

The Hong Kong successful entrepreneurs and high-flyers exhibit a distinctive educational profile from the Hong Kong general population, and the entrepreneurs and high-flyers reported in other studies (Cox and Cooper, 1988, Jennings, Cox and Cooper, 1994), they achieved higher level of education. In particular, the Hong Kong high-flyers saw professional qualifications as an asset and liked to pursue management training.

All of the high-flyers received post-secondary education, whereas most of them (93 percent) have at least a bachelor degree, and one-third of them have even a master's degree. In the case of the successful entrepreneurs, success in careers appear to correlate less strongly with educational level when compared with the high-flyers. Only 63 percent of them have post-secondary qualifications. Many of them did not start off their careers with a degree.

The level of education achieved by the successful entrepreneurs and high-flyers is considered rather high bearing in mind they received education in a generation when educational opportunities were not widely available. Primary education in Hong Kong was only made free and compulsory in September 1971. Free and compulsory education was extended to junior secondary level in 1978. The majority of the successful entrepreneurs and a smaller number of the high-flyers were born shortly after the War and received primary and secondary education in the 60s and early 1970s, hence they had not quite benefitted from the free and compulsory primary and junior secondary education policy. Nevertheless, the successful entrepreneurs and high-flyers achieved not only a minimum of junior secondary education, but they also have obtained a higher percentage than the general population in achieving post-secondary/university level. Sixty-three percent of the Hong Kong entrepreneurs and 100 percent of the Hong Kong high-flyers have received post-secondary education and above, but only 6.7 percent of the general population in 1981 could attain post-secondary education as indicated in Table 5.4. Tertiary educational opportunities were extremely limited at the time when the successful entrepreneurs and high-flyers were supposed to enter university. Until the early 1980s, there were only two universities in Hong Kong. University education was designed for the elites. However, they were not deterred from pursuing higher education, even if the cost of studying overseas posed an immense financial pressure to their families.

Table 5.4   Educational Level of the Hong Kong Population*

Year	(in percentage) No Schooling/ Kindergarten	Primary	Secondary/ Matriculation	Post- Secondary/ University	Total
1971					
Male	9.9	49.6	34.5	6.0	
Female	35.9	38.4	22.9	2.8	
Total	22.7	44.1	28.8	4.4	100.0
1981					
Male	7.6	36.8	47.5	8.1	
Female	25.5	31.5	37.9	5.1	
Total	16.1	34.2	43.0	6.7	100.0
1988					
Male	5.5	31.9	50.0	11.8	
Female	20.2	27.3	43.4	9.4	
Total	12.7	29.7	47.2	10.4	100.0
1990					
Male	6.8	28.9	51.7	12.6	
Female	20.2	25.4	45.0	9.4	
Total	13.3	27.2	48.4	11.1	100.0

* Figures confined to population of age 15 and over.

Source: General Household Survey Section, Census and Statistics Department, Hong Kong Government, Hong Kong.

Apart from academic qualifications, many of the Hong Kong entrepreneurs and high-flyers had suggested in the interviews that they liked to become members of a professional body and participate in its activities because all these could provide opportunities to meet people in the field and establish personal and organizational connections, which is important for career advancement and business development.

The successful entrepreneurs and high-flyers realized as their businesses expanded or as they progressed up the career ladder, they would have to engage in management tasks and that some kind of management education would help. Nearly half of the successful entrepreneurs and high-flyers (40 percent and 57 percent respectively) have received some kind of management training, ranging from short courses to formal management degree education. These ratios are much higher than those obtained in various studies (Firth, 1987; White, 1992; Jennings, 1994). There is not one exclusively popular form of management training for the entrepreneurs, whereas more than half of the high-flyers had management training (7 out of 17) through MBA programmes.

The figures reflect another interesting phenomenon that most of the entrepreneurs and high-flyers received their management training in the course of their career development. Only one of the entrepreneurs and two of the high-flyers had a bachelor's degree in business administration, whilst the rest started off their careers with no specialized training in management. Instead they came to realize the need for management training when they gradually took up management responsibilities. A study by the British Institute of Management (Firth, 1987) suggests that few of the 90,000 managers entering management each year have had any prior formal management training at all. Many of the high-flyers used their own money to pay for the management training and used annual leave to attend courses and complete coursework.

Management training is seen as important, though not necessarily essential, to the entrepreneurs and high-flyers. This is particularly so for the entrepreneurs. It is due to the their role in the organization. Entrepreneurs are more like the navigator of a ship. They steer the overall direction and policy of the organization. They would consider the execution of the company policy and the management of the organization the responsibilities of senior staff.

On the other hand, high-flyers would see management knowledge and skills more imperative for their job. They are responsible not only for themselves, but also to the organization. They are held accountable for the management and performance of the organization. No matter how senior they are in the organization, they are still employees. Their career prospect is linked with how well they can get the job done. Hence high-flyers are more in need of professional qualifications and management training.

That the successful entrepreneurs and high-flyers reached much higher educational levels than the general population can be explained by at least two possible reasons:

1.   The successful entrepreneurs and high-flyers were intelligent individuals. They excelled others in the educational process and were able to reach the top of the pyramid of the educational system.
2.   Education is perceived to be important by the entrepreneurs and high-flyers and/or by their parents. Hence a belief that they should strive for as much education as possible.

The Hong Kong successful entrepreneurs and high-flyers are generally rather intelligent. Their mean sten scores on the Intelligence Factor (Factor 2) of Cattell's 16PF is 7.2, higher than that of the British general population which is 4.4. Since no means or norms of the 16 PF have been established for the Hong Kong population, the hypothesis that the successful entrepreneurs and high-flyers are more intelligent people is yet to be confirmed.

Regarding the second hypothesis, the emphasis on education was clearly conveyed by the successful entrepreneurs and high-flyers, and this emphasis is actually rooted in their parents' view of education. The parents of the successful entrepreneurs and high-flyers insisted that their children received good and as much education as possible, which can be seen in their efforts to send their children overseas for study. As one of the high-flyers mentioned, it would cost the family a fortune to send family members, even just one, to overseas countries for study. 59percent of the high diplomas and bachelor's degrees were obtained in overseas institutions. Apart from creating a financial burden for the family, studying in a foreign country required great adjustment and hence strong commitment on the part of the successful entrepreneurs and high-flyers. This commitment would have to be supported by a strong belief that they were doing something important and worthwhile. The resulting experiences in studying abroad did prove to the successful entrepreneurs and high-flyers that they were worthwhile because they brought significant changes to the course of their lives.

Education and social mobility Education has been assigned great value by Chinese parents due to the aspiration of becoming a learned scholar, but more importantly the upward social mobility it promises. The parents of the successful entrepreneurs and the high-flyers were all emigrants from China. In order to establish their own standing in the new society, they were found to be working very hard. And in order to secure their descendants' standing in the society, they emphasized they received education so that they could advance in the conventional paths. Entry to and promotion in the civil service system in Hong Kong followed a qualifying-by-examination system. Historically, and also in their generations, being part of the officialdom commanded great respect. Hence the parents of the successful entrepreneurs and the high-flyers saw education as a route to respected groups in the society, and they tried their best to provide education for their children.

Education and perceived structure of opportunities The parents' values on education were well internalized by the successful entrepreneurs and high-flyers. They perceived a strong link between their educational background and the kind of job they would like to have, hence choosing their subject of study accordingly. Educational decisions in relation to the choice of the subject of education can to a very large extent reflect what Astin (1984) calls the perceived structure of opportunity which is a determining factor affecting career decision and work behaviour. The pursuit of professional qualifications, management training or further study are also considered in the context of the perceived structure of opportunities which varies at different periods of time.

At the time when most of the successful entrepreneurs and high-flyers had to make career-related educational decisions, Hong Kong was well on its economic take-off and moving towards professionalization and modernization. There was a need for professionals in various areas. This structure of opportunities partly explains that more than half of the high diploma/undergraduate qualifications obtained by the successful entrepreneurs and high-flyers are related to professional subjects such as engineering, law, business administration, banking and marketing. In some cases, the degree itself is already a licence to practice in the profession. In others, the degree can spare at least part of the professional qualification requirement. The decision to study a professional subject was part and partial based on an assessment of the prospect of that particular profession in terms of social status and financial returns, as one entrepreneur stated:

> I like fine arts but I chose electrical engineering because I had to eat. (E20)

However, the perceived structure of opportunities is not the sole determinant of career-related educational decisions. Not everyone make the same decision in the face of a clear structure of opportunities. The individual's self-concept functions to determine the extent to which he/she is influenced by the structure of opportunities in making educational decisions. One of the functional constituents of self is self-efficacy, meaning that the successful entrepreneurs and high-flyers would also assess their ability to study a particular subject apart from recognizing that subject would bring career prospects.

Educational Experiences as Watershed Events in Life

A total of ten entrepreneurs and high-flyers claimed their educational experiences as their watershed events in life. Six of them regarded going abroad for study is their watershed event. Among the others were experience in boarding school enabling the learning about people, the opportunity to get in an elite boarding school receiving good education and an excellent set of values. These experiences had developed a strong sense of independence and self-reliance, high sensitivity to the social environment, skills in leadership and a set of excellent values.

Link to Success - Education as Increasing the Chances of Success

The educational experiences of the successful entrepreneurs and high-flyers were related to career success in a number of direct and indirect ways:

1. Education provides general knowledge and technical know-how which is essential for job-related tasks and management.
2. Education increases the chances of social mobility. Education and training provides the entry requirements for a post in a particular profession.

3. Education enhances personal competence. Bruce (1976) suggests that the influence of education on the career of any individual is not simply confined to technical understanding. The educational process enabled the entrepreneurs and high-flyers to develop wider perspectives and critical thinking crucial for handling an increasingly complex business world.

Similar to the childhood experiences, the educational experiences which were regarded as watershed events had nurtured essential qualities for success in careers.

6   Career History

Successful entrepreneurs and high-flyers are, by definition, noted for their career achievements.   This chapter is aimed at identifying the key elements of successful careers by reviewing relevant studies.

Career Patterns

Clements (1958) suggests five basic patterns in managerial careers:-

1.   The crown prince - the person is a member of the family owning the business
2.   The ex-managerial trainee - the person is usually a university graduate recruited specifically to be trained for, ultimately, a managerial position
3.   The expert trained before entering industry - these are people who enter industry after taking specialist training and qualification most often in accountancy.   They tend to be promoted initially in their specialized area, but may transfer into general management later in their careers
4.   Rising from the bottom - these are people who have literally started their careers at the lowest level of the organization, often as either clerks or manual workers
5.   The special entrant - this is somewhat miscellaneous category of people who did not fit the other classifications.   They include sales trainees, specialist apprentices and those who have negotiated some special form of entry to a company, such as being headhunted.

The above categories provide a classification of the different ways in which an individual starts his/her career.   However, the categories do not further consider career development which certainly requires more detailed accounts of how an individual goes from his/her starting point.

Much of the career-development literature is dominated by Erikson's (1968) view of development. His psychosocial stages of development postulate that an individual has changing tasks as a result of changing genetically-based psychological needs as well as social demands as he/she develops in age.

Ego strengths emerge when the individual fulfils his/her developmental tasks. Therefore the individual may be seen to produce his/her own development through behavioural intervention or behavioural agency. In terms of career development, one can overcome adverse factors in the environment to pursue successful careers. Erikson suggests that identity formation including occupational identity is the central task of an individual entering adulthood. Marcia (1966) developed an identity-status theory which is intended to allow measurement of Erikson's central concept of identity. It is suggested that there are four different modes of identity formation and that anyone over eighteen years of age should fall into one of the categories:

1. *Identity achievement*. Individuals experience a period of decision-making and are pursuing a self-chosen occupation and ideological goals.
2. *Foreclosure*. Individuals are committed to their occupation and ideological goals, but these have been parentally chosen. These people show no evidence of crisis.
3. *Identity diffusion*. Individuals who have no set occupation or ideological direction, regardless of whether or not they have experienced a decision-making crisis.
4. *Moratorium*. Individuals who are currently struggling with occupational and/or ideological issues - that is, they are in crisis.

Examining career development with the notion of identity formation has fostered a school of thought emphasizing career stages. Levinson et. al. (1978) premise that no matter what one's occupation is, he/she will grow through specific life stages. The nature, duration and exact timing of certain events may differ, but certain developmental tasks are thought to be predictable. In dealing with these developmental tasks, certain issues will emerge in chronological order and therefore the mean age of the individuals when dealing with a particular developmental task is given. Figure 6.1 shows Levinson's model of life development.

Figure 6.1 Levinson's Model of Life Development

Early Adulthood
  Early adult transition, 17-22
  -     start thinking about place in the world separate from parents and educational institutions
  -     test initial preferences for living
  Entering Adult World, 22-28
  -     develop sense of personal identity in work and non-work
  Thirties Transition, 29-33
  -     evaluate accomplishments of their ties and make adjustments
  Settling Down, 34-39
  -     strive towards achieving personal goals
  -     make commitments to family and work
Middle Adulthood
  Mid-life Transition, 40-45
  -     review life structure adopted in thirties
  -     recognize mortality limits on achievement
  Entering Middle Adulthood, 46-50
  -     develop greater stability as questions raised in mid-life transition are answered
  Fifties Transition, 51-55
  -     raise questions about life structure previously adopted
  Culmination of Middle Adulthood, 50-60
  -     answer questions raised and adjust life choices
Late Adulthood (over 60)

The concept of identity and its associated concept of age-linked stage is useful for understanding career behaviours because it explains career decisions in the context of the individual's self and his/her overall life development, though further research is required to test the validity of the age-linked structure. The life histories of many successful entrepreneurs indicate that their career success is very much related to how they have overcome crises at critical stages in life (Cox and Cooper, 1988).

Early Responsibility

The career history of successful managers show that they hold positions of responsibility at an early age. The British CEOs interviewed by Cox and Cooper (1988) evidenced this career characteristic. They were given an assignment early in their career with complete responsibility and very little outside support. Often this was to manage an overseas subsidiary, where they were very much on their own and had to cope.

Wide Exposure

Many successful entrepreneurs and top managers have reported that they had often been moved from one post to another when working in a company. These moves were not necessarily a job advancement but had certainly helped them gain valuable experience across a range of functions so that they could see business in all its aspects. Those who worked in a small organization were in an even better position because they had to master different functions at different levels within a very short period of time. Among the various kinds of experience, the experience of working abroad is of particular significance and relevance for heading and managing a successful business.

Taylor (1985) summarizes from existing studies that varied business experience is a considerable advantage to a business owner. A generalist rather than a specialist can better understand a broad range of responsibilities - in finance, in personnel, in marketing, and in production.

Mentoring

Mentoring can be formal or informal, which offers guidance on work and management by a role model at the workplace. The career and psychological benefits of mentoring increase the likelihood of success at work through enhancing the levels of aspiration and self-efficacy. Successful managers, both male and female, often reported to have had a mentor in their careers (Cox and Cooper, 1988; White, 1992).

Career History of Hong Kong Successful Entrepreneurs and High-Flyers

Mentoring

Five successful entrepreneurs reported having experienced mentoring in their first job. Interestingly none of the high-flyers reported similar experiences.

> I did not receive any mentoring. I learnt through mistakes and I might have taken many unnecessary steps. One can still be successful without mentoring but it may take a longer time. (HF10)

The fact that the majority of the entrepreneurs and high-flyers had no mentoring is because mentoring is a rather new concept and practice in organizations even at the present time, not to mention in the 1970s. In fact, two of the five entrepreneurs who claimed they had mentoring were going through apprenticeship training which they might have considered as mentoring.

Nevertheless, many more entrepreneurs (10) and high-flyers (14) suggested there were significant persons who had influenced their career development. They are:

1. Father (2 entrepreneurs)
2. Peers (1 high-flyer)
3. Colleagues (2 entrepreneurs)
4. Boss (6 entrepreneurs and 13 high-flyers)

The fathers, peers and colleagues were influential in offering advice and encouragement particularly at times of crisis, whereas the influence from the boss came in a number of ways:-

Gave insight to how to manage (5 entrepreneurs and 8 high-flyers) One high-flyer had the following remarks about her boss:

> Most people I met at work had been negative models, except the boss when I was in a travel business. He taught me to be flexible, when to hit hard and when to leave things alone. (E14)

Another male high-flyer made similar remarks:

> When I was promoted to be in charge of a team of engineers, I did not quite
> know what to do. My background had been on the technical side and I used
> to work on my own. My senior at that time gave me a lot of advice and
> showed me how to build the team. I began to appreciate the importance of
> teamwork. (HF4)

Willing to give opportunities for development (3 high-flyers)

> We (I and my boss) went to a world conference on banking. My boss was
> supposed to deliver a speech. Ten minutes before the speech, he asked me
> to present the speech for him because he thought I was more appropriate to
> tell others about the state of the art in Hong Kong. I was so unprepared for
> this that I rushed to the bathroom and prayed for five minutes. The speech
> I made was more like sharing my banking experience with friends. The
> audience was attentive and looked interested. They gave me the greatest
> applause of the day and later I received lots of congratulation telegrams.
> That was a turning point in my life. I became much more confident of
> myself. I really appreciate my boss for not keeping all the credits to
> himself but letting others take the opportunities.

Served as a model (1 entrepreneur and 2 high-flyers) One woman high-
flyer expressed her admiration to her previous boss:

> The boss of my first job is a woman. We only worked together for one
> year but she had influenced me much. I was very green then and it was
> really quite an experience to see a woman at such a senior position. I was
> very impressed by what she did and what she achieved. She set a direction
> for me, I wanted to follow her path. Her experiences gave me a lot of
> confidence, that women could be as successful as men. She was a role
> model for me. (HF7)

It is interesting to note the gender difference in reporting significant
persons in careers. Seven of the thirteen high-flyers having significant
persons in careers are female constituting 78 percent of the total woman
high-flyers. Whereas only six male high-flyers (30 percent) reported
having such persons in their careers.

Early Responsibility in Career

A number of the entrepreneurs (7) and high-flyers (17) were assigned, through promotions, responsibilities at an early stage of their careers, which was regarded as significant for career success.

> As soon as I had graduated, I worked in the controls department of a bank in Canada. I analysed business and banking results of its branches all over the world, and provided reasons for its gains and losses. I worked at the headquarters and reported directly to the board of directors. It was rare for a fresh graduate, and a foreignor, to be given such responsibility. I had chances to work with the top management. (H17)

> I had only been in the post for six months and they asked me to be the acting head of the division. I was not prepared for this. I knew it would be hard but I took it as a challenge. I did work very hard to perform. (H28)

> I had only started as a management trainee for two months when the manager of the division left. They asked me to take up the vacancy. I did not know anything about paper but I told myself it's no harm trying. This is the turning point in my career which set me on the road to doing paper business.(E21)

> Two years after being an engineer, in fact just a trainee, I was promoted to be the project engineer in charge of a team of engineers. This was considered in the field a rather rapid advancement. (H4)

> Before I graduated, I already had six job offers. Two years after I started work, I was headhunted to be the operations director of a declining plant. I was the youngest director they ever had.(E22)

Ten of the entrepreneurs and twelve of the high-flyers did not experience such rapid progression as representing early responsibility in careers. Instead they stayed in a job for a relatively long period of time during which they acquired the basics of that particular trade or profession.

> That's why (starting from the bottom and knowing every loop in the business) they are afraid of me and respect me. They can't bullshit me. I can cheat you easily but you can't cheat me. I'm not born to be a boss. I've been through the stages at which they are now at. I started from the

bottom. I know the processes and I always update the information. You know the problem only if you know the processes. I know the new production process well. (E8)

There's no shortcut to the top. You have to go through each and every stage (of work) so that you know what it takes to have the job completed. They (colleagues) will not follow your leadership even if the company gives you a nice title. They want you to show them you can do what they cannot do. Therefore it all goes back to experience, to see whether you have experience in this field. (H13)

Six of the entrepreneurs worked in their family business before they started their own business. The experiences acquired were also seen as important for their entrepreneurial success.

I joined my father's company after graduation. I had worked in different units to develop practical experience. It was good to have the opportunities to try out what I had learnt at university. There were many colleagues to help me learn the frontline job. I am interested in the technical job. I remembered the days when I started working in the plant. The big fire, melting hundreds of tons of steel. You never got that from studying in university. The books do not tell you how it feels, the heat. You have to be there to feel the real thing. I was sweating. (E13)

I helped in the family business after I returned to HK. There was not a lot of salary but I was pleased with what I learnt. As experience accumulated, I started my own restaurant. (E7)

Seven entrepreneurs decided from the start to have their own business. The remaining one high-flyer, being well-liked by his boss, entered the organization at a very senior position as soon as he got his Ph D.

Wide Career Exposures

The successful entrepreneurs and high-flyers have very wide exposure to different job experiences, if the number of career moves is an indicator. Table 6.1 indicates the number of job moves taken by the entrepreneurs and the high-flyers including those within the same organization and across different organizations.

Table 6.1   Number of Job Moves of Entrepreneurs and High-Flyers Within and Across Organizations

No of Job Moves	Entrepreneurs	High-Flyers
1	11	-
2	8	-
3	5	4
4	2	14
5	3	10
6	-	-
7	1	2
Total subjects	30	30

It is seen from Table 6.1 that the entrepreneurs changed jobs less often than the high-flyers. Most of the entrepreneurs (63 percent) had only one to two job moves while majority of the high-flyers (80 percent) had four to five job moves. The fact that the entrepreneurs had lesser job moves is because these entrepreneurs made their decisions to start their own business at an early stage of their career history. For the high-flyers, it was found that ten of them followed a corporate path in moving jobs, that is, their job moves represent promotions in the same organization. Whereas the other nineteen high-flyers moved jobs across organizations for better career prospects.

Apart from being viewed as advancement, job moves expose the high-flyers to different work contexts, work functions and requirements. The exposure was important in terms of both personal and career development.

My career history is quite interesting because I always changed jobs. I started off as a nutritionist in the US. Then the company transferred me to marketing. I thought marketing might take me into management which was definitely better than being a nutritionist. Then I went to Singapore to join the Ministry of Health. I returned to HK a few years later and joined another company responsible for marketing. At present I am responsible for manufacturing. Manufacturing was totally new to me when the MD of the present company approached me. I thought it worth taking a risk. (H14)

At first I worked in the travel business because I wanted to meet people. Then I moved to work in a hotel and again I could meet people from all walks of life. I returned to the travel business doing commission-based sales which gave me much immediate satisfaction. From that I joined the marketing department of a Swiss food products company. After a short time, I joined an American bank doing retail banking and loan marketing. Soon afterwards I was headhunted to join the insurance field. So here I am. (H15)

When I look back, all the jobs I had are important in their own right. If I lack any one of the exposures, I could not be a well-balanced manager. (HF7)

I spent about 2 to 3 years in every job I had, then I changed to another job. I think I had to widen my scope by working in different areas. (E6)

Risk Taking

The successful entrepreneurs and high-flyers were asked to rate themselves in the Questionnaire in relation to their risk taking at work by circling the appropriate number on a five-point scale.

Table 6.2   Degree of Risk Taking of the Successful Entrepreneurs and High-Flyers

Degree	Entrepreneurs	High-Flyers
1 (Low Risk Taker)	-	1
2	12	8
3	10	10
4	7	11
5 (High Risk Taker)	1	-
Total subjects	30	30

It is observed from Table 6.2 that the successful entrepreneurs as a group have a similar risk-taking pattern to that of the high-flyers. There is quite an even distribution of high and low risk takers in both groups, and with the exception of one successful entrepreneur and one high-flyer, there are no extremely high and low risk takers.

Watershed Events in Career

Twenty entrepreneurs and fourteen high-flyers recognized some kind of watershed events in their career history. These events can be classified as follows:-

1. Promoted to a position for which they were not quite ready in terms of experience and training (5 high-flyers)
2. Asked to reorganize family business (4 entrepreneurs) or set up/reorganize a local business (2 entrepreneurs and 2 high-flyers)
3. Came across an opportunity and changed job (3 entrepreneurs and 4 high-flyers)
4. Sent overseas to take charge of a branch business (1 high-flyer)
5. Turning a crisis situation into success (2 entrepreneurs and 2 high-flyers)
6. Worked in a worldwide company gaining invaluable experience (1 entrepreneur)
7. Set up own business (6 entrepreneurs)
8. Made the first deal in business, which proved oneself was capable (1 entrepreneur)

One entrepreneur recalled a negative experience which became the turning point of his career,

> I worked as an apprentice when I was 17. One day I was carrying out a routine check on a passenger lift and was clearing away the rubbish underneath the lift. A woman and her son happened to see me removing the rubbish. The woman told her son, "You'd better study hard or else you will have to be a cleaner one day". This was a big insult to me. I can still remember this very clearly. I told myself that I would not be checking lifts forever. (E6)

Summary

Based on the career experiences of the successful entrepreneurs and high-flyers, three career patterns can be identified: professional, opportunist and true entrepreneur. These career paths are so called because the names are indicative of the themes that differentiate one from the others. Those who follow the professional path anchored their careers at a very early age in one specific profession and advanced in the same profession, in the same or different organizations. Those who follow the opportunist path, on the other hand, did not show this early anchor in one profession. Instead they moved between functions and professions whenever there were opportunities for career advancement. The salient feature of this career path is taking career opportunities as they come. The true entrepreneur path defines those who chose to be entrepreneurs right at the beginning of their careers. This differentiates them from those who made a decision to start their own business at a later stage. The true entrepreneurs have been entrepreneurs throughout their career history.

It is noted that no two individuals experience exactly the same career history, hence the three categories are general summarizations of very similar career experiences of individuals. All individuals are classified under one of the three career paths on the basis that an individual's career experiences reflect the defining characteristics of that particular career path. The three career paths and the number of successful entrepreneurs and high-flyers falling onto each of the career paths are shown below.

Pattern 1 Professionals

		Leaving school or university
		↓ ↓
		Apprenticeship first job
		↓ ↙
Crystallization		professional qualification
		↓
		rapid learning, proving ability
		↓
Establishment		becoming established in the firm
		consolidating professional reputation
		↓
Advancement	Within or across	gaining practice experience, exposures
	organizations	and social reputation
		↓
Achievement		realization of goals
		↓
Rebalancing		reassessment of personal/family priorities
		reassessment of fit with organizational goals
		↓ ↓
		entrepreneur intrapreneur

Eleven entrepreneurs (37 percent) and seventeen high-flyers (57 percent) followed this pattern. Ten of the high-flyers progressed through a corporate path, that is, they advanced within one organization.

The entrepreneurs and the high-flyers who advanced through this pattern basically started off and progressed in similar ways. Both groups began their careers in professions by either having achieved a relatively high academic level or obtained the required qualifications through apprenticeship. Both groups advanced fairly quickly, some within the same organization with others moving from one organization to another.

Crystallization The prerequisite for advancement in this career path is possessing professional qualifications which were obtained upon graduation with a few years' working experience or apprenticeship. This implies that the professionals anchored and crystallized in a particular career direction at quite a young age.

Establishment, advancement and achievement   These three stages represent a period in which the professionals develop and consolidate themselves in the profession in terms of practice wisdom and social recognition, particularly for those who later became entrepreneurs who had to take care of everything in the business.

> I didn't have much experience in many big organizations. I should have stayed and learnt more in big organizations before I started my business. (E20)

> I have to deal with different government departments and to avoid sensitive issues which may provoke them. My previous working experiences in the Government are definitely very helpful. (E19)

Rebalancing   At the rebalancing stage, the professionals reviewed their achievements in considering what they would be going next. Those who perceived their career development was blocked decided to quit their paid jobs to join the self-employed. Career development was perceived to be blocked under two situations: feeling bored because there was no further challenge and learning (3 entrepreneurs), and no further advancement prospects (3 entrepreneurs). These individuals became entrepreneurs at an older age than the true entrepreneurs described in Pattern 3 below.

> The jobs I had were well-paid and status jobs. But I was not excited about that and still felt I had missed something in life. I began to realize that I had been working for my husband, not for myself. I started to ask myself what I wanted in life, and I decided to pursue my own career. I knew it was hard for both of us but I went ahead to start my business. (E17)

> The most important motivation (for starting own business) was that I could develop my own specialty, because in the government, I was restricted to do what I could do. My prospects in the government is very limited ... Not money, I might lose money when I ran my own business. (E18)

> Many MBAs were joining the company and I realized I could not compete with them because I simply lacked the proper qualifications. Without the qualifications, I didn't think I could go further. Not before long, these newcomers with MBAs would surpass me and became my boss. Having no future prospects in the company, the only alternative was to leave and start my own business. In a way I was forced to be an entrepreneur. (E26)

Two entrepreneurs highlighted that age was one of the considerations in deciding to become an entrepreneur.

> I felt I was at an age that I should try something challenging. I might lose that gist after that age. (E21)

> I thought that was the time for change, that I should go out and do my own thing. (E19)

Three entrepreneurs decided to follow their fathers' footsteps of being self-employed.

> My father always advised me that I need to rely on myself in the long run, being one's own boss is the safest, and I quite agreed with him. (E22)

> There was a British managing director and the company was British, I wouldn't be further promoted and I wouldn't learn much more. At that time my father had a factory. He had sold out his business but we still kept the factory. I've seen him (father) doing the business for 20 years, I had the idea of reactivating his business, so I resigned. (E21)

> My father came across a business opportunity at that time. The supplier of ninja turtles was looking for a manufacturer in Hong Kong, but my father's company did not have sufficient capital, equipment and manpower to compete for the deal. I stopped working as a lawyer and went to contact some of his friends and staff to raise money and manpower, and I formed a new company. Because I had the best people in the industry, I got the contract. This is the turning point in my career. (E24)

One entrepreneur mentioned family was his main consideration for giving up his well-paid job and started his own business:

> I wanted to be closer to my family, so I decided to return (from Canada) and started my own business. I thought if I failed, I might just find a job again. Perhaps the experience in operating a business can be my strength for securing an ideal job. (E23)

Those professionals (16 high-flyers) who decided to remain as salaried employees had the following professed reasons which are considered typical:

Many have this fantasy (of starting own business) and so do I, but I will seriously consider the pros and cons. At the moment, I do not see there are more pros than cons, and the opportunity cost is high, so I won't take any concrete action in the near future. (HF18)

Who's going to support my family? I can't afford to give up the high pay while I am still repaying the mortgage and looking after two babies. (HF16)

The following high-flyer considers not only his own vested interests but also the interests of his colleagues in facing a career choice:

It is indeed very tempting to have one's own business. I think I have very favourable conditions in starting my own business. But I am also concerned about my followers. I cannot ask them to share the risk I take. They have been working for me for a long time. They will be out of jobs or they will get into a difficult position if I quit now. I simply do not want them and their families to starve because of me. (HF23)

Pattern 2   Opportunists

	Leaving school or university
	↓
Exploration	first job
	↓
	changing jobs
	↓
Crystallization	clearer ideas about own capabilities and work areas, but may not have occupational preferences
	↓
Establishment	seeking opportunities to develop in chosen work areas
	↓
	proving ability in chosen areas developing reputation
	↓
Advancement	taking new opportunities changing to other work functions
	↓ ↓
	intrapreneur entrepreneur
	↘ ↙
Achievement	deepening and widening experience

Six entrepreneurs (20 percent) and thirteen high-flyers (43 percent) followed this pattern.

The following interview transcripts illustrate how the opportunists explored, crystallized, established and advanced in their career path. The stages are not separated because they are highly intertwined. In addition, if the stages are shown in continuity, salient characteristics of the opportunist career path are more easily discerned.

The individuals who progressed through this career pattern did not have clear career orientation when they were engaged in their first full-time paid job.

> I wasn't quite sure what I wanted to do (as a job). I got a job as a trainee but did not like the way I was treated. Then I happened to know the Hong Kong Polytechnic was receiving applications for courses and I applied to study in marketing. Actually I didn't quite know what marketing was, I guessed it was about selling things and bargaining. After graduation, I joined the present company and worked all the way to now being the managing director of its branch company. (HF18)

> After graduation, I stayed in California doing part-time jobs. After returning to Hong Kong, I worked in the travel business and found it interesting. Then I went to work in a hotel but returned to the travel business two years later. I changed to do marketing in a food company for some time, then went to a bank doing retail banking and loan marketing. It was there I was headhunted for the present post and so I got into the insurance profession. (HF15)

> My career history is very interesting because my background was totally not related to what I am doing now. My first job was a research assistant in a food company in the States, but very quickly I switched over to being a management trainee doing marketing in the same company. One year later, I went to Singapore working in the Ministry of Health for a year. When I returned to Hong Kong, I first worked in marketing and then I joined the present company responsible for manufacturing. (HF14)

Pattern 3   True Entrepreneur

Leaving school or university

Crystalization	Entrepreneur

↓

accumulating   seeking
experience in   opportunities
family business   to set up own business

↓   ↙

Establishment	proving ability in trade and profession

↓

developing reputation

↓

Advancement	expanding business

↓

Achievement	realization of goals

13 entrepreneurs (43 percent) followed this pattern.

The following transcripts illustrate what the considerations in pursuing a true entrepreneur career path.

> My father has four sons, but my brothers were not interested at all in the shipping business (the family business). The only one left is me. Actually I quite like ships, building models and doing repairs. When I went to university, I chose mechanical engineering and then worked in the (family's) company after graduation. My interest in shipping actually increased. I even did a Ph.D. in nautical engineering. (E2)

> I had never thought of working for somebody. I guess my family had influenced me a lot. We used to support one another in the family business. Everything was sorted out within the family. It was very natural for me to have my own business and be my own boss. (E30)

> At that time I always told myself I could do what Li Ka Shing (a multi-millionaire in Hong Kong) could do. I didn't think the successful people

were particularly wiser people. So I started my business in order to prove I could do it too. (E1)

I always wanted to get rich. With my qualifications I didn't think I could get a decent job. The only way to get rich is to rely on myself: my gist and my hands. (E14)

Very soon after I had started work I realized I could never work for someone else. I was fired for four times, because I liked to do things my own way which annoyed my boss. In the end I borrowed money from my mother and started a small trading business. (E29)

The only thing I was concerned in work was to make money. You don't get rich if you work for someone else. That's why I only thought of working for myself, and earning for myself. (E28)

Career History and Career Success

This section discusses, with reference to the career history of the successful entrepreneurs and high-flyers, the career decisions they made as to be one's own boss or be a salaried employee. The career history is also examined with a view to identifying conditions of career success.

Career Decisions

The successful entrepreneurs and high-flyers are found to have followed one of the three career paths which are outlined in the last chapter. The career paths are: professionals, opportunists and true entrepreneurs. It is found that eleven entrepreneurs (37 percent) and seventeen high-flyers (57 percent) followed the professionals career path. Ten of the high-flyers progressed through a corporate path, that is, they advanced within one organization. Six entrepreneurs (20 percent) and thirteen high-flyers (43 percent) followed the opportunists pattern. Thirteen entrepreneurs (43 percent) followed the true entrepreneurs pattern.

The true entrepreneurs differ from the professionals and the opportunists in that they decided to start their own business right at the beginning of their career, whereas the others decided to get a paid job. Those successful entrepreneurs and high-flyers who followed the professional and opportunist career patterns have very similar career history except that they made different career decisions at a later stage of their career development. Hall (1976) claims that career decision is not just the choice of an occupation, but any choice affecting one' career. Theories of occupational choice fall into two basic categories: 'matching theories', which describe what kinds of people enter what kinds of occupation, and 'process theories', which describe the manner in which people arrive at an occupational choice. It is the latter category - the process of occupational decision - which is the focus of concern.

The three career paths were constructed to show the order of the career stages and their associated tasks. The rationale of using career stages is that individuals' vocational attitudes and behaviours change in relation to their life development, and that stage-related issues can be identified in understanding individual behaviour in organizations, which may lead to more effective planning.

Those who followed the professionals and the true entrepreneurs career patterns anchored their career in a particular direction rather early in life. The pre-requisite for pursuing the professional career path is a professional qualification obtained through formal education or apprenticeship. Hence these successful entrepreneurs and high-flyers had made a vocational decision when they chose their subject of study in university, or when they chose to specialize in a particular area in their first job. It is observed that these successful entrepreneurs and high-flyers were more influenced by the perceived structure of opportunities or by significant others in developing a preference for a particular profession.

Similarly, the true entrepreneurs anchored themselves in a particular career orientation as soon as they started work, some even earlier. Six of these entrepreneurs have self-employed fathers and they in fact were well prepared to take over the family business. They were encouraged to study a particular subject, they were arranged to acquire particular work experiences and they were clear of where they would end up in the organization. Although one of them decided to have his own business, the career orientation was largely affected by their significant others. The remaining three true entrepreneurs who did not have families engaging in business possess average educational qualifications. Perhaps the path for them to embark on a brilliant career must be one that can allow them to use their other personal assets such as hard work and wittiness. Wong's (1988) Shanghai industrialists who were emigrants to Hong Kong were very conscious of the peculiar opportunity structure of the society in which they realized small entrepreneurs could prosper through hard work.

In contrast to the professionals and the true entrepreneurs, the opportunists did not anchor in a particular career until a later time. The opportunists at their late adolescence experienced what Marcia (1966) called identity diffusion. They showed a less well-defined self-identity hence vocational identity, and they were less directed by the existing structure of opportunity, which are shown in their experimentation of jobs in the initial stage until they found the right job and crystallized in it. However, these individuals were good at taking opportunities to advance their career.

After a series of job moves, a few of the individuals decided to start their own business, which often occurred at the rebalancing stage of their career. Both the professionals and the opportunists experienced a rebalancing stage in their career which is absent for the true entrepreneurs. The latter do not consider other career alternatives. It is at the rebalancing stage that a small number of the professionals and the opportunists decided to start their own business and became successful entrepreneurs. These entrepreneurs are different from the true entrepreneurs because they made such career decision at a much later age, and because of their history of working as salaried employees, it is thought that they share more common characteristics with the high-flyers than the true entrepreneurs. The highly similar childhood experiences of the successful entrepreneurs and the high-flyers may have predisposed more than half of the entrepreneurs (57 percent) to initially pursue a career path which was also followed by the high-flyers. Since this majority of the successful entrepreneurs have a career history similar to that of the high-flyers, they may develop personality, management approach and values very close to those of the high-flyers in general. In fact, only small differences were identified in the personality and the management approach between the successful entrepreneurs and the high-flyers, which shall be discussed in later sections.

The decision to stay as a paid employee or to be one's own boss is a complex one which cannot be reduced to a simple formulae. The successful entrepreneurs and high-flyers who followed the professionals and the opportunists patterns experienced conditions that favoured the starting of own business, but they had different assessment of these conditions resulting in different career decisions.

The emigrant industrialists studied by Wong (1988) provided some insight to understanding what is involved in the decision to be one's own boss. These industrialists represented two groups of directors: owner-director and salaried director. As one group, nearly two-thirds of them indicated a preference to become owners. However, there is no significant correlation between the owner-directors and the salaried-directors regarding their preference for independent ownership. The chief motives for choosing to be independent owners were the lure of self-advancement and the abhorrence of self-subjugation. It is generally believed that the Chinese value individual autonomy[1] hence have a greater tendency to work and earn for themselves (Ryan, 1961; Redding, 1986; Wong, 1988). The developmental background of the successful entrepreneurs and the high-flyers also suggest a higher likelihood for them to be one's own boss, considering the strong sense of independence and self-reliance that have emerged. In spite of these, the high-flyers chose to work for others. The professed reasons are lack of initial capital and risks that are too high to bear. It is thought that the security and stability guaranteed in a familiar environment and an attractive salary package are what the high-flyers aspire at their present stage of life, hence they gave the status quo a higher priority.

Those who decided to start their own business mentioned they perceived no further prospects in the organization in terms of learning and advancement, and they had done enough for the organization and it was time they should earn for themselves. Wong (1988) observed that many managers in large companies are accumulating knowledge, skills, and contacts with a view to starting their own businesses whenever the opportunity arises. Some of its implications are that in any large company, the relationship between many key personnel and the organization is likely to be utilitarian, that employees may be treated with suspicion of their loyalty to the organization, and that organizational growth may be constrained by the high staff turnover it causes. As a result, in many Chinese companies, centralization and autocracy are used as part of the defensive strategy to counteract the centrifugal tendency of their executives to desert the company. These implications will be further discussed in later sections in relation to management approach.

In examining what influenced the decision to be one's own boss or not, the following factors are identified and presented in a 'general to specific' order:

1. Value bestowed to individual autonomy and self-reliance. Chinese tend to value the ability to earn and accumulate wealth for oneself and one's family.
2. Unique parental influence particularly for initial career decision when the individual is at a stage where independence from parents is not yet achieved in many aspects such as psychological, emotional and financial.
3. Perceived structure of opportunities in relation to self-identity and self-efficacy. An individual assesses an occupation based on not only the opportunities it offers, but also with reference to his/her self-identity and self-efficacy. Higher congruence of self-identity with requirements of a particular occupation, and higher self-efficacy in that occupation will strengthen the decision to choose that occupation. Those who refuse to compromise their self-identity, or perceive low self-efficacy will decide not to make occupational choices according to the existing structure of opportunities.
4. Being blocked in conventional paths at the beginning of career, or being blocked in further career development at a later stage. Such individual will have to explore viable means of employment and usually starting own business provides an alternative.
5. Personal needs arising from present life situation. An individual constantly evaluates his/her career development in relation to his/her other personal needs as well as the needs of significant others usually family members.

The consideration of present life situation in making occupational decisions is indeed the focus of concern for stage theories of career development (e.g. Levinson et al., 1978). Stage theories postulate that no matter what an individual's occupation is, he/she will go through specific life stages. The nature, duration and exact timing of events may differ, but certain developmental tasks are predictable. However, these stage theories considers the individual's development in isolation as if he/she lives in a vacuum. Even those which describe stages from a psychosocial perspective combine career and family roles only. The experiences of the successful entrepreneurs and high-flyers inform us that the opinions and needs of people other than immediate family members have a significant impact on their career decisions. These people include colleagues and friends, which is indicative of the Confucian emphasis on collective interests rather than those of the individual. The individual assesses the consequences of his/her career decisions on the interests of significant others, which affects the perception of his/her personal needs and hence the final career decision. In this way, current stage models of career development which considers personal needs merely arising from individual developmental stages is not adequate to account for the reasoning behind which the successful entrepreneurs and high-flyers made their career decisions. Their career decisions need to be viewed from a collective perspective and analysed within a wider social context, which can then be explained in the light of themes of continuity in development in addition to stage-specific issues.

Conditions for Career Success

The career history of the successful entrepreneurs and high-flyers strongly suggest two conditions for career success: early responsibility and wide exposure.

Most of the successful entrepreneurs and high-flyers took up, at a very early stage of their career history, posts involving organizational responsibility. They were trained to be independent, decisive, conscientious and had a strong sense of accountability.

The Chinese particularly realize the importance of starting from the bottom in doing business.

> I joined the company after graduation. I had worked in different units to develop practical experience. It was good to have the opportunities to try out what had been learnt in university. There were many colleagues to help me learn the frontline job. I am interested in the technical job, but had to gradually take up administration. I remembered the days when I started working in the plant. The big fire, melting hundreds of tons of steel. You never got that from studying in university. The books do not tell you how it feels, the heat. You have to be there to feel the real thing. I was sweating. (E13)

However, early responsibility may not be an important condition for a successful entrepreneur because some of the successful entrepreneurs went to start off their own business right from the beginning of their career. However, wide exposure appears to be a universal condition for career success of the entrepreneurs and the high-flyers alike.

One of the ways the successful entrepreneurs and high-flyers obtained wide exposure is through moving jobs, which was made possible by the abundance of opportunities for career development in Hong Kong. Due to its centrality in location in the Asian region and easy access to Mainland China, many international corporations have set up regional headquarters or branches in Hong Kong. These corporations are gathered in a small area, facilitating easy physical access, thereby people change jobs without experiencing too many problems, such as change of residence, change of social affinities. What is more important is that one changes jobs without having to be uprooted from the business circles one has tried so hard to establish. The business connections can still enable the entrepreneurs and high-flyers in their business/career development.

While it is difficult to conclude whether the successful entrepreneurs and high-flyers changed jobs more often than the general population, their frequent job-moving behaviours indicate their ability to take risk and opportunities. Job move represents leaving a familiar environment, hence involving a degree of uncertainty and adjustment, which requires risk-taking. However it should be noted the successful entrepreneurs and high-flyers were rather cautious in taking up opportunities. They are not extreme high risk-takers. Rather their decisions were based on calculated risks. The opportunists are believed to be higher risk-takers compared to the professionals. Many opportunists changed to a different job function or even to a different business when they changed jobs, whereas the professionals in general had job moves in the same profession or only in the same organization. The professionals experiences less drastic changes, hence less adjustment.

As an outcome of many job moves, the successful entrepreneurs and high-flyers were exposed to various business and work settings. They became more knowledgeable about the dynamics of the business world increasing their efficacy as the mastermind of an organization.

The true entrepreneurs, while not having as many job moves as the other successful entrepreneurs and high-flyers, also experienced wide exposure due to the need for building up business connections. All in all, wide exposure is a very obvious characteristic of career success. Underlying this wide exposure is the individual's willingness to have himself/herself being exposed to risk.

Link to Success - Career Experiences as Developing Practice Wisdom[2] in Business and Management

The successful entrepreneurs and high-flyers, through their career experiences, developed practice wisdom about dealing with business and people. They developed a management philosophy that is shown to be 'worldly'. They emphasized a contingent management approach which is certainly an outcome of much hands-on management experiences. The ability to apply the contingent management approach requires the ability to judge what is right in what situation for what people, thus the ability to differentiate and discriminate.

On the other hand, the successful entrepreneurs and high-flyers also know where to position themselves in the organization. They know what they are personally good at and what the organization requires of him/her, hence deciding their functions in the organization. All these require the successful entrepreneurs and high-flyers to have good knowledge of themselves, their colleagues, the organization and the environment. This knowledge is built up from education and training, from experiences in the family and in work.

Notes

1   Ryan makes an important distinction between 'individualism' and 'self-reliance' indicating that the former is not appropriate but the latter is in understanding what motivates the entrepreneur.

2   Practice wisdom is a term used in social work literature, referring to the knowledge gained from direct practice experience.

7 Personality

Personality is a rather encompassing term including numerous aspects of the individual. It can refer to the individual's intrapsychic dynamics as conceived by the psychoanalysts, or one's overt observable behaviours as believed by the behaviourists, or represent the cognitive behaviours of the individual, etc. In the present context, personality refers to the traits exhibited by the individual as are measured on psychometric instruments. The motivational aspects of personality are treated separately and discussed in Chapter Eight on work motivation.

The trait approach has often been used to describe the personality of successful entrepreneurs and managers. Among the various possible ways to identify and measure traits, type A/B personality and 16PF are selected for review.

Type A/B Personality

The notion of type A/B personality and behaviour patterns was developed by Rosenman, Friedman and Strauss (1966) during a study of patients with coronary heart disease (CHD). They found that these patients exhibited similar behavioral characteristics, for example, they were extremely competitive, high-achieving, aggressive. Rosenman et. al. hence described such patterns as type A personality as opposed to the type B personality which refers to individuals who are more relaxed and easy-going. Rosenman et. al. also hypothesized that individuals who are type As may be more prone to coronary heart disease. On the basis of large-scale prospective epidemiological research, they found that this behavioral pattern in all groups of people, executives as well as car assembly workers, was a significant precursor to coronary heart disease and other illnesses; indeed, they have found a 6.5 times greater probability of heart disease in type A than the opposite type B. Their results are also confirmed by many other studies. Type A men have been found to have symptoms or risk factors of heart disease such as raised blood pressure and high cholesterol levels.

The popular stereotype of the successful entrepreneurs and top executives includes many type A characteristics. One study that looked at 943 white-collar, middle-class males in Buffalo, New York, shows that job status and type A personality are related. The men came from five different work settings. The findings indicate that not only was the type A behaviour patterns related to occupational status as measured by rank, level of occupational prestige and income, it was found to be significantly related to rapid career achievement as reflected by rank and income relative to age. Though type A tended to describe their jobs as having more responsibility, longer hours and heavier workload, they did not in general report more job dissatisfaction, anxiety than did type B. In one study on British managers (Marshall and Cooper, 1979), it was found that the most successful and satisfied executives are the typical type A.

Cooper and Cox (1988) interviewed forty-five managing directors, and found that 27 out of the 30 subjects who completed the Type A/B Behaviour Questionnaire scored very highly on type A behaviour (17 type A1s, 10 type A2s). This percentage (90 percent) is much higher than the distribution in the general population, that is, 50 percent are type As and 50 percent type Bs. Regarding individual type A/B personality characteristics, most of the MDs are never late, very competitive, going all out, fast at eating, hard driving and ambitious.

Among the high-flyers studied by Firth (1987), twelve of them were type A1, nine type A2, only three type B3 and no type B4. This was found to be higher than the population norm. The distribution of the high-flyers' scores on the individual scales showed that they were never late, very competitive, going all out, wanting a good job recognized by others, fast eating and walking, and had many outside interests. Whereas the distribution of their responses on other scales was rather equal between type A responses and type B responses. Hence it could be said the high flyers were generally type A but there was some evidence to suggest they have to learn to cope with stress to avoid illness.

Managerial Stress and Its Management

The above review of type A/B personality clearly suggests that successful business people tend to be type A, hence they are likely to be prone to stress. There is a large literature on the sources of managerial stress and how stress is managed. Much of this is also applicable to understanding entrepreneurial stress, because both entrepreneurs and managers face the same demand to excel in the competitive business world. Brummett, Pyle and Framholtz (1968) note that managers are suffering extreme physiological symptoms from stress at work, such as disabling ulcers or coronary heart disease. Other stress-related effects include anxiety and tension, affecting the individual's ability to manage family life and social relations. Hence the physical as well as mental effects of job stress pervades the whole quality of managerial life.

In the present context, the focus of examining managerial and entrepreneurial stress is in relation to an individual's personality and ways of thinking. In current literature, one of the major approaches to understanding stress, in general and work-related, is to conceive an individual's cognitive appraisals of events and situations as mediating between his/her environment and stress (Lazarus, 1966). Stress is a result of the perception that external demand exceeds an individual's ability to cope with it and the perception that he/she does not have the resources to manage the resulting problems. Hence stress involves the evaluation of oneself in relation to the environment and one's ability to cope with the demands of the environment. High self-efficacy and expectation of adequate coping resources will reduce the impact of stress on the individual.

With regard to stress management, Cooper (1976, 1981a, 1981b) identifies various coping methods employed by managers and that social support is found to be an important coping mechanism for managerial stress. In view of the centrality of family in Chinese society, it is thought that family is a major source of support for its members when coping with stress.

16 Personality Factors

Constructs of traits are always employed in conceiving what oneself is like and how individuals differ from one another. Traits, according to Cattell (1970), are relatively permanent and broad reaction tendencies and serve as the building blocks of personality.

In his process of theory building and research, Cattell had identified through factor analyses 16 major source traits initially labelled factors A, B, C, D, E, and so on. Figure 7.1 gives a summary of the bipolar traits represented by each scale on the 16PF.

Figure 7.1 Descriptions of Cattell's 16 Primary Personality Factors

Factor	Low Score Direction	High Score Direction
A	*Reserved*, detached, critical, aloof	*Outgoing*, easygoing, participating
B	*Less Intelligent*, concrete-thinking	*More Intelligent*, abstract-thinking, bright
C	*Affected by Feelings*, emotionally less stable, easily upset	*Emotionally Stable*, faces reality, calm, mature
E	*Humble*, mild, accommodating, conforming	*Assertive*, aggressive, stubborn, competitive
F	*Sober*, prudent, serious, taciturn	*Happy-go-lucky*, impulsively lively, enthusiastic
G	*Expedient*, disregards rules, feels few obligations	*Conscientious*, persevering, staid, moralistic
H	*Shy*, restrained, timid	*Venturesome*, socially bold, uninhibited, spontaneous
I	*Tough-minded*, self-reliant, realistic, no-nonsense	*Tender-minded*, clinging, overprotected, sensitive
L	*Trusting*, adaptable, free of jealousy, easy to get along with	*Suspicious*, self-opinionated, hard to fool

M	*Practical*, careful, conventional, regulated by external realities	*Imaginative*, wrapped up in inner urgencies, careless of practical matters
N	*Forthright*, natural, artless, unpretentious	*Shrewd*, calculating, worldly, penetrating
O	*Unperturbed*, confident, serene	*Apprehensive*, self-reproaching, worrying, troubled
Q1	*Conservative*, respecting established ideas, tolerant of traditional difficulties	*Experimenting*, liberal, free thinking, radical
Q2	*Group Oriented*, a 'joiner' and sound follower	*Self-sufficient*, prefers own decision, resourceful
Q3	*Undisciplined Self-conflict*, follows own urges, careless of protocol	*Controlled*, socially precise, following self-image
Q4	*Relaxed*, tranquil, unfrustrated	*Tense*, frustrated, driven, overwrought

The scores on each of the sixteen scales can range from one to ten. The scoring is arranged so that an average score of five to six is obtained by about 40 percent of the population.

Cox and Cooper (1988), from the 16PF results obtained from their managing directors, found that there is no one personality profile indicative of managerial success because the scores are distributed very widely over most of the scales, except that there is clearly a strong tendency towards being outgoing (factor A) and assertive (factor E), and a slight tendency towards being emotionally stable (factor C), trusting (factor L), imaginative (factor M), experimenting (factor Q1), self-sufficient (factor Q2) and shrewd (factor N).

High-flyers exhibit both similar and different 16PF patterns when compared to the top executives. The high-flyers in Firth's study (1987) were emotionally mature (factor C), assertive (factor E), towards the tough-minded and self-opinionated end of the scale (factors I and L). These factors point to the ability to push for power, be less affiliative in behaviour and retain self-control - all of which reflecting McClelland's (1975) pattern of achievers. The distributions of scores on other factors are fairly even. In another study of high-flyers by Fisher (1990), they are found to skew towards the high end of factors B, C, E, H and M and towards the low end of factors N and O, meaning they tend to be intelligent in abstract thinking, emotionally stable, assertive, venturesome, imaginative, forthright and unperturbed.

It can be seen that being emotionally stable (factor C) and assertive (factor E) are traits consistently related to managerial success. Similar correlation with success, however, is absent in other factors, suggesting that some of these factors may not be good indicators of success, especially those with very widespread and even distribution of scores. Besides, there is an apparent contrast of scores in factors like L and N, suggesting that these factors may correlate to success in different forms such as entrepreneurial and managerial success, and at different levels such as top-level and middle-level management.

Notwithstanding the relative lack of consensus in the 16PF findings, one of the contributions of the 16PF to understanding organizational behaviours, according to Cattell (1970), lies in the advantage of having a vocational guidance system based less on crude empiricism and more on test scores which represent known temperament or dynamic structures. Much can be brought to bear in the latter system from our knowledge of the natural history of the traits, and the sociology of the occupation. For instance, it is known that some source traits, like cyclothymia, intelligence, and threctic (Factor H) are largely constitutionally given, while others, such as premsia (I factor), super-ego strength, change. To know from the scores which of these traits account for the person fitting the occupational profile or criterion at a given moment is important.

The Chinese Personality

There are numerous studies on Chinese personality, the majority of which are based on western concepts and instruments to measure the Chinese personality, partly with a view to comparing Chinese with westerners.

With regard to using Cattell's 16PF for Chinese, only one study is traced. Chiu (1963) obtained a lower average score on Cyclothymia (easy going, warm-hearted) and Surgency (talkative, cheerful) for Chinese university students in Taiwan, than that of American university students.

Yang (1986) gives an excellent summary of the Chinese personality through a review of relevant studies particularly those published in Chinese which had not been accessible to the western scholars and readers. From the review, Yang identified the following patterns of the Chinese personality which had remained rather consistent:

1. Collectivist orientation
2. Other-orientation
3. Relationship orientation
4. Authoritarian orientation
5. Submissive disposition
6. Inhibited disposition
7. Effeminate disposition

Yang suggests that these patterns make up a social-oriented character. This national character is actually encouraged by Confucian ideals[1] and reinforced by family upbringing and socialization for generations. To examine the link of Confucian social philosophy to Chinese personality, one must begin with the fundamental Confucian assumption that man exists in relationship to others (King and Bond, 1985). The western starting point of the anomic individual is alien to Chinese considerations of man's behaviour, which see man as a relational being, socially situated and defined within an interactive context (Hsu, 1981; Bond and Hwang, 1986). Certain relationships are accorded a position of paramount importance, namely, those between sovereign and subject, father and son, elder brother and younger brother, husband and wife, and friend and friend. These relationships are constructed in hierarchical patterns. In each case, the senior member is accorded a wide range of prerogatives and authority with respect to the junior.

Both parties to the relationship are circumscribed by rules of correct behaviour, which entail both rights and responsibilities for each. Harmony will be realized if each member of the duality is conscientious in following the requirements of his/her role. Subsequently, this interpersonal harmony brings forth a political and social order.

The Confucian view of man and its expectations of man's behaviours has immediate implications for the daily functioning of Chinese people.

Hence it is necessary to consider the social or the relational dimension in understanding Chinese personality in general and Chinese work behaviour in particular.

In the same review, Yang (1986) discovered changing patterns of Chinese personality from the studies carried out since the 1970s. The traditional social-oriented character is changing in the direction towards an individual-oriented character, with an individualistic orientation that emphasizes competition, equalitarian values, enjoyment, autonomy and expression of oneself. It should be noted that these traditional and changing personality patterns are derived from studies of overseas Chinese, mostly in Taiwan and the US, hence the changes in orientation is a result of exposures to western values and influences associated with economic and societal modernization. As the People's Republic of China is now moving towards modernization, changes in personality orientations are expected. The Chinese national character will become less fixed and clearcut.

To summarize, the traits which have been found associated with career successful people are those typical of type A personality such as never late, fast, very competitive and going all out. In terms of the 16PF, they showed strong tendencies to be assertive, tough-minded. However, information concerning type A/B traits and 16PF characteristics of Chinese, particularly Chinese successful career people are not available. From the existing literature on Chinese personality, it is seen that Chinese are basically social-oriented in personality but are adopting a more individualistic orientation typical of westerners. It is suspected that Chinese people including Chinese successful career people exhibit different but not too drastically different type A/B and 16PF patterns from those reported in studies on western successful entrepreneurs and high-flyers.

Personality Characteristics of Hong Kong Successful Entrepreneurs and High-Flyers

This section identifies the personality traits of the successful entrepreneurs and high-flyers, with reference to the constructs of type A/B personality and the 16PF. Twenty-five entrepreneurs and twenty-eight high-flyers completed and returned the two questionnaires used to measure the type

A/B personality and the 16PF. The findings from each questionnaire will be presented separately and then analysed. In addition, there are some findings concerning stress and its management which will be analysed in relation to the type A/B personality.

Type A/B Personality

Borland's version of the type A/B Behaviour Questionnaire was used in the present study. Twenty-five successful entrepreneurs and twenty-eight high-flyers completed and returned the questionnaires which were then scored. The individual's total score was then classified according to types. The highest possible score is 140 and the lowest zero. A type A1 person is one with a total score of 140 to 111, type A2 110 to 71, type B1 70 to 31 and type B2 30 to zero. Table 7.1 shows the types of the successful entrepreneurs and the high-flyers.

Table 7.1 Type A/B Personality

Type	Entrepreneurs	High-Flyers	Total
A1	-	-	-
A2	22	20	42
	(88%)	(71%)	(79%)
B1	3	8	11
	(12%)	(29%)	(21%)
B2	-	-	-
Total subjects	25	28	53

It is easily discerned from Table 8.1 that the majority of the entrepreneurs and high-flyers fall into the Type A2 personality category. A quarter of all the entrepreneurs and high-flyers belong to Type B1 but no one is found to be extreme Type B2. The results suggest a pattern that the successful entrepreneurs and high-flyers tend to be moderate Type As.

Figure 7.2 Distribution of Type A/B Scores of Entrepreneurs (Total Respondents: 25)

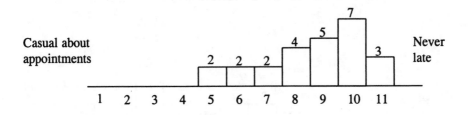

Casual about appointments — Never late

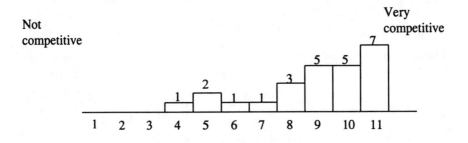

Not competitive — Very competitive

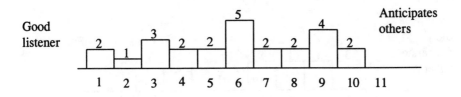

Good listener — Anticipates others

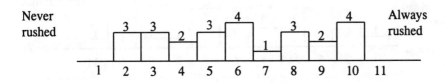

Never rushed — Always rushed

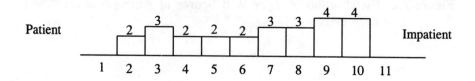

Patient ... Impatient

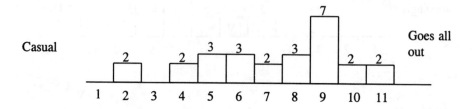

Casual ... Goes all out

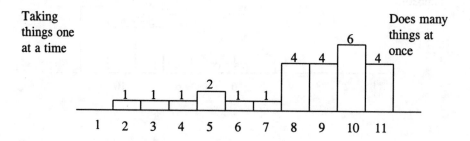

Taking things one at a time ... Does many things at once

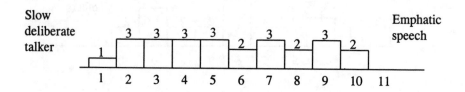

Slow deliberate talker ... Emphatic speech

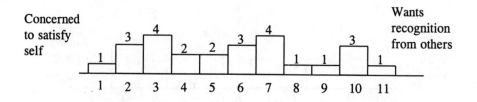

Concerned to satisfy self ... Wants recognition from others

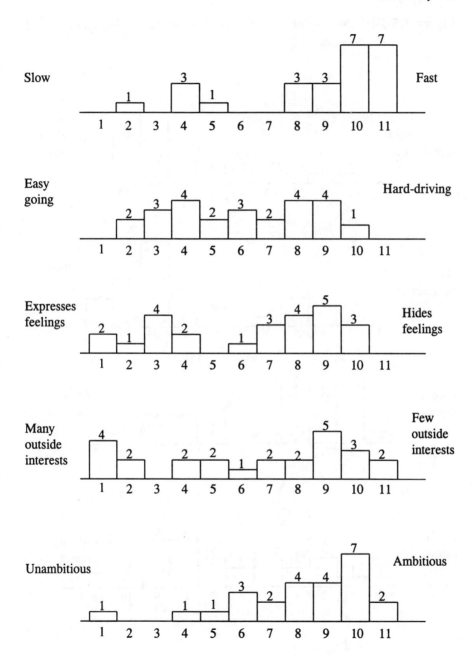

Figure 7.3 Distribution of Type A/B Scores of High-Flyers (Total Respondents: 28)

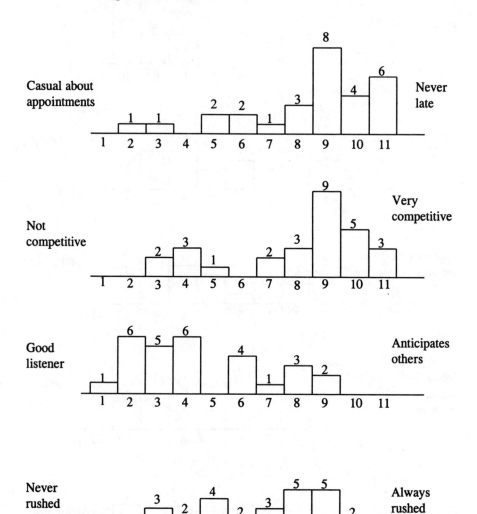

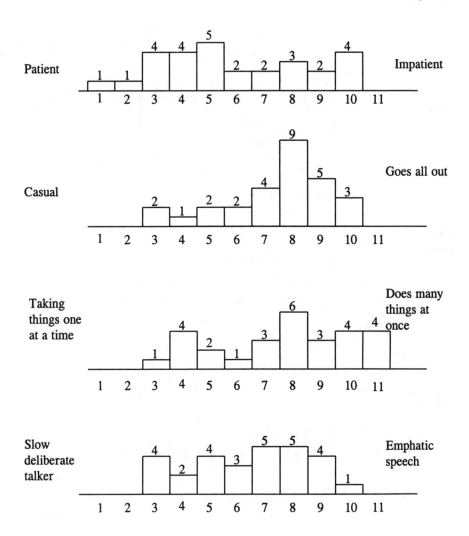

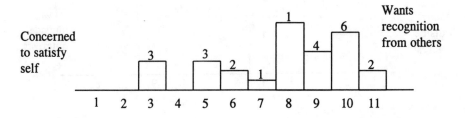

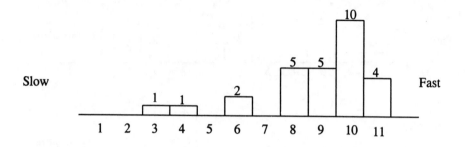

Slow ... Fast

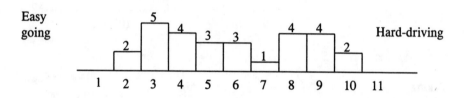

Easy going ... Hard-driving

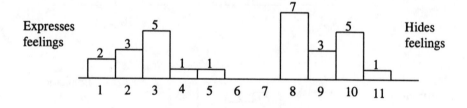

Expresses feelings ... Hides feelings

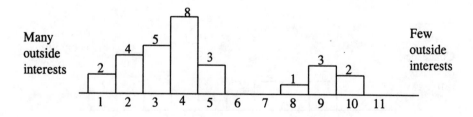

Many outside interests ... Few outside interests

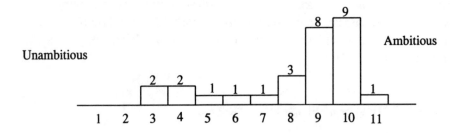

Figure 7.2 illustrates the distribution of scores of the Hong Kong entrepreneurs on the type A/B behaviour. The entrepreneurs are found to be never late, very competitive, going all out, trying to do many things at once, fast eating and walking, and ambitious, all of which are typical of type A traits. The distribution of scores on the remaining scales appear even, inclining towards both type A and type B ends.

The pattern of scores for the high-flyers on the type A/B behaviour is presented in Figure 7.3, showing strong tendency to the type A traits such as being never late, very competitive, going all out, trying to do many things at once, being fast and very ambitious. In addition, they also score high on wanting their good jobs to be recognized and such type B traits as being good listeners and having many outside interests. The patterns of scores on the other scales appear fairly even.

The major difference in the patterns of scores between the successful entrepreneurs and the high-flyers lie in the latter having a stronger tendency in traits such as being good listeners, wanting goods jobs to be recognized and having many outside interests. The entrepreneurs do not show a distinctive tendency to either end on these scales.

Both groups are never late, very competitive, fast, very ambitious, wanting to do many things at the same time and going all out. All these traits display an image of the person being highly efficient with an exacting time concept and always working full-stretched. The entrepreneurs and high-flyers recognized hardwork as one of the most essential work attributes, but it is important that the work is done in an efficient manner in order that time and energy is optimized. This explains why the entrepreneurs and high-flyers achieved more, both in quantity and quality, than the average person.

Stress and its management The successful entrepreneurs and high-flyers were asked to assess how stressful their work is, on a five-point-scale from one (not at all stressful) to five (very stressful). Their responses are shown in Table 7.2.

Table 7.2 Degree of Stress in Work

Degree of Stress	Entrepreneurs	High-Flyers
1 (not stressful)	-	-
2	7	11
3	10	13
4	10	6
5 (very stressful)	3	-
Total Subjects	30	30

As shown in Table 7.2, more entrepreneurs experienced greater stress. There are three entrepreneurs who rated themselves on the top of the scale. One of them is the owner of a giant multinational courier business. One is a small business owner. It is thought that being the person ultimately responsible for the life and death of the business, the entrepreneur has more anxieties.

> I always need to be alert to the global economic environment so that I can make strategic planning which is important for an international corporation. I am concerned with not only the overall strategic planning, but also the local planning to make sure the foundation vision of the company is not lost. (E11)

> I have to oversee many things, staff recruitment, people management, financial management, quality of service, marketing. The most worrying is about the liquidity of the business. I have to make sure there is no problem in the cash flow. (E19)

Facing varying degrees of stress, the entrepreneurs and high-flyers have developed ways of coping which were considered to be effective in view of the good health they enjoyed. Only one entrepreneur who rated himself as very stressful was undergoing a stress management programme on his recovery from a serious illness. The subjects were asked in the Questionnaire to indicate, from a list, the ways they cope with stress. It is noted that only those who rated themselves at 3 or above on the stress scale are asked to give such indication. Their responses are shown below, which are substantiated by interview transcripts.

• *Pursue personal interests or hobbies (11 entrepreneurs and 16 high-flyers)*

> I devote 2/3 of my time (waking hours) to work and 1/3 to charity. I do not have regular working hours. I work when required no matter where I am. But when I am with my family and friends, I will forget work and enjoy myself. (E7)

> Everybody has stress. It's how you deal with it. I work hard and I play hard. I relax when I play, then I can work hard again. (E22)

• *Talk to someone who understands (20 entrepreneurs and 14 high-flyers)*

> When I go home and tell my parents the difficulties I have at work, they will listen patiently and not ask me to quit. I think that is encouraging. If I am mad at somebody, they will say something "yeah, he's really bad". They give me an outlet. I get more relaxed after speaking out. (H1)

• *Find out what is causing the stress and deal with it (2 entrepreneurs and 8 high-flyers)*

• *Put aside the stressful job for a while (4 entrepreneurs and 3 high-flyers)*

> When I'm off, even if I have to bring work home, I will take some time before going home just to stroll around to relax myself. When I arrive home, I have something to eat, take a shower. Then I start working again. When I get stuck, I simply go to bed and sleep. If there is anything that cannot be solved for the time being, just put it aside. (H2)

• *Take a holiday (3 high-flyers)*

• *Give up on the stressful task (1 high-flyer)*

More entrepreneurs tended to talk to someone and pursue personal interests in managing stress. Whereas the high-flyers employed the same strategies as the entrepreneurs did, they also coped with stress through some other ways such as taking a holiday and dealing with the causes of stress. The high-flyers' coping styles are rather consistent with their type B trait of having many outside interests.

It is interesting to note that only a few considered taking a holiday or giving up. Given their heavy workload and importance in the organizations, it is simply unrealistic for the entrepreneurs and high-flyers to leave or withdraw.

Though taking different measures to manage stress, the entrepreneurs and high-flyers display a common characteristic which is their attitudes to stress. They showed high acceptance of stress as part of life, that it is inevitable in the kind of work they were doing given their roles and positions in the organizations.

> No, there's no pressure. If there is, it's surely an excuse. Everybody in the world... perhaps not everybody... but people at a position like mine should have great pressure. I had no money in the beginning. I was very worried about the cash flow. Our expenditure was over 10 million per month. But I'm never worried. I believe there's a solution for every problem. We shouldn't add pressure onto things to increase our burden. Basically, every job has pressure. If you think it's something, it is something. If you think it's nothing, it is nothing. Is there any pressure? Yes, there is. But if you ignore it, it's nothing. I think pressure is an excuse. I also believe that you can't improve if there's no pressure. Can't always be easy-going. (E14)

> You don't have the solution to every problem, so take the problem as it comes. You have to think this way, otherwise you end up neurotic. (H1)

> I have stress but I won't quit because of it. I take it as it comes. I treat it as part of my life. If you don't talk about it, it is not stress to you any more. I think stress is related to ability. If you always find yourself stressful, first ask yourself whether you are capable enough. Find out your own problem first. Don't say it is the other people who have problems. (E9)

These attitudes to stress bring positive ways of managing stress, positive in the sense that the entrepreneurs and high-flyers take initiatives to deal with the difficulties rather than allowing themselves to be driven by the difficulties. As a result, work performance and personal well-being is maintained, even growth and development in some cases.

> Pressure is different to different people. I work better under pressure. I won't do anything if I've no pressure. I always tell others that I love examinations. I can do really well because I know there's a goal and I have to achieve it. Now when I need to hand in a report, I tell my client to give me a deadline. I work to the deadline. Under pressure I would perform. (E17)

Stress can be constructive depending on how it is perceived and handled. The successful entrepreneurs and high-flyers perceive pressure and difficulties as a challenge, hence an opportunity for improvement. Even when stress is truly felt, they have effective ways to deal with it such that the negative impact of stress is allayed.

> I did not realize I had been under intense stress until one day I found myself seriously ill. After leaving the hospital I decided to do something about my stress. I went to a stress-management workshop and was much encouraged by the instructor. He said 'Don't let stress hit you. You are not the only one who has stress. Look at the people who are here. You are people in the same boat'. I have become more self-aware, and health-conscious.(E21)

Family support That the successful entrepreneurs and high-flyers experienced little negative impact of stress is very much related to the support they gained from their family.

The successful entrepreneurs and high-flyers claimed they had the support from their family in what they are doing. On a five-point scale ranging from one (not supportive) to five (very supportive), they rated the degree of family support they have. Table 7.3 summarizes the findings on family support.

Table 7.3   Degree of Family Support

Degree of Family Support	Entrepreneurs	High-Flyers
1 (not supportive)	-	-
2	3	-
3	6	5
4	11	15
5 (very supportive)	10	10
Total Subjects	30	30

It is seen from table 7.3 that the entrepreneurs and high-flyers received a high degree of family support. Only three entrepreneurs suggested they received less than average support (3 is the rating of average support).

There are three sources of family support:-

1.   Principal source is spouse (16 entrepreneurs and 26 high-flyers)
2.   Principal source is parents (3 entrepreneurs and 2 high-flyers)
3.   Both from spouse and parents (8 entrepreneurs and 2 high-flyers)

Support from spouse All the high-flyers who were married (28) claimed they had a very supportive spouse. Twenty-four of the twenty-seven married entrepreneurs also reported having a supportive spouse, whereas the other three did not find their spouse and other family members particularly supportive. Those who were not married (two women high-flyers and three entrepreneurs) received support from their parents.

The support from spouse mainly comes in the form of financial contributions to the family, giving emotional support, and offering advice. The support is seen as vital by the entrepreneurs and high-flyers for their career development, particularly at critical points of their careers.

Five entrepreneurs started their business with small capital after they had married. Support from the spouse became decisive. Leaving a well paid job to take up an adventure with unstable income has important implications for the whole family, since men are the traditional breadwinners in Chinese families. One male entrepreneur suggested that his wife is the most significant person in his career history:

The significant person in my career? I would say it's my wife. She gave me unreserved support when I decided to have my own business. At that time we only had $10,000 savings and we agreed to put it all on the new venture. As a result we had to cut short on everything. I used to have $8,000 housing allowance, so at that time we moved to Cheung Chau to live in a smaller flat for $2,000. She also worked to help the family finance, and we had to travel a long way each day to and from work. Not long after she was pregnant, but we had confidence that we could go through the difficult time. It would only be a short while. In fact we did persist through the beginning stage of the new venture, soon afterwards it was very smooth. Nowadays my wife does not work any more. She stays at home looking after the kids. She does not feel bored at all. It helps me put full concentration onto my work. (E19)

I did not encounter any objection when I decided to quit my well-paid job to start my business. My wife had a job but she was about to give birth to our son. We only had $10,000 which we thought was enough for three months' expenditure. We were so worried that there were many sleepless nights. Yet we had passed through that period. My wife was a great support to me. (E20)

The turning point in my career was to start my own business. The decision was inspired by my wife who was a businesswoman. I learnt many things from her and thought I could realize my goals through running my own business. (E9)

Encouragement from the spouse was also decisive for the high-flyers (4) when they changed job or function.

When the managing director of my present company approached me and asked me to switch over to (overseeing) manufacturing, I was much encouraged by my husband. His attitude was that it worth taking a chance, taking a risk. It wouldn't do any harm if things did not turn out right. (HF14)

Apart from being supportive at critical moments, the spouse continually rendered their support to what the entrepreneurs (14) and high-flyers (22) did.

I am glad I do not have a nagging wife, so that when I return home, I do not have to be bothered by trivial things that happen in the family. (E18)

> My wife has her own job, which I think is favourable for our understanding each other. She knows what it's like in the business world. It is important that she knows what I am doing, so that we have mutual understanding. (E8)

A strong image of a supportive spouse emerges from the above transcripts. In traditional Chinese society, it is rather natural to find supportive wives. A wife is supposed to be subservient to her husband and is expected to give support to him when he is in difficulty. However, the experiences of the married female entrepreneur (1) and high-flyers (7) indicate the supportive spouse was also there. As suggested at the beginning of this chapter, women may still be seen as alien in the business world. If women are to succeed in this environment, they may need to take greater effort than their male counterparts. A supportive husband will surely help to sustain the successful female entrepreneurs and high-flyers in their course to excel in a male-dominant environment.

> I came from a family where women were supposed to stay at home. My husband thinks the other way. He is very positive about my pursuing my own career. (HF15)

> My father-in-law doesn't really like me having a job. Fortunately I have the support of my husband. He thinks I should not waste what I have learnt from schools. (HF17)

One woman entrepreneur started her business after she had divorced. The reason for divorce is related to her husband not giving her the space and support she wanted in pursuing her own life goals.

Support from parents Eight entrepreneurs and two high-flyers claimed they had the support from their parents as well as from their spouse. The parents' support came when they decided to start their own business, in the form of financial assistance and concrete advice. They continued to offer advice on business matters. The spouses supported the entrepreneurs and the high-flyers through looking after the family and giving encouragement.

One entrepreneur and two woman high-flyers who were single said their parents were their principal source of support, so did the woman entrepreneur who had divorced. One other single entrepreneur indicated he had the both psychological and practical support of his parents:

> I cannot say whether our (my parents and I) relationship is intimate, all I can be sure is that we have been very close. We talk about almost anything. We share all we have in mind. Even now when I have a problem in business, I will consult my parents. Like what others say, I have a family to fall back on. (E21)

The entrepreneurs and high-flyers still maintained close contacts with their family of origin though they did not live under the same roof. The close contacts were also made possible by geographical proximity given the small area of Hong Kong. The extended family is found to be able to carry out a mutual-help function for its members. Individual stress can be reduced through this family support.

It is noted that more high-flyers obtained the support from their spouses whereas more entrepreneurs tended to seek support also from their parents. This may be related to the fact that the entrepreneurs have parents who themselves run business, hence being in a better position to offer support in terms of experience, advice and encouragement.

Children The children of the successful entrepreneurs and high-flyers also exert their influence on their parents. Many of the entrepreneurs (8) and high-flyers (12) have young children who still need much attention from them.

> I insist that I have breakfast with my son, and walk him to school. We save this period of time exclusively for each other. Then I start my day's work. (E19)

> I used to work very late. But after I had given birth to my baby, I realized family is much more important. One day I will retire, all that is left is my family. It does not mean I don't work hard any more, it's just that I am striking a right balance between work and family. (HF2)

The entrepreneurs and high-flyers, in order to make a good parent, try to reserve time for family functions and they seldom take work home. In this way they maintain quite a clear dividing line between work and family, which may have helped them to relax from work and stay healthy.

16 Personality Factors

Cattell's 16 Personality Factors (16PF) Questionnaire (Form A) is another psychometric instrument used in this research to measure the personality characteristics of the successful entrepreneurs and high-flyers.

Twenty-five of the successful entrepreneurs (83 percent) and twenty-eight high-flyers (93 percent) completed and returned the 16 PF questionnaire. It should be noted that all the raw scores were converted to stens according to the British General Population Means (Male + Female), because there has not been any norms established on the 16PF for any population types in Hong Kong. The mean scores of the successful entrepreneurs and high-flyers on the sixteen scales are presented in Table 7.4 and the distribution shown in Figure 7.4 and 7.5 respectively.

Table 7.4 Mean Sten Scores of 16PF of Successful Entrepreneurs and High-Flyers

Factor	High-Flyers	Entrepreneurs
A	6.9	5.6
B	7.1	7.6
C	5.8	6.3
E	7.5	8.0
F	5.6	5.0
G	6.9	6.3
H	7.2	6.9
I	4.4	3.4
L	6.1	4.9
M	7.0	7.2
N	4.8	2.9
O	4.4	4.0
Q1	6.0	7.2
Q2	4.2	5.9
Q3	5.8	6.8
Q4	3.7	3.2
Total Subjects	28	25

It is found that the mean stens of the 16PF obtained by the successful entrepreneurs and the high-flyers as shown in Table 4.18 are mostly very close. Slight differences are observed in relation to the following factors:-

1. Factor A. The high-flyers are more outgoing than the successful entrepreneurs.
2. Factor I. The successful entrepreneurs show a stronger tendency to be tough-minded.
3. Factor L. The high-flyers are more suspicious than the successful entrepreneurs.
4. Factor N. The entrepreneurs are more forthright than the high-flyers
5. Factor Q1. The entrepreneurs are more unperturbed than the high-flyers.
6. Factor Q2. The high-flyers are more group-oriented than the successful entrepreneurs.

Concerning the similarities, both the successful entrepreneurs and the high-flyers obtained rather high mean stens on factor B, E, H and M, suggesting both groups are more intelligent, assertive, venturesome and imaginative whereas the two groups obtained rather low scores on Factor Q4 suggesting they are relaxed.

In spite of its precision hence usefulness for comparison purposes, the mean sten may at times be skewed by rare cases of extremely low or extremely high individual scores. Hence examining the distribution of scores on the 16PF is also useful. The distributions of the scores obtained by the twenty-one successful entrepreneurs and the twenty-eight high-flyers are shown in Figure 7.4 and Figure 7.5 respectively.

Figure 7.4 gives a clear view of the 16PF patterns obtained by the successful entrepreneurs. They show a tendency to the high score direction on factors B, E, H, M and Q3, which suggests they are more intelligent, assertive, venturesome, imaginative and controlled. On the other hand, they show a tendency to the low score direction on factors I, N, O and Q4, implying they tend to be tough-minded, forthright, unperturbed and relaxed.

Figure 7.4 Distribution of Stens of Entrepreneurs on the 16PF (Total Respondents: 25)

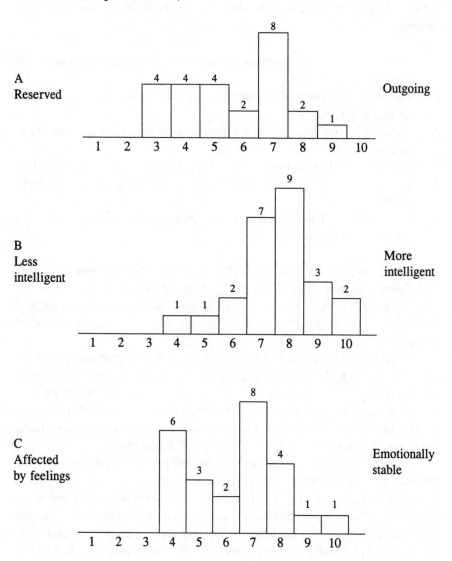

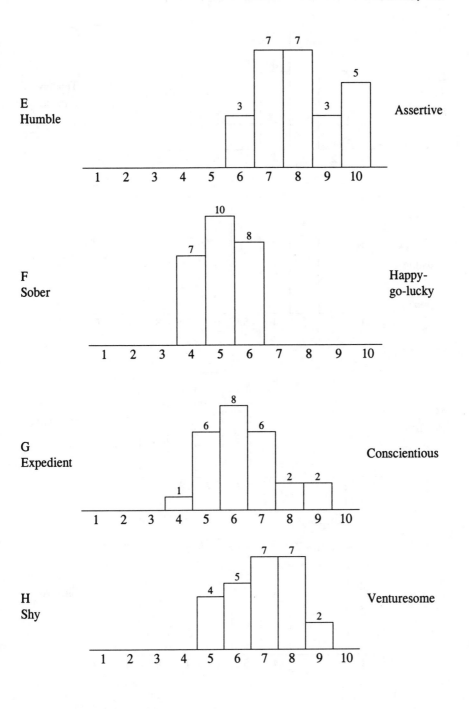

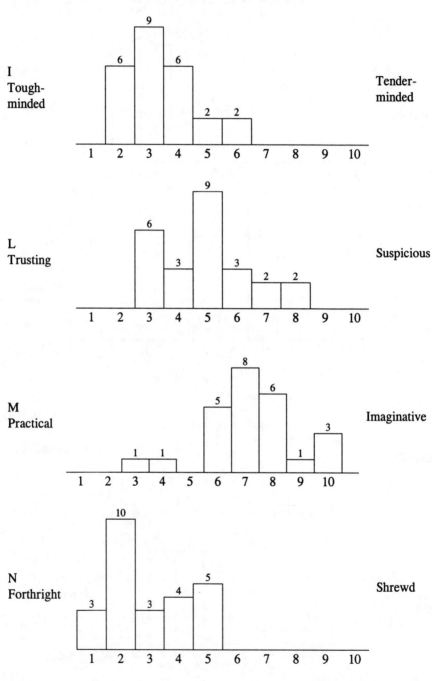

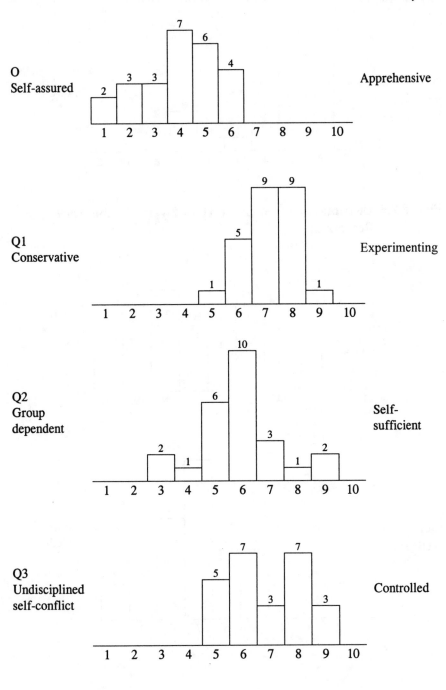

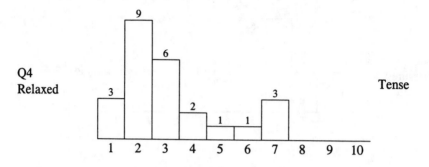

Figure 7.5 Distribution of Stens of High-Flyers on the 16PF (Total
Respondents: 28)

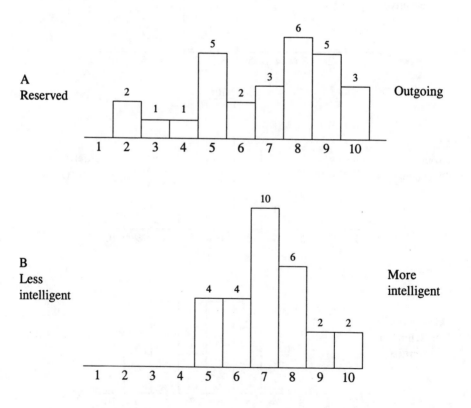

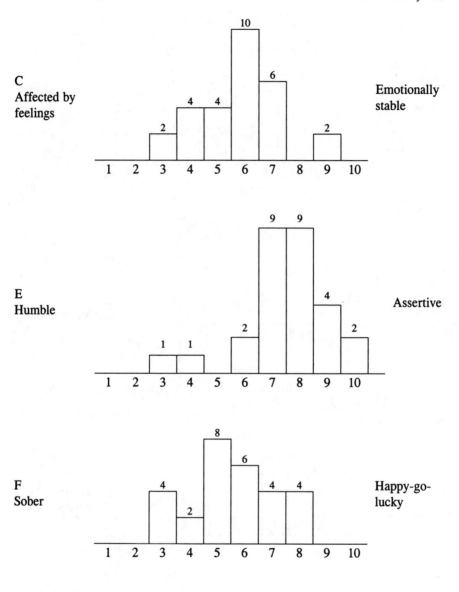

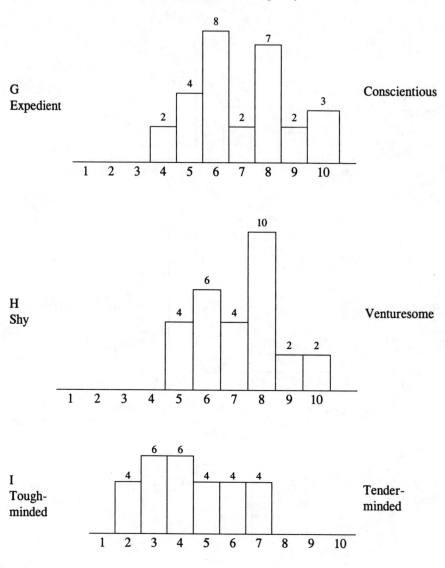

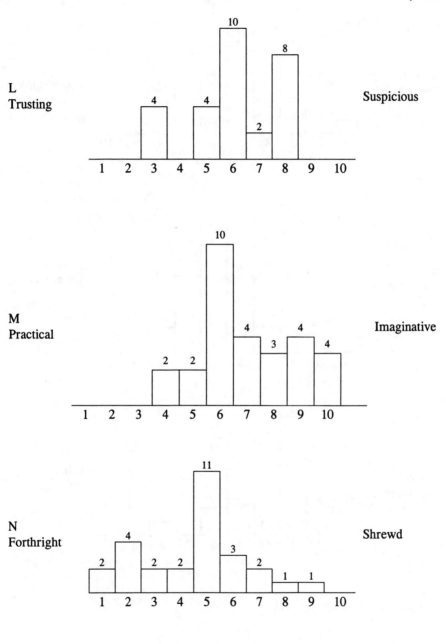

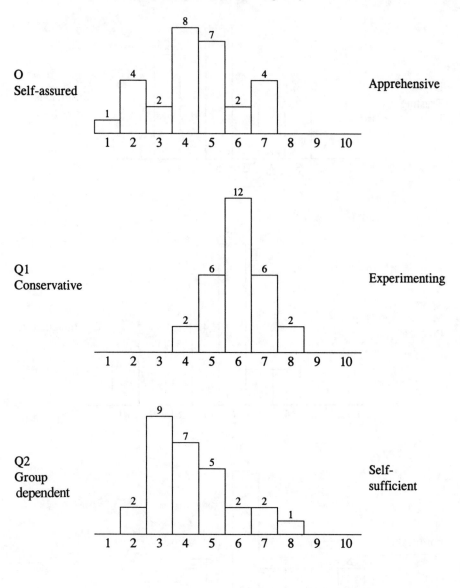

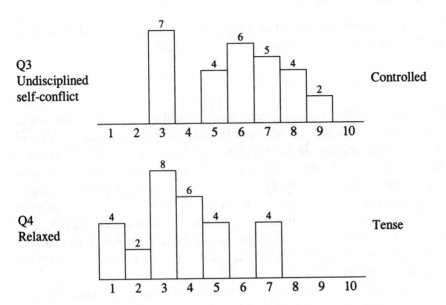

The high-flyers' 16PF patterns look more spreadout than those of the successful entrepreneurs. Most of the scores cluster around the average stens. Nevertheless, they show a tendency to the high score direction on factors A, B, E, G, H, M and to the low score direction on factors I, N, Q2 and Q4, suggesting they tend to be warmhearted, more intelligent, assertive, conscientious, venturesome, imaginative, tough-minded, forthright, group-oriented and relaxed.

In summarizing the findings on the 16PF so far, it can be said that both groups tend to be more intelligent, assertive, venturesome, imaginative, tough-minded and relaxed, whereas the successful entrepreneurs are found to be more tough-minded and forthright than the high-flyers. In addition, the successful entrepreneurs also tend to be controlled and unperturbed whereas the high-flyers tend to be outgoing, conscientious and group-oriented.

From the tendencies they exhibit on the 16PF, it can be suggested that the successful entrepreneurs as a group portray a personality that is consistently tough, confident (assertive, tough-minded, controlled) and sophisticated (intelligent, venturesome, imaginative) whereas the high-flyers in general portray a personality with contrasting characteristics such as being venturesome and yet conscientious and group-oriented, assertive, tough-minded and yet forthright and warmhearted.

Summary

The majority of the successful entrepreneurs and the high-flyers are found to be type A2 and the rest of them B3, suggesting their personality and life style can possibly bring stress-related health problems. However, though stress was reported, the successful entrepreneurs and high-flyers have effective ways of coping with stress including a positive attitude towards stress. In addition, many of them have strong family support which helps reduce the impact of stress in both practical and affective ways. As a result, all except one successful entrepreneurs and all the high-flyers reported good health and that both groups tend to be relaxed as measured by the 16PF.

The 16PF results also suggest that both the successful entrepreneurs and the high-flyers exhibit a tendency to be more intelligent, assertive, venturesome, imaginative. The major differences though very small are that the high-flyers are more outgoing, conscientious and group-oriented whereas the successful entrepreneurs tend to be tough-minded, forthright, unperturbed, experimenting and controlled. These differences are congruent with the differences identified in their type A/B patterns that the high-flyers tend to be good listeners and have more outside interests.

Personality and Career Success

Type A/B Personality

The majority of the successful entrepreneurs (88 percent) and high-flyers (71 percent) fall into the type A2 personality category, whereas 12 percent of the entrepreneurs and 29 percent of the high-flyers belong to Type B1 and no one is found to be extreme Type B. The normal distribution in the general population is that 10 percent of them are A1s, 40 percent each of A2s and B3s, and 10 percent B4s. The results indicate that successful entrepreneurs and high-flyers are more type A than the average population.

As observed from the patterns on the fourteen type A/B characteristics, the successful entrepreneurs and high-flyers are found to have a stronger tendency to be very ambitious, competitive, strict about time, act very fastly, which all seem to fit in with the general perceptions of a successful person.

1. Ambition is considered a prerequisite for career success. They must be highly ambitious in order to be motivated for working towards certain goals.
2. In addition to being ambitious, they must also have the behaviour repertoire and determination to realize their ambitions.
3. To succeed in the business world which is highly competitive, the entrepreneurs and high-flyers must be able to move ahead of others. Having a strict time concept is important because it means time is not wasted and that being punctual brings good reputation.

The high-flyers also tend to be good listeners, wanting their good jobs to be recognized and having many outside interests. The first two tendencies are thought to be related to the nature of their work.

1. The jobs the high-flyers do require them to be good listeners because they are supposed to be the links between top management and frontline operational staff. The high-flyers need to attend to the interests of both or more levels in the organization. In turn, those who are good listeners will be more likely to advance on the career ladder.
2. When job promotion is decided by someone else which is what happens to the high-flyers, they certainly wish themselves to be recognized and given credit for their good jobs.
3. It seems to be a matter of personal preference that the high-flyers have many outside interests because both the successful entrepreneurs and the high-flyers have similar treatment of work and personal life. Sixty-seven percent of the entrepreneurs and 50 percent of the high-flyers make clear distinctions of work and personal life. The high-flyers are no less work-centred than the successful entrepreneurs to make them have more outside interests.

Apart from the abovementioned stronger type A/B tendencies, the successful entrepreneurs and the high-flyers are found to be moderate on the other type A/B characteristics, suggesting they tend not to go to extremes in life when seeking career success. In fact, striking a balance in life in the pursuit of harmony is a Confucian aspiration.

High tolerance of stress The majority of the successful entrepreneurs and high-flyers are type A2, hence theoretically speaking their proneness to coronary heart disease is not low. In addition, the successful entrepreneurs and the high-flyers did report feelings of stress at work. However, with the exception of one successful entrepreneur who mentioned record of serious illness, the remaining successful entrepreneurs and all the high-flyers seem to enjoy good health. There are some possible reasons for the successful entrepreneurs and high-flyers not being hit by the negative impact of stress.

1. They have developed a high tolerance of stress since childhood. Many of the successful entrepreneurs and high-flyers came from low socioeconomic status families which faced many difficulties in life. Through their parents' and their own experiences of coming through the difficulties, they developed positive attitudes towards stress and learnt to live with it.
2. Apart from directly tackling the problems that may cause stress, the successful entrepreneurs and high-flyers have developed various effective ways to prevent or reduce the negative impact of stress.
3. A majority of them have strong support from their family members. If stress is shared, its impact on the individual will be much lessened.

The ability of the successful entrepreneurs' and the high-flyers' ability to tolerance stress is related to their past experiences of coping with difficult situations, their values and attitudes towards problems and difficulties, and the skills and resources they have to cope with them. It is postulated that their high tolerance of stress is mediated by a high expectancy of reward in difficult situations as well as a high self-efficacy to achieve the reward from these difficult situations. If expectancy of reward is high, stress can be tolerated. If self-efficacy is high, stress is less utterly felt.

The 16 Personality Factors

Cattell (1970) believes that traits are developed out of a process of cognitive learning in interaction with the environment. The traits as measured by the 16 PF are hence thought of as resulting from childhood experiences as well as developmental experiences in later life.

The 16 factors represent the following personality traits:-

A   Reserved/Outgoing
B   Less Intelligent/More Intelligent
C   Affected by Feelings/Emotionally Stable
E   Humble/Assertive
F   Sober/Happy-Go-Lucky
G   Expedient/Conscientious
H   Shy/Venturesome
I   Tough-Minded/Tender-Minded
L   Trusting/Suspicious
M   Practical/Imaginative
N   Forthright/Shrewd
O   Unperturbed/Apprehensive
Q1   Conservative/Experimenting
Q2   Group-Dependent/Self-Sufficient
Q3   Undisciplined/Controlled
Q4   Relaxed/Tense

Since 68.2 percent of the adults in the British general population obtained sten scores from four to seven (Cox and Cooper, 1989), it is more meaningful to consider those factors with mean sten scores which are around four or below and around seven or above. In such case, findings on the 16PF suggest that both the successful entrepreneurs and the high-flyers are more intelligent (factor B), assertive (factor E), venturesome (factor H), imaginative (factor M), and relaxed (factor Q4). In addition, the successful entrepreneurs also showed a tendency to be tough-minded (factor I), forthright (factor N), self-assured (factor O), experimenting (Q1) and controlled (factor Q3) whereas the high-flyers showed a tendency to be outgoing (factor A), conscientious (factor G) and group-oriented (factor Q2).

In order to test whether these traits are unique to successful career people, their 16 PF scores are compared to those of thirty-two social work students who have work experience. The mean stens of the three groups are shown in Table 7.5.

Table 7.5   Mean Sten of 16PF of Hong Kong Successful People and Social Work Students

Factor	Entrepreneurs	High-Flyers	Social Work Students
A	5.6	6.9	5.6
B	7.6	7.1	6.3
C	6.3	5.8	5.1
E	8.0	7.5	5.7
F	5.0	5.6	5.0
G	6.3	6.9	5.6
H	6.9	7.2	4.9
I	3.4	4.4	6.6
L	4.9	6.1	5.9
M	7.2	7.0	5.8
N	2.9	4.8	5.2
O	4.0	4.4	6.4
Q1	7.2	6.0	5.3
Q2	5.9	4.2	5.0
Q3	6.8	5.8	5.3
Q4	3.2	3.7	5.8
Total subjects	25	28	32

When compared to social work students, both the successful entrepreneurs and high-flyers show a stronger tendency towards the high score direction on factors B, E, H, M, Q1 and Q3, and the low score direction on factors I, O and Q4. These suggest that the successful career people are more intelligent, assertive, venturesome, imaginative, experimenting, controlled, tough-minded, self-assured and relaxed.

Among the successful career people, the entrepreneurs have stronger tendency to being trusting (factor L), forthright (factor N), experimenting (factor Q1) and controlled (factor Q3), whereas the high-flyers show stronger tendency to being warmhearted (factor A) and conscientious (factor G).

A summary of career-success traits and their brief definitions are given below:-

Successful entrepreneurs and high-flyers

More Intelligent	Abstract-thinking, bright
Assertive	Aggressive, authoritative, competitive, stubborn
Venturesome	Socially bold, uninhibited, spontaneous
Imaginative	Careless of practical matters, unconventional, absent-minded
Relaxed	Tranquil, torpid, unfrustrated

Successful entrepreneurs

Tough-minded	Self-reliant, realistic, no-nonsense
Forthright	Natural, artless, unpretentious
Unperturbed	Confident, secure, serene, self-satisfied
Experimenting	Liberal, free thinking, radical
Controlled	Socially precise, following self-image, compulsive

High-flyers

Outgoing	Easy-going, participating
Conscientious	Persevering, proper, moralistic, rule-bound
Group-oriented	A "Joiner" and Sound Follower

Studying the brief and the substantive descriptions of the abovementioned traits which characterize the successful entrepreneurs and the high-flyers, it is proposed that the successful entrepreneurs tend to be consistently confident, spontaneous and self-centred whereas the high-flyers are equally confident, spontaneous but less self-centred. The difference in the degree of self-centredness and other-centredness is often conceived as what distinguishes the entrepreneurs and the managers. Porter and Lawler (1968) described such great individuals like Henry Ford, John Rockefeller as 'self-made men' of single-minded dedication, forcefulness and imagination. They were self-directed, independent persons who generated their own values in life. However, Riesman (1950) argues that with the advent of the 1950s, success was more likely to be achieved by the 'outer-directed' person, the individual who is super-sensitive to the thinking and desires of others, the individual who complies with the norms of a situation and adheres to the values of the organization. Whyte (1956) calls such individual the organization man. Riesman suggests that inner direction is typical of the 'old entrepreneur' while other direction is becoming the typical characteristic of the 'new middle class as exemplified by the bureaucrat and the salaried employee in business', and that the inner-directed person is being replaced by the outer-directed person. Whyte contends in a similar way that the social ethic and the kind of behaviour it requires of an individual who is to succeed in the modern American firm, especially the large firm, is one which demands a type of conformity and a go-along-with-the crowd behaviour. However, Whyte observed that top executives were still motivated by the old individualistic values of competition and creativeness representing an inner-directedness.

The successful entrepreneurs interviewed in the present study clearly exhibit the kind of inner-directedness these writers described. And the fact that these inner-directed entrepreneurs are still prospering thirty years after Riesman and Whyte suggested the eclipse of the entrepreneur gives a reassurance that the entrepreneur is not dead and has not been replaced by the organization man/woman. In fact, the entrepreneurial spirit is infiltrating the minds of the organization men/women who aspire success in modern bureaucracies as salaried employees. The high-flyers are found to have a tendency to exhibit rather contrasting personality traits, in the sense that these traits do not exemplify merely one particular personality disposition such as inner-directedness or outer-directedness. Instead, the high-flyers show tendencies of both directions. Their type A/B behaviour patterns indicate that they are assertive, competitive and they also are good listeners and like to be recognized. In addition, their 16PF patterns suggest they are assertive, competitive, spontaneous and yet they are also aware of rules and other people. Hence it is observed that while the entrepreneur is not dead, the organization man/woman is taking on an entrepreneurial spirit which is becoming crucial for success in modern organizations. Similar conceptions of the high-flyers are found in Toffler (1971)'s notion of associative man and Pinchot's (1985) notion of intrapreneur.

The abovementioned personality characteristics of the successful entrepreneurs and the high-flyers are attributed to the cognitive learning that has been taking place in their course of life development. It has been seen that their childhood experiences had encouraged an independent, self-reliant and socially sensitive personality. Their educational experiences and achievement had reinforced their competitiveness and independence, whereas their career exposures had taught them to be assertive and creative in order to survive and excel in the business world. The observed difference in the self-directedness (inner-directedness) of the successful entrepreneurs and the high-flyers is conceived to be a result of the difference in the kind and the extent of the cognitive learning the individuals have acquired from their unique experiences in childhood, education and career. Examining the nature and the extent of learning from experiences involves a heredity-environment discussion. The sets of traits found in the successful entrepreneurs and the high-flyers which initiate and guide their behaviours, are genetically based but often subject to modification by learning experiences. While recognizing the significance of heredity in forming personality disposition, the present study focuses on the influence of the developmental environment in shaping the personality of the successful entrepreneurs and the high-flyers.

As a result of the cognitive learning acquired in life experiences, the successful entrepreneurs and high-flyers have formed a set of personal constructs with which they use to guide their actions. The various personalities of the successful entrepreneurs and the high-flyers are viewed by the personal construct theorists as their having *different* constructs which are organized in a hierarchical order. There is a focus of convenience and a range of convenience for every construct. Hence different constructs, based on their respective conveniences, are used to define different relationships and situations so that a high predictive efficiency can be obtained. The personal construct theorists conceive the ability to use different constructs according to varying circumstances as the best way to deal with the environment. The apparently contrasting personality characteristics found in the high-flyers can be conceived as their using different constructs in dealing with different people and different situations, implying a flexible personality.

The flexible personality can be seen as a manifestation of the networked self developed from the childhood experiences of the high-flyers. The networked self implicates a concern with relationships. With this comes the notion of differential order developed by Fei (1948) to explain the structure of relationships in the Chinese society. In this view, the individual is at the centre of a series of concentric circles, the closest having the strongest blood ties. What is significant is that rights and obligations differ according to the relative positions of people in such circles. In this context, the individual may find himself/herself relating to a number of significant others simultaneously. This tapestry of dualities may seem unmanageable, as it may call forth seemingly incompatible patterns of behaviour of superordination and subordination from the same person. However, Fei argues that multiple standards of morality may well operative and be seen as perfectly acceptable. Similarly, the apparent contradiction in differential standards is not considered by Bond and Hwang (1986) as an important issue when it is seen from a relational perspective on the nature of social life; one is human in one's relationships and develops the skills necessary to fulfil all one's responsibilities. Hence, adaptability,[2] not consistency, becomes a focal issue in considering personality.

Adaptability occurs throughout the life of the successful entrepreneurs and the high-flyers but is considered particularly critical when they entered the world of work since they encountered a lot more differences than those presented in family and in schools. Relationships in the business and the work contexts are more diverse, rules of the games also get more complicated. Between the successful entrepreneurs and the high-flyers, the issue of adaptability is much more critical for the latter because of the difference in authority attached to their status in the organization.

Though being members of the senior management, the high-flyers remain salaried employees and are subject to the sanctioning of top management. On the other hand they are managing people who in fact are most direct in meeting the organizational targets and carrying the organization's image.

The high-flyers are almost required to develop a flexible personality to deal with this diversity of relationships and tasks. In turn, they who possess a flexible personality and a wide behavioral repertoire advanced more rapidly than others in their organizations.

Notes

1   See for example Fung, Y. L. (1948) *A Short History of Chinese Philosophy*. New York: Macmillan, for details of the philosophy of Confucius.

2   Adaptability is a core concept in many psychological theories, particularly in Jean Piaget's theory of cognitive development. Adaptability is essentially resulted from two complementary processes: assimilation and accommodation. The basic meaning of assimilation is to take in, absorb or incorporate as one's own. In Piagetian terms, it is the application of a general schema to a particular person, object or event. Accommodation generally refers to adjustment, and according to Piaget, it is the modification of internal schemes to fit a changing cognizance of reality. In essence, cognitive development is a result of both assimilation and accommodation, the individual modifies both himself/herself and the environment in order to adapt. For details, see Cohen, D (1977) *Piaget: Critique and Reassessment*. London: Routledge.

8 Work Motivation

Although existing studies have not yet been able to demonstrate a clear-cut relationship between a particular type of motivation and success, they do suggest that success and achievement is positively related to intrinsic motivation.

Intrinsic and Extrinsic Motivation

Motivating factors have traditionally been classified into extrinsic and intrinsic type. The dividing line between extrinsic and intrinsic factors is determined by whether the source of the incentive is internal to the individual or coming from the external environment.

According to Maslow (1954), physiological needs and shelter needs are considered as basic human needs but they are low-level needs in the sense that human beings will not just be satisfied with these and will strive for higher-level needs such as love and self-actualization. Maslow's model of hierarchy of needs implies that high-level needs provides a stronger motivating force for human behaviours. In validating his model, Maslow had chosen successful people in the society to identify their common characteristics, and discovered they all possessed creativity. All in all, Maslow does not recognize material needs as having a strong motivating drive for human behaviours, particularly behaviours leading to success.

A lot of other researchers have also shown that success or achievement are more related to intrinsic motivation than to extrinsic motivation. Haywood (1968) argues that individuals differ in their response to intrinsic and extrinsic motivators. This is extended from Hertzberg's dual factor theory (1959) which suggests that there are two groups of factors affecting one's job satisfaction. Existence of motivating factors lead to job satisfaction while the improvement of hygiene factors will only serve to reduce job dissatisfaction. His list of motivating factors seem to parallel the internal/personal causes and hygiene factors look very similar to external/environmental influences.

The weakness of judging intrinsic needs and extrinsic needs as higher level needs and lower level needs respectively is that it has ignored the meaning of the motivator to the individual. A motivator becomes a motivator only when it is perceived by the individual to have an incentive value. Hence what is motivating depends on one's perception. Such perception forms the basis of one's behaviours. Intrinsic motivators and extrinsic motivators can be equally important in bringing about behaviours relating to success.

The patterns of motivation identified by Cox and Cooper (1988) for their fifty British chief executive officers include interest and involvement (enjoy doing the job), achievement, ambition (determination to do it), and developing the business. Among these motivators, achievement has been systematically studied.

The Need for Achievement

The first formal study in using the achievement-motive as a construct was the work of Murray (1938) in which he conducted an in-depth study of fifty men, and from which he developed a taxonomy of personality needs. He defined these personality needs as hypothetical constructs reflecting psychological forces which direct behaviour. One of these forces was the need for achievement.

Murray described this motive as

> the desire or tendency to do things as rapidly and/or as well as possible. (It is) also a desire to accomplish something difficult. To master, manipulate and organize physical objects, human beings or ideas. To do this as rapidly and independently as possible. To overcome obstacles and attain a high standard. To excel one's self. To rival and surpass others. To increase self-regard by the successful exercise of talent.

McClelland (1951) took this a further step in using the achievement-motive construct to explain individual differences in tendencies towards striving for success in life. He has identified three different socio-motivational drives which people possess or not in different quantities.

These are Need for Achievement (nAch), Need for Power (nPow) and Need for Affiliation (nAff).

Need for Achievement is identified as an intrinsic drive to achieve something. McClelland (1951) characterised individuals with high nAch as those preferring to be personally responsible for solving problems, for setting goals, and for reaching those goals by their own efforts. Such persons also have a strong desire to know how well they are accomplishing their tasks. People with a low nAch need money as an incentive to work harder corresponding with Hertzberg's hygiene factors and Maslow's lower level needs. Those people who have a high nAch need only money as a symbol of what they have achieved.

McClelland (1951) argues that nAch is of most importance to those people who run a small business where success depends upon one key person. He hypothesized that entrepreneurs should have high nAch. He carried out three major studies in 1961, 1965 and 1969 respectively to validate the hypothesis. Generally his results suggested that high nAch would influence a young man to select an entrepreneurial position, and increasing the level of nAch had subsequently increased entrepreneurial efforts (Brockhaus, 1982). McClelland's hypothesis that entrepreneurs have high nAch is supported by the work of Komives (1972) and Margerison (1980). Komives (1972) in his study of 20 high-technology entrepreneurs found that they were high in achievement and decisiveness. The chief executives interviewed by Margerison (1980) clearly showed that they were very result-oriented. They liked to talk about how they personally had set and achieved targets which other people felt could not be done. They were proud of their achievements.

However, all of McClelland's early studies used a rather loose definition of entrepreneurial occupations, and he did not directly connect nAch with the decision to own and manage a business. In addition, Kets de Vries (1977) cited a number of studies which all suggest that the need for achievement is not the sole motivational factor of entrepreneurial efforts.

Recent work by Carsrud, Olm and Eddy (1986) on a uniform group of male entrepreneurs found that despite being high on competitiveness as a group, the trait was a negative predictor of business success.

Gasse (1982) also pointed out a few methodological shortcomings in the achievement motivation approach:

1. It does not take into account the historical and holistic structure in which motivation takes place. To McClelland, the economic, social, and political determinants of the distribution of power and the direction of achievement are negligible. Researchers such as Gunder, Kunkel, Weber and Tawney have stressed the importance of identifying the determining social and historical structures because entrepreneurial decisions are inevitably constrained by the cultural milieu.

2. Another shortcoming concerns the nebulous aspect of the concept itself. Achievement, for McClelland, is a way of thinking. However psychologists have given different interpretations to the concept, so employed varying measurements, hence given rise to many constructs that look similar, such as independence, desire for prestige, desire for power, internal locus-of-control belief, drive, high involvement, moderate risk-taking, etc.

3. McClelland confined his studies to economic activity. However, people who excelled in other areas of activities can also be characterized as achievers. Even within economic activities, his concept of entrepreneurship may be applied to a wide range of people, let alone business owners. Therefore the specificity and the distinctive power of the concept is largely lost.

The causal link between ownership of a small business and a high need for achievement is not proven. The success experienced by owners in their business may contribute to their high need for achievement, rather than the reverse.

McClelland shifted his emphasis from achievement to power in his later study (1975). He argues that for organizational effectiveness power motivation is required. An interest in power demonstrates the individual's desire to have an impact on other people. McClelland (1975) proposes that successful top level managers have 'the leadership motive pattern'. The leadership motive pattern consists of a moderate to high nPow, a moderate to low nAff and a high degree of self-control (socialized power) as opposed to high nPow and low self-control (personal power). Need for Achievement is not seen as associated with managerial success. McClelland and Boyatzis (1982) state that people with a high nAch are primarily interested in how well they personally are doing, not in influencing others to do well. Managerial success, however, depends on how well he/she can influence his/her staff to achieve organizational goals. Hence nAch is not so important to managerial success in large organizations as the leadership motivation pattern.

Regarding nAff, a high nAff would result in a manager more concerned with creating warm and friendly relationships and less concerned with task performance. A low nAff means that a manager can make difficult decisions without worrying about being disliked. High self-control is important because it suggests that someone can follow systems and abide by rules and procedures.

The high nPow for a successful manager would seem to conflict with Ghiselli's (1968) findings that successful managers no more or less desired power than the general employed person. It thus appears that the nPow is constructive when used to influence people in terms of long-term organizational goals but is not effective when used as personal power. Cox and Cooper (1988) remarks that nPow seems to be a necessary but not sufficient condition for successful management. An individual's nPow would need to be tempered by other qualities in order to achieve success.

In fact the 'right' balance between need for achievement, power, and affiliation seems to be a more important factor. Research by Spence and Helmreich (1978) showed that achievement motivation is not unidimensional but multidimensional.

The Chinese Achievement Motivation

Studies on Chinese achievement motivation have obviously been strongly influenced by the work of McClelland and his associates. Two related studies (Lewis, 1965; McClelland, 1963), relying on content analysis of educational materials, examined efforts to foster the development of independence and achievement motivation in children in Mainland China.

Lewis selected for analysis teachers' manuals for kindergartens in a Chinese province. He found that 'the manuals reveal a highly sophisticated program of training conducive to individual achievement motivation' (Lewis, 1965, p.425). Efforts were directed towards training children to become active, self-reliant, competent, intellectually critical, and achievement oriented.

McClelland (1963) compared three sets of Chinese stories used to teach children in public schools: one from Republican China (1920-29), one from Taiwan (1950-59), and one from Mainland China (1950-59). The stories were objectively scored for need for achievement (nAch), need for affiliation (nAff), and need for power (nPow). The results showed that the pattern of scores for Republican China corresponded to that found very frequently in static, tradition-oriented societies governed by an authoritarian regime - low nAch, very low nAff, and very high nPow. Both Taiwan and Mainland China, however, showed an increase in nAch and nAff, but the increases were much greater in Mainland China. For Mainland China, nAch rose above the world average (based on comparative sets of stories from studies of over forty countries for the period 1950-59), whereas that for Taiwan was still below the average. McClelland interpreted an increase in nAff as indicating movement in the 'modern' direction, since nAff tends to rise in the contractual type of society which he believed is necessary for a modern economic order, whereas in a tradition-oriented society affiliative relationships do not require special effort or concern over their maintenance. With regard to nPow, there was a decrease for Taiwan but a dramatic increase for Mainland China when compared with Republican China. Stories from Mainland China dealing with authority or power relationships were, however, of a different sort from those of the past. McClelland (1963, p.17) stated:

> In contrast to the Chinese stories of the 1920's, the emphasis here is clearly on everyone assuming responsibility insofar as he can for the welfare of others. The power to help, to guide, and control others is not now way off somewhere else, as a kind of dangerous impersonal force, but resides in every person at least in some degree ... So the motivational concerns which favour economic and social modernization are more prominent in the Communist Chinese stories than in the China-Taiwan stories at nearly every point.

McClelland's findings, though interesting in its own right, must be interpreted with great care. Yang (1986) cautioned that the writing, editing, and publishing of public-school reading books are usually under the strict control of the government in most South-east Asian countries. Therefore the stories in these books cannot be regarded as spontaneous expressions of the inner desires of the populations of these countries. This is especially true of the Chinese Communist stories. Yang's remarks serve as an important reminder that apart from parents and traditions, a government can intentionally instil in its people through education a particular, perhaps different, motivational orientation, be it moral or economic. If the children were continually exposed to the contents of their school books, their motivational patterns would be made to orientate towards those ideals advocated in these books and they might experience an inconsistency of values with the values upheld by their parents and families.

A number of scholars (Yang and Liang, 1973; Yu, 1974; Yang, 1982) developed their studies on Chinese achievement motivation based on the work of McClelland, and they found it necessary to refurbish his need for achievement construct. Yang (1986) argued that McClelland's conceptualization of the achievement motive as a well-internalized predisposition in the self-reliant individual as a result of independence training is probably only one variety of achievement motivation. Dissatisfaction with this highly individualistic conception of achievement motivation as a cross-cultural research variable has been voiced among investigators (such as Kubany, Gallimore, and Buell, 1970; Yang and Liang, 1973; Yang, 1982) studying people in Japan, Taiwan, and the Philippines. A strong and pervasive preoccupation with achievement and accomplishment is commonly observed among people in the family and related social settings in Chinese and Japanese societies. In order to do justice to this observed preoccupation, Yang and Liang (1973), Yang (1982), Yu (1992) proposed to distinguish between two basic types of achievement motivation: individual oriented and social oriented. Individual-oriented achievement motivation is defined as a kind of functionally autonomized desire, in which the course of achievement-related behaviour, the standards of excellence, and the evaluation of the performance or outcome are defined or determined by the actor himself/herself. The social-oriented achievement motivation is defined as a kind of functionally unautonomized (hence still extrinsic and instrumental) desire in which the course of the achievement-related behaviour, the standards of excellence, and the evaluation of the performance are defined or determined by the significant others, the family, the group, or the society as a whole. The former type is conceived of as resulting mainly from independence-emphasizing socialization in an individualistic society and the latter type from dependence-emphasizing socialization in a collectivistic society. Yang and Liang (1973) demonstrated empirically that these two types of achievement motivation are related in different ways to other variables such as socio-economic status. Yang and Liang (1973), Yu (1992) also found that the Chinese are prone to being motivated by a social achievement orientation.

Yu (1974) replicated McClelland's procedures in a study of achievement motivation and its relations with filial piety and familism in Chinese teenagers in Taiwan. It was found that: (a) teenagers upheld filial peity; (b) verbal statements on achievement were uncorrelated with nAch as measured by Thematic Apperception Test (TAT) stimuli; (c) nAch was not significantly correlated with filial piety, the Familism scale, or with either the Extended Familism or the Nuclear Familism subscales; (d) verbal statements on achievement were, however, significantly correlated with both filial piety and the Familism scale; the correlation was higher with the Extended Familism subscale than with the Nuclear Familism subscale, with or without any control variable. Yu interpreted the findings as support for the argument about the saliency of the collectivist orientation among Chinese, on the basis of the presupposition that nAch is rooted in the individualistic perspective, whereas filial piety and familism encompass a non-individualistic collectivist orientation. The finding that verbal statements on achievement correlated more highly with the Extended Familism subscale than with the Nuclear Familism subscale suggests that Chinese achievement motivation is rooted more firmly in the collectivist than in the individualistic orientation.

Further support for this contention is provided by Li, Cheung, and Kau (1979) in an experimental study indicating that Chinese children in both Hong Kong and Taiwan showed greater cooperation with increasing age, even when the cooperative reward condition was changed to the competitive reward condition, in contrast to a similar American study (Madsen, 1971) which showed more non-adaptive competition with increasing age.

Redding (1980) surveyed on a group of Chinese and Western (European and Anglo-American) middle managers on their perceptions of need importance. A comparison of the results of the two groups is summarized in Figure 8.1.

The results evidence a downplaying of the individual and the upgrading of relationships by Chinese people in the organizational context. In addition, the Chinese case displays a concern for the importance of social needs which is fairly close to the salience attached to autonomy and self-actualization. For the large sample of Western managers, the gap between the two levels is wide and the importance of the self is clearly dominant.

This also corroborates the differences in collectivism-individualism scores shown in Hofstede's data collected from a major international study on values. According to Hofstede (1980, p.83):

> Individualism stands for a preference for a loosely knit social framework in society wherein individuals are supposed to take care of themselves and their immediate families only. Its opposite, Collectivism, stands for a preference for a tightly knit social framework in which individuals can expect their relatives, clan, or other in-group to look after them in exchange for unquestioning loyalty (it will be clear that the word 'Collectivism' is not used here to describe any particular political system.) The fundamental issue addressed by this dimension is the degree of interdependence a society maintains among individuals. It relate to people's self concept: 'I' or 'we'.

It is clear from Figure 8.2 that the Overseas Chinese as represented in the scores for Hong Kong, Singapore, and Taiwan are consistently collectivist as societies. Although they are not so to the most extreme degree, they are clearly so in a way which separates them virtually all Western cultures.

Figure 8.1 Comparative Perceptions of Need Importance, Chinese and Western Managers

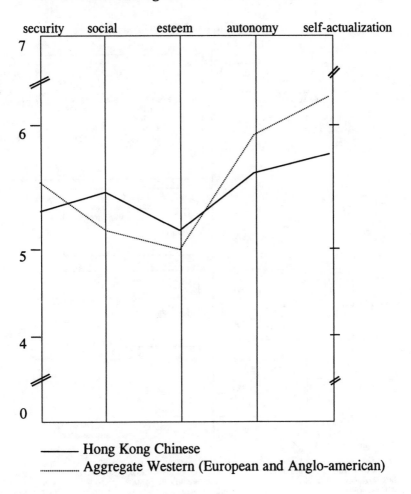

——— Hong Kong Chinese
.... Aggregate Western (European and Anglo-american)

Source: Redding 1980

Figure 8.2 The Core Values of Power Distance and Individualism/ Collectivism in Different Societies

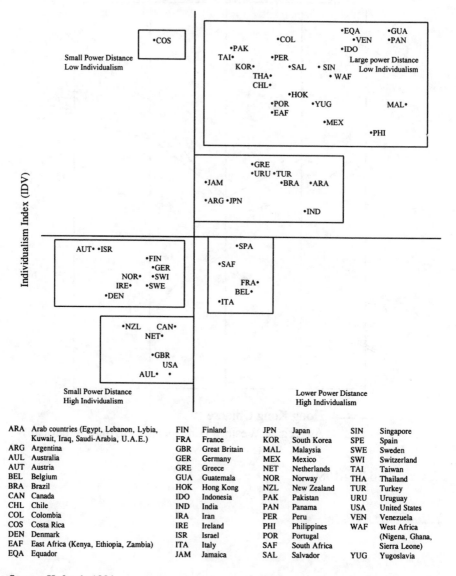

ARA Arab countries (Egypt, Lebanon, Lybia, Kuwait, Iraq, Saudi-Arabia, U.A.E.)
ARG Argentina
AUL Australia
AUT Austria
BEL Belgium
BRA Brazil
CAN Canada
CHL Chile
COL Colombia
COS Costa Rica
DEN Denmark
EAF East Africa (Kenya, Ethiopia, Zambia)
EQA Equador

FIN Finland
FRA France
GBR Great Britain
GER Germany
GRE Greece
GUA Guatemala
HOK Hong Kong
IDO Indonesia
IND India
IRA Iran
IRE Ireland
ISR Israel
ITA Italy
JAM Jamaica

JPN Japan
KOR South Korea
MAL Malaysia
MEX Mexico
NET Netherlands
NOR Norway
NZL New Zealand
PAK Pakistan
PAN Panama
PER Peru
PHI Philippines
POR Portugal
SAF South Africa
SAL Salvador

SIN Singapore
SPE Spain
SWE Sweden
SWI Switzerland
TAI Taiwan
THA Thailand
TUR Turkey
URU Uruguay
USA United States
VEN Venezuela
WAF West Africa (Nigena, Ghana, Sierra Leone)
YUG Yugoslavia

Source: Hofstede 1984

The collectivist orientation in general, and the social-oriented achievement motivation, in particular characterizes the Chinese motivational patterns. The cultivation of such motivation is largely through the socialization of parents. It has been pointed out that in a Chinese society, family is the primary unit around which the life of an individual is organized. Parents play a predominant role in socialization and development of the individual's self. It is generally recognized that modern Chinese parents place great emphasis on the achievement of their children. In the study of child-rearing attitudes and practices in Hong Kong (Ho and Kang, 1984, Study 2), the most frequently mentioned personal characteristics expected of the child when grown up were those concerned with competence and achievement, followed by those concerned with moral character, sociability, and controlled temperament.

Insofar as the studies on the Chinese achievement motivation are concerned, the Chinese motivational pattern can be summarized as one that is high on social-oriented achievement. While this need characteristic is essentially a continuation of the traditional Chinese motivational proclivities with a collectivistic orientation, it is expected to be flavoured by new elements which convey the modern individualistic outlook which is particularlyassociated with the capitalist economy.

Locus of Control

Rotter (1966) believed that need for achievement is related to the belief in internal locus of control. He hypothesized that individuals with internal beliefs would more likely strive for achievement than would individuals with external beliefs. Entrepreneurs who are believed to have a high *n*Ach (McClelland, 1975) have been described as 'internals', that is, they believe their own behaviour to be relatively decisive in determining their business success. Anyone who does not believe he/she controls the outcome of a new business venture is unlikely to expose himself/herself to the uncertainty associated with starting a business. Brockhaus et. al. (1986) quoted a number of studies which support Rotter's hypothesis, including that of Berlew (1975) who founded that entrepreneurs perform best in situations where they have personal responsibility of results; they tend to be internally rather than externally controlled.

Liles (1974) suggests that it is the potential entrepreneur's perception of a specific situation, rather than the actualities involved, that influences his decision to start a business venture. Therefore it is important to study the perception of control.

Shapero (1975) used Rotter's scale to determine the locus-of-control of a group of entrepreneurs, and founded they tended to be on the 'internal' end of the scale. Brockhaus and Nord (1979) compared the locus-of-control beliefs in entrepreneurs and managers. The scores on Rotter's scale did not differ significantly between the owners of new businesses and managers.

Borland (1975) examined locus of control, nAch and entrepreneurship with the purpose of discovering what characterized her university students who intended to become business owners. There were significant differences in internal locus of control between the students who expected to start a company and those who did not. Among those with low nAch, those with higher internal locus of control were found to have a greater expectancy than others of starting a company. The level of internal locus of control made no difference in expectancy of starting a company among those with high nAch. This would seem to indicate that the combination of personality traits might be more crucial than the possession of any single trait. It should be noted that Borland employed a different instrument in measuring internality-externality. He used the Levenson's (1972) Locus of Control Scale which essentially extends Rotter's Internal-External Scale. The Levenson inventory consists of three sub-scales: Internality (I) measures the extent to which one believes in self-control over one's life; Powerful Others (P) measures the extent to which one believes that powerful significant others control his life; Chance (C) measures the extent to which one believes that chance or luck controls his life.

Procuik and Breen (1975) suggest that the relationship between locus of control and success can be further clarified by exploring the dimensional structure underlying the trait. Three dimensions have emerged from factor-analytic studies:-

1. *Internality*   The belief that one has control over one's career
2. *Powerful Others* The belief that career is under the control of powerful others

3. *Chance*   The belief that career is controlled by luck or fate.

While the causal relationship between locus of control and success is still open to contention, the results obtained by Andrisani and Nestel (1976) do support that an internal locus of control is related to occupational success. They found that over a two-year period internals experienced more favourable employment circumstances, that is, they achieved a more pronounced advancement in their annual earnings and job satisfaction. They also reported cross-sectional data which suggested that internals are in higher-status occupations, they earn more money and tend to be more highly satisfied with their work than externals.

With regard to the Chinese, the earliest cross-cultural study on locus of control involving Chinese subjects is that by Hsieh, Shybut, and Lotsof (1969). These investigators administered Rotter's I-E Control of Reinforcement Scale to two hundred and thiry-nine Anglo-Americans, three hundred and forty-three Hong Kong Chinese and eighty American-born Chinese, and found that Americans exhibited a stronger belief in internal control of reinforcement and the Hong Kong Chinese a stronger belief in external control of reinforcement, with the American-born Chinese in between. This higher externality of the Chinese was later confirmed by Tseng's (1972) study using the Rotter Scale with sixty-seven Asian and sixty-one American students at an American university. While the Chinese in general exhibit a weaker belief in internality, the link between business success and locus of control orientation is yet to be established.

Lao (1977) employed the multidimensional I-E Scale developed by Levenson to measure the belief in internal control, in powerful others, and in chance of five hundred and seventeen Chinese (243 males and 274 females) and four hundred and twenty-three American college students (180 males and 243 females). The Chinese were reported to be stronger in their belief in powerful others than Americans of either sex. While Chinese females had a weaker tendency to believe in internal events than American females, the two male groups were not significantly different from each other on this factor. Finally, no significant cross-cultural difference was found on the chance factor in either sex.

From the above review and discussion of literature on work motivation, it is seen that traditional approaches to understanding the motivation of career successful people tend to view motivational factors as either intrinsic or extrinsic. Success is related to a need for achieving internal standards, although the notion of Need for Achievement requires further conceptual and empirical review. The intrinsic-extrinsic distinction also applies to beliefs of control. Rotter believes that achievers have internal locus of control orientation. His hypothesis is supported by a number of empirical studies which found that successful entrepreneurs and managers are high internals. Studies of motivational characteristics of Chinese reveal that they are externals in locus of control, and are influenced more by external factors in striving for achievement as a result of their collectivist orientation.

Work Motivation of Hong Kong Successful Entrepreneurs and High-Flyers

Motivational Factors

Anything can become a motivator to the successful entrepreneurs and high-flyers, depending on the perception they hold about what is important and the unique reinforcement experiences they have.

The successful entrepreneurs and high-flyers were asked to identify, from a list, three factors or less which they thought were important motivators in their career. They could also give motivating factors not found in the list. The purpose is to understand motivation in the perspectives of the subjects themselves rather than assuming a certain factor is important and to measure the factor in different individuals. Table 8.1 shows the number of counts of all the motivating factors the entrepreneurs and high-flyers had mentioned.

Table 8.1 Motivational Factors for Entrepreneurs and High-Flyers

Source of Motivation	Entrepreneurs	High-Flyers
Need for achievement	15 (11)	11 (6)
Achieve self-set goals	7 (3)	6 (3)
Prove oneself	8 (5)	5 (2)
Monetary rewards	8 (4)	20 (9)
Enjoy doing the job	12 (3)	5 (2)
Developing reputation	12	8 (3)
Desire to excel	6 (3)	7 (2)
Organizational goals	-	6 (2)
Sense of responsibility	1	4 (1)
*Family well-being**	4	3
Job security	-	-
Mastery of job skills	-	-
*Give meaning to life**	1 (1)	-
Please significant others	1	-
Total Subjects	30	30

Note: Figures shown in brackets represent first counts of the motivational factor

* *factors not listed in the Questionnaire but mentioned by the respondents themselves*

What motivates our entrepreneurs and high-flyers varies a great deal, and there is no one single motivator that is important to all successful people. By merely counting the number of times each of the motivating factors was mentioned, the need for achievement is clearly a very strong motivator for most entrepreneurs (11), whereas proving oneself and monetary rewards is most motivational for five and four entrepreneurs respectively. Though many of them (12) mentioned developing reputation as also motivational, these are seen as one of the factors instead of the most important factor. The need for achievement, proving oneself, achieving self-set goals are intrinsic motivators, and a majority of the successful entrepreneurs (19, 63 percent) are motivated by these intrinsic factors. The high-flyers showed a somewhat different pattern of motivation. Monetary rewards and the need for achievement provide the strongest motivation for the majority (9 and 6 respectively). The pattern of motivational factors for the rest of the high-flyers is rather spreadout. Both intrinsic and extrinsic motivators are important for the high-flyers.

Each of the motivational factors will be examined below by means of analysing interview transcripts so that their exact motivational meaning for the successful entrepreneurs and high-flyers is revealed.

The need for achievement Achievement means different things to different entrepreneurs and high-flyers. In fact, proving oneself and achieving self-set standards are found to be related to the general need for achievement. Hence the need for achievement covers three aspects:

1. *Being successful in what one is doing (15 entrepreneurs and 11 high-flyers)*

The sense of achievement derived from being successful in what one is doing is the basic motivating force to one-third of the high-flyers.

2. *Proving oneself (8 entrepreneurs and 5 high-flyers)*

This is the sense of achievement secured from seeing oneself is correct or capable, which can be seen from the following transcripts.

> What is important to me is 'I've done it'. It gave me much satisfaction when I succeeded in making the first business deal which amounted to about three million dollars. It was not the money, but to show that I could do it. (E27)

> I was very happy indeed that I was given the patent to produce the toys. No one ever thought we would be able to get that contract because we had less capital and manpower. I had the same feeling when our company was allowed to be listed on the market because it is not common for a new company with just one year's history to go up market. That is a proof of the company's success. (E24)

3.   *Achieving self-set standards (7 entrepreneurs and 6 high-flyers)*

This is the sense of achievement obtained from meeting one's goals, which is illustrated by the following transcripts.

> The work environment has changed, but my expectations towards my work has not changed.   Maybe because I want to be a winner, I have high expectations towards myself.   I am a perfectionist, I expect a 100 percent commitment to my work and a 100 percent output.   I think this is a big driving force to me.   (HF7)

The goals the entrepreneurs and high-flyers wish to achieve may not merely be related to work goals.   In fact, the goals often represent their life goals:

> My motivation comes from my goals.   There are four goals I would like to achieve in business: to be of contribution to mankind; to improve the global management system, that's why I am doing a Ph D in corporate governance; to help develop the third world countries; and to pass on the family name, I am all ready for going up market. (E10)

> (My motivation) I think, if you only live once.   Someone may spend his/her life as it goes but some can make the best out of it.   For example, environmental protection is my calling, my life.   I play a part in creating a better environment.   There are so many advancements that we can't forever keep up with, so that's what keeps me going.   The more you can do for the environment the better. (E17)

Monetary rewards (8 entrepreneurs and 20 high-flyers)

The importance of monetary rewards can be primary and secondary. Some entrepreneurs and high-flyers regarded monetary rewards as an indication of social status and personal competence.   These cases are classified under other factors such as the need for achievement or social recognition.   There is a significant difference in importance for the entrepreneurs and the high-flyers.   Nine high-flyers indicated that monetary rewards are their primary motivators but only one entrepreneur did so.   Staying in a well-paid job gives a more predictable guarantee of stable income than taking on an adventure.   The two individuals below are simply interested in having more monetary returns from their work:

> My value concept is money. When I was promoted to assistant manager, manager and now senior manager, I didn't feel really great. My first response was to know how much salary I'd get. My family was not so well-off. My mother always said how much was spent, etc. She always counted. So when I went out to work, title does not mean much to me. The most important thing to me is how much more money I'll get. If the increment is satisfactory, I will do it. If the increment is not satisfactory, it's meaningless even if you offer me the post General Manager. I don't mind the title. (HF1)

> What motivates me? I like spending money, so I make money. (E9)

Although there are entrepreneurs and high-flyers who claimed that money is not their major motivator, it seems likely that money had once important to them but it had lost its motivational power at their present stage of life.

> Money is not important any more for senior managers like myself. (HF11)

> When I first started, I was not too concerned with money and titles. I simply wanted to learn more. But after five years or so, money and title became an issue. I wanted to get promoted. (HF13)

Enjoy doing the job (12 entrepreneurs and 5 high-flyers)

> This is my area of interest. (HF17)

Develop reputation (12 entrepreneurs and 8 high-flyers)

This is the wish to be recognized particularly within one's profession.

> I was headhunted for the present job. I still feel proud of it. (HF6)

> I work hard to develop my reputation in the profession. My credibility is my asset. (HF8)

> My motivation was to become the head of the most prestigious company in the field. (HF10)

The desire to excel (6 entrepreneurs and 7 high-flyers)

The desire to be better than others has generated a great determination for our entrepreneurs to be successful. The founder and director of a fashion chain store claimed:

> No, (driving force is) absolutely not money. I just want to do something and do it better than the others, faster than the others. You need 50 years to establish a company. I want to do it within 15 years. (E12)

The competitive work environment also demands our high-flyers to outstand themselves among others in an organization in order to pursue a successful career. There are always many equally well qualified, and equally competent persons working in the same organization, at the same grade. Being good is necessary (and presumed), but may not be sufficient any more to gain others' recognition. One has to have the craving to excel in order to improve and accomplish continually. An entrepreneur recalled his life as an employee:

> Within a short period, 6 months, I was promoted to be in charge of a division. Yes, it was very fast. At that time, the company gave us some targets and I always surpassed the targets. I was famous for being number one for doing anything: receiving orders, creating problems, taking the blame ... but the boss was fond of me ... Whatever I do, I want to do it better than the others, faster than the others. (HF22)

Organizational goals (6 high-flyers)

Six high-flyers mentioned achieving organizational goals was motivational for them.

> I'd like to see the business goals being met, my staff being developed. This is what my job is about. (HF3)

The fact that no entrepreneurs mentioned meeting organizational goals as motivating does not mean they did not perceive these goals as unimportant. In fact, their organizations represent themselves. Henceforth, achieving organizational goals is closely related to achieving self-set goals which was discussed above under The Need for Achievement.

Sense of responsibility (1 entrepreneur and 4 high-flyers)

> I am investing on behalf of my clients. The money is their money, so I have to be accountable for what I do. I put my clients' interest before that of the bank. I need to be honest with my clients, I will not create false hopes in them, otherwise they only get disappointed and lose their trust in me and the bank. (HF17)

Family well-being (4 entrepreneurs and 3 high-flyers)

Three entrepreneurs and three high-flyers mentioned that they worked hard for their family and children. Apart from providing their family members with a comfortable life, they wished they would not disappoint those who are significant figures in their lives.

> I hope when I get old, I can tell my children, or perhaps grandchildren, what kind of things I have done for which they can be proud of me. (E11)

> One of the reasons why I decided to return (to Hong Kong) was to be closer to my family, especially to help my brother who took good care of me when I was young. (E23)

> My family is one of my motivational force. I want them to have a happy life. (E24)

> I think my family would be pleased to see I am doing well. (HF30)

Giving meaning to one's limited life (1 entrepreneur)

> I guess everyone will want to live one's life to the fullest, at least I want my life to be meaningful and that I would have no regrets when I die. (E27)

Changing motivation The above patterns of motivation indicate what the successful entrepreneurs and high-flyers saw as their driving force at the time they were interviewed. It is noted that what motivates the successful entrepreneurs and high-flyers change over time. This is illustrated by one high-flyer who said the following,

> When I was younger, it (motivation) was achievement. I didn't want to be looked down upon by others ... I didn't graduate from a formal university.

I had to be much better than people joining the company in the same period to get same increment ... I've said I started (my job) with the difficulty of closing down. So the initial motivation was survival, to secure my job here. Now, it's more on the side of-self-actualization. I've been in the industry for so long. You may think I'm proud but others do say I am good. I can't lose. My colleagues have been working with me for many years and again I can't lose in front of them ... My view (about source of motivation) is that it is different at different stages. (HF18)

A similar perception of motivation was shared by another high-flyer:

What motivates me? I think people change. The motivational drive when you start working at 22, and then at 30, at 40 and so on is very different. As you get older, you see things differently. When I started working, I was very anxious to prove myself, to prove to my boss what I could do. Money and titles were not big deal. But after three to five years, I wanted promotions. Money and titles became important. What about now? I don't look for promotions any more. In fact I had turned down further promotions. I just want to do my job to the best of my capability, make as much money as possible for the company and myself, and try to enjoy life with my family. (HF13)

It can be seen that motivation, the perception about what is important, has its fixed and variable qualities. Motivation is related to the development of the entrepreneurs and high-flyers and will change according to the needs of a particular stage of development. On the other hand, motivation is also rooted in past experiences.

Locus of Control

The present study has employed the three-factor (internality, powerful others, chance) scale developed by Levenson (1973). Twenty-five entrepreneurs (83 percent) and 28 high-flyers (93 percent) completed and returned the IPC instrument. Table 8.2 shows their results on the three scales. The lower the score on the scale, the more the person believes his/her behaviours is under the control of that factor. Henceforth a true internal will score low on internality scale while score relatively high on the powerful others scale and/or the chance scale.

Table 8.2   Locus of Control: Internality, Powerful Others and Chance

Scale	Entrepreneurs Mean	SD	High-flyers Mean	SD
Internality	19.40		20.64	
		3.29		4.21
Powerful others	36.04		32.14	
		4.44		4.41
Chance	35.56		33.36	
		3.92		4.60
Total Subjects	25		28	

By comparing the results of the successful entrepreneurs with the high-flyers, it is noted that the scores of the successful entrepreneurs on the internality and chance scales are very similar to those of the high-flyers, with the high-flyers more believing in the control by powerful others. T-test results show that the differences between the means of the two groups on all the three scales are not significant. Tests of correlation show that there is a significantly strong negative correlation between the high-flyers' internality and powerful others scores ($r=$ -.41, $P=0.032$), other correlations are weak, suggesting that the successful entrepreneurs are not 'true' internals, they also have tendency to believe in the control of powerful others and chance. Similarly the high-flyers tend also to believe in chance.

Summary

The entrepreneurs are motivated by intrinsic factors. Though their degree of internality found on the Locus of Control Scales is not significantly higher than that of the high-flyers, they are motivated by the need for achievement and job satisfaction which are internal in nature. These two factors together explain why the entrepreneurs took the course of starting their own business in order to satisfy their personal goals and interests, whereas the high-flyers' concern with achievement and monetary rewards explain why they chose to pursue their goals in an organizational context which provides a stable environment and income.

Both the successful entrepreneurs and the high-flyers have a stronger internal locus of control. However, when considering the correlations between internal, powerful others and chance orientations, only the correlation between the high-flyers' internal and powerful others orientations is found to be strong in a negative direction. This suggests that the successful entrepreneurs in particular and the high-flyers do not have a significantly overwhelming orientation towards internality.

Work Motivation and Career Success

The Need for Achievement

There exists a strong link between success and the need for achievement which comes in several forms for the successful entrepreneurs and high-flyers:

1. Being successful in what one is doing
2. Proving oneself
3. Achieving self-set goals

These three forms of achievement are in fact very similar. Among the three forms of the need for achievement, achieving self-set goals appears to have a more individualistic orientation. Individual-oriented achievement motivation is defined as a kind of functionally autonomized desire, in which the course of achievement-related behaviour, the standards of excellence, and the evaluation of the performance or outcome are defined or determined by the actor himself/herself (Yang, 1986, p.114). The successful entrepreneurs and high-flyers were concerned with accomplishing the goals set by themselves and not someone else. However when the entrepreneurs and high-flyers were asked to elaborate what their personal goals were, these goals were sometimes found to be related to the wishes of people other than themselves. One entrepreneur stated that his goal of achieving business success was to honour his father as a way to show his admiration for him.

Proving oneself is somewhat linked to social recognition in that the individual is demonstrating his/her capabilities in return for the appreciation by himself/herself as well as others. Similarly, being successful in what one is doing can mean being successful according to personal or objective criteria or both, hence entailing either an individualistic or collectivist orientation or both. As far as the findings of the present study are concerned, it is far from conclusive to state whether the achievement motivation of the successful entrepreneurs and high-flyers is individual-oriented or social-oriented or otherwise.

Monetary rewards

Monetary rewards are particularly motivating for the high-flyers, although some successful entrepreneurs and high-flyers claimed they found monetary rewards and social recognition motivating only at the beginning stage of their career development. Monetary rewards lost their incentive value as they progressed up the career ladder. They became satiated with these extrinsic rewards. Furthermore, the successful entrepreneurs and high-flyers, at their present stage of life, should have already developed the ability of self-regulation, that is, they are able to judge their own success and self-reinforce without having to rely on external rewards as an indication of their success. One of the high-flyers stated that money is not important for senior managers. Attitude surveys among Chinese workers often find that monetary rewards are high on the list of priorities (Chau and Chan, 1984; Lui, 1985). However, Turner (1980) noted from a large sample survey that those most concerned with pay were the less skilled workers, casual employees, those in smaller private firms, and those in manufacturing industry. A few other entrepreneurs and high-flyers echoed similar remarks that what is motivating varies at different stages of their career development, perhaps as well as at different stages of their life development.

Notwithstanding the above discussion, the fact that one-third of the high-flyers and two successful entrepreneurs regarded monetary rewards as their principal motivator needs to be explained. The general wage level of the Hong Kong workforce is among one of the highest in the world. The high-flyers enjoyed high salaries together with very comprehensive fringe benefits. The financial rewards increase with seniority in the organization, and they are sufficiently attractive to become the major motivator for the high-flyers.

Lau (1982) finds 'emphasis on material values' as the first of the major normative orientations of the Hong Kong people and suggests the followings reasons for this infatuation with money:

1. A historic tradition of commercialization and business shrewdness in Guandong (the nearest Chinese province to Hong Kong), which antedates exposure to the West;
2. The freedom of a migrant class from traditional moral constraints on acquisitiveness, and the related absence of a gentry class to set alternative values;
3. The blocking of upward mobility through political channels in a colonial society, and the use of economic mobility as the only viable alternative;
4. The stimuli of visible inequality and conspicuous consumption;
5. The openness of the economy and the resulting inability of any elite to monopolize economic opportunities.

In short, Lau suggests the search for wealth mentality present in the Hong Kong people is a result of the need of security in a threatening environment with no certainty of its political future.

The search for wealth can be also inferred from the number of small businesses established each year. It is assumed that one of the major reasons for setting up one's own business is to have more financial returns than can be secured from a paid job, although only four successful entrepreneurs affirmed this belief. Hong Kong has a very high proportion of small businesses, compared to the rest of the world. In Hong Kong at present, there is one business unit for 18 people, compared with one for 36 people in the United States. Cheng (1977, p.57) reasons that this high Hong Kong figure may be seen to reflect the strong pecuniary drive of the local inhabitants as well as the relatively lenient laws governing the formation of business.

In addition, the Chinese are respectful of those who are self-reliant in making wealth. Due to the centrality of the family as the basic survival unit and its dependence on its members for contribution, anyone who creates burden on the family will come under intense social pressure. Redding and Wong (1986) claim the implication of this respect for independence is that many managers in large companies are accumulating knowledge, skills, and contacts with a view to starting their own businesses whenever the opportunity arises. This claim is affirmed by many of the successful entrepreneurs who followed the professional and opportunist career paths. They found the experiences they gained from working in large corporations were invaluable for running their own businesses.

Changing Values In comparing the values the Hong Kong entrepreneurs and high-flyers inherited from their parents and the values they hold towards work, it is found that their values to work are somewhat different from the life values inherited from their parents. On one hand, some of the parental values are no longer held. On the other hand, they developed their own values which were not conveyed by their parents.

As a general pattern, most of the successful entrepreneurs and high-flyers stress achievement. Yang (1986), by studying Taiwan university students, observed the need for achievement (social-oriented) is decreasing while the need for achievement (individual-oriented) is increasing as a result of societal modernization influence on the Chinese personality. The increasing stress on achievement and social recognition by the successful entrepreneurs and high-flyers can be seen as a result of secondary socialization during their course of development. Entering adolescence, they began to experiment with their roles and test their abilities outside the home. Parental values were questioned. The influence of peers, school, and the larger society assumed more weight in the individual's identity formation which is the central developmental task in adolescence. According to Erikson (1968), a large part of our identity rests on what we do for a living, on the support we receive from society, and on our internalization of the ideals of our class, our nation, and our culture. The development of an identity enables an individual to be loyal to his/her commitments in the face of the inevitable contradictions of value systems.

Most of the successful entrepreneurs and high-flyers reached their adolescent stage in the 1970s during which the Hong Kong society witnessed many changes as a result of the economic take-off. Bond (1993) claims that economic prosperity has further increased the internationalization of Hong Kong. Local people interact with foreigners of many cultures, communicate across national boundaries, travel widely, and enjoy access to a variety of media conveying information about foreign places and cultures.

The successful entrepreneurs and high-flyers, in going through an English educational system, being exposed to many more different cultural norms and values, observing how others succeeded in an increasingly capitalist society, gradually developed their own goals. The orientation to occupational choice is particularly closely related to the socioeconomic development and the changing modes of production in the society, that is, the perceived structure of opportunities.

Internal Locus of Control

The successful entrepreneurs and the high-flyers are internals as measured by Levenson's IPC Inventory. In addition, the internality scores of both groups are almost identical, no one group is more internal than the other. The two groups also show low beliefs in chance, whereas the high-flyers are slightly more inclined to beliefs in the control of powerful others, which is explicable by the fact their careers are still partly determined by their seniors.

That the successful entrepreneurs and high-flyers have a greater internal control orientation is not quite congruent with the locus of control data obtained elsewhere on Chinese subjects (Hsieh, Shybut and Lotsof 1969, Tseng, 1972) who were found to be externals. The Chinese subjects in these studies were university students while the entrepreneurs and high-flyers in the present study are successful career people, hence internal orientation and success in career are related. The successful entrepreneurs and high-flyers are also compared to a group of seventy-nine social workers studying a postgraduate social work course in terms of their IPC scores which are shown in Table 8.3. Surprisingly their IPC scores come very close. The postgraduate social work students are themselves full-time practising social workers, some of whom are supervisors. One purpose of their pursuing postgraduate study is striving for professional development, leading to career advancement or simply personal satisfaction. Hence the internal control orientation can be seen as related to the need for achievement rather than career success as such, falling in line with Rotter's (1966) hypothesis that individuals with internal beliefs would more likely strive for achievement than would individuals with external beliefs.

Table 8.3   The Mean IPC Scores of Hong Kong Successful Entrepreneurs, High-Flyers and Social Workers

Scale	Entrepreneurs	High-Flyers	Social Workers
Internality	19.40	20.64	21.90
Powerful Others	36.04	32.14	31.67
Chance	35.56	33.36	31.35
Total subjects	25	28	79

A note should be taken in analysing the above IPC results of the successful entrepreneurs, the high-flyers and the postgraduate social work students. The results were obtained using Levenson's IPC scales which asked highly transparent questions with the result that the respondents can easily infer what the instrument aims to measure. It becomes tempting for them to rate themselves in a socially desirable direction, in this case towards internality. Hence the results obtained by this instrument need to be treated with caution and verified by other data on control beliefs.

Changing locus of control orientations   The childhood experiences of the successful entrepreneurs and high-flyers are considered conducive to the development of an internal orientation as well as a powerful others orientation.   The present IPC results suggest that they have a stronger internal control orientation.   Later experiences in education and work had a reinforcing effect on internality, and these experiences were related to economic and societal modernization which were already shown to have changed the work values of the successful entrepreneurs and high-flyers. Similar changes in beliefs of control were reported by Liu, Chen, Chen and Yang (1973) who identified those who scored high on modernity[1] had lower tendencies to consult parents when they were in trouble or had a problem.   In Yang's (1976) study concerning fertility psychology, individual modernity was observed to be negatively related to Rotter's Internal-External Control Scale, with the more modernized having a greater tendency to believe in their own skill, effort, foresight, and acceptance of responsibility as major determinants and punishments.

These more recent research findings indicate the long-time image of the Chinese as externals is being replaced by the modern Chinese as more internally-controlled.

However, the apparent change from an external to a more internal orientation in personality and motivation should be treated with caution. The IPC results of the successful entrepreneurs and high-flyers do not affirm their overwhelming tendency to be internal in all situations. They also exhibit tendency to believe in control of powerful others and chance. In addition, internality and externality are not mutually exclusive constructs. Bandura (1978) theorizes that an individual's internal standards, the basis of self-regulation, are developed out of a process of internalization[2] of external standards, usually the standards of significant others. Hence it is difficult, both conceptually and empirically, to separate inner beliefs and external influences. In the Chinese case, their strong collective orientation makes it even more difficult to isolate the individual's self from the environment, hence divide his/her orientation into internal and external.

Link of Personality and Motivation to Success

The successful entrepreneurs and high-flyers exhibit largely similar motivational and value orientations, resembling an individual-oriented character proposed by Yang (1986). The major departure lies in the high-flyers showing at the same time social-oriented or outer-directedness character. The emerging personality and motivation patterns are believed to be a result of the interplay of the individual and his/her social and work environment, each shaping the other.

An individual's personality and motivation orientation influence the career choices he/she makes and continues to influence behaviours at work. The successful entrepreneurs portray the traditional great man/woman of self-determination, whereas the high-flyers image the well-balanced person. They have their own goals but are aware that the realization of these goals are related to external forces, such as their obligations to the organization and other work-related parties. They maintain a balance of achieving their internal needs and fulfilling their responsibilities to others.

It is proposed that in a society where changes are taking place at a rapid pace but traditional influences still remain strong, individuals who are flexible, sensitive to others and the environment but with a high internality will be more able to balance traditions and innovations, hence more likely to succeed. Kelly (1984) suggests a similar view of the person who is best equipped to deal with the environment. He argues that such person should be capable to differentiate the circumstances under which propositional thinking and preemptive thinking[3] is required. Piaget (1978) regards flexibility as the ability to adapt is central in cognitive development, which acquired through both assimilation and accommodation. In essence, both Kelly and Piaget suggest that in learning to deal with the environment, an individual modifies the environment to match his/her existing thinking and behavioral modes, but at the same time allows himself/herself be modified by new experiences.

For those who refuse to compromise themselves with the environment, becoming an entrepreneur is an alternative. However, the sensitivity to the environment and others is still essential for achieving entrepreneurial success, as several successful entrepreneurs coincidentally quoted the same Chinese maxim 'Know yourself and know your enemies, and you win in all the hundred battles you fight'.

Notes

1   Modernity is measured by the Chinese Individual Traditionality/Modernity Scale (CITMS), an instrument developed by Yang and his associates to assess the degree of modernization at the individual level. See Yang, K. S. (1981) The formation and change of Chinese personality: a cultural-ecological perspective, *Acta Psychologica Taiwanica, 23* (In Chinese).

2   Internalization is the acceptance or adaptation of beliefs, values, attitudes, practices, standards, usually those of parents, as one's own. Within traditional approaches to social psychology and personality an important issue is the degree to which a person attributes his/her behaviour to such internalized motives. It is differentiated from introjection where the values are 'borrowed' rather than adopted, and from socialization where the behaviour may conform to societal values without commitment or belief. See Reber, A.S. (1995) *Dictionary of Psychology*, p.383. Penguin Books.

3   Propositional thinking is flexible thinking. It allows existing constructs to be open to as well as modified by new experiences. However, exclusive reliance on propositional thinking makes a person become immobilized because he/she is continually reevaluating and reconstructing experiences. Preemptive thinking refers to thinking according to a well-established and well-defined sets of constructs which are resistant to changes.

9   Management Approach

Management approach refers to the orientation and methods of management.   Orientation is determined by one's perception of what he/she does.

Managerial Work

Mintzberg (1993) suggests a framework for describing what affects manager in approaching his/her managerial work, with the two central tenets being the person in the job and the frame of the job.   Management approach is indicative of how a manager carries out what he/she conceives his/her functions require.   His conception of the manager is illustrated in Figure 9.1.   He contends that the manager approaches his/her jobs with a set of values, probably rather firmly set by this stage in life.   The manager also brings a body of experiences, including managerial skills or competencies partly developed through training, which provide the base of knowledge in managing.   This knowledge is used directly, and is also convertible into a system of mental models by which the manager interprets the world around him/her to construct management plans and actions.

Figure 9.1 The Person in the Job

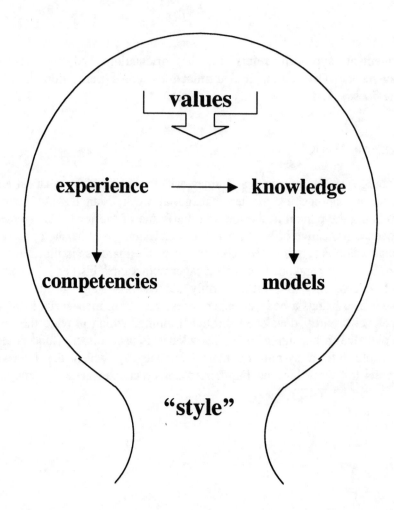

The manager depicted in Figure 9.1 carries out his/her job and we get managerial work, and the manager carries out the job with a frame for the job. The frame is the mental set guiding the manager as to how he/she carries out what the job requires. As the manager carries out the job, his/her management style will gradually come to life.

Leadership Styles

One of the themes of leadership studies is identifying leadership styles and then developing measures to classify individuals into types of leader. Leadership style is revealing of an individuals' assumptions about human nature, what he/she believes are right and desirable in leading, and what he/she actually does in practice. Since there is often cognitive dissonance between an individual's attitudes, and between his/her attitude and his/her actual behaviour (Festinger, 1957), it is unrealistic to classify individuals into very discrete leadership types. As an alternative, Tannenbaum and Schmidt (1958) developed a Continuum of Leadership Styles on which four types of leadership styles are identified, namely Tells, Sells, Consults and Joins. These four styles vary in terms of the amount of authority and control the leader either retains or shares with subordinates, from a very authoritarian style (equivalent to theory X) at one end to a highly participative style (equivalent to theory Y)[1] at the other end.

Tells

This is an authoritarian style. The leader/manager sees himself/herself as having all the control, with the necessary information and power simply to make decisions and issue instructions. The role of the subordinate(s) is to follow these instructions. This style is based on the assumption that the subordinate has no useful role to play in decision making; possibly because of lack of knowledge, ability or motivation.

Sells

It is arguable whether this is really any less authoritarian than the 'telling' style. The leader still takes control and makes the decisions but takes the additional step of trying to persuade the subordinate to accept what is proposed. The objective is to get willing compliance rather than simply imposing the decision.

Consults

The leader/manager consults the subordinate(s) and obtains their views on the issue in question and will take these into account, but reserves the right to make the final decision which may, or may not, be in line with the views of the subordinates.

Joins

This is a totally participative style. The leader joins with the subordinates to make a decision in which all views are represented.

The Chinese Way of Managing

One way to understand management behaviours and processes can be made through studying leadership behaviours. Silin (1976) provides an unusual metaphor in describing Chinese leadership style as 'didatic'. The meaning is that the leader holds information, and thus power, and doles it out in small pieces to subordinates, who thus remain more or less dependent. The leader's role has some overtones of that of the teacher. At the same time, the leader does not normally commit himself/herself openly to a line of action, but rather keeps his/her options open, leaving the direction of his/her organization or department to follow the lines detected by a somewhat nebulous but nevertheless powerful set of personal intuitions. Hence it depends somewhat on the leader's sense of responsibility, his/her authority and his/her capability to intuit the right strategy. Silin also pointed out that in Chinese firms there was a common but accepted lack of corporate planning which was more obvious in Western firms.

In such case, leadership style within Chinese companies tend to be directive and authoritarian. Redding and Casey (1976) compared the Chinese beliefs about management behaviour with those found in the West and found the Chinese clearly indicated a distinctly more autocratic approach, especially in sharing information with subordinates and allowing them to participate in decision-making. Their findings are supported by the studies carried out in Taiwan by Bond and Hwang (1986). In addition, the Overseas Chinese as represented in Singapore, Taiwan and Hong Kong are found by Hofstede (1980) to be constituting a 'high power distance' culture. As described by Hofstede (1980, p.83):

Power distance is the extent to which the members of a society accept that power in institutions and organizations is distributed unequally. This affects the behaviour of the less powerful as well as of the more powerful members of society. People in large power distance societies accept a hierarchical order in which everybody has a place which needs no further justification. People in small power distance societies strive for power equalization and demand justification for power inequalities. The fundamental issue addressed by this dimensions how a society handles inequalities among people when they occur. This has obvious consequences for the way people build their institutions and organizations.

A high power distance culture is one in which people express in their behaviour and attitudes, a strong sense of vertical order. They understand that they fit naturally below some people, and, just as significantly, above others. Living on a form of ladder is not a cause for resentment as that is how their social world has always been designed, and, in any case, a superior position carries obligation.

Similar results to those of the three Chinese groups studied by Hofstede were found in Mainland China. Chong, Cragin and Scherling (1983) administered the Hofstede survey in the People's Republic of China to a wide variety of managerial groups. There is a close correspondence in results among all the four Chinese groups on the dimensions of individualism/collectivism and power distance.

Up to this point, it can be seen that leadership styles and management approaches are very much related to the concept of man/woman and his/her relationship with other people. Chinese leaders tend to see themselves and subordinates in a hierarchical relationship defined in authority terms, as a result, Chinese management practices tend to be leader-centred. However, as pointed out in the earlier sections on personality and motivation, with increasing modernization and its associated values, Chinese are experiencing changes in orientation including their outlook to management. It is expected that Hong Kong Chinese business leaders, particularly those with exposures to western management practices, will show both Chinese and western leadership and management styles.

Management Approach of Hong Kong Successful Entrepreneurs and High-Flyers

This section examines the successful entrepreneurs' and high-flyers' management approach which is hypothesized to be related to how they perceive their functions in the business or organization and what managerial skills they perceive important.

Functions

The entrepreneurs and high-flyers were asked to identify from a list in the Questionnaire, the most important aspects, up to a maximum of three, of their present job. Table 9.1 summarizes their total responses.

It is observed from Table 9.1 that developing policy is an important function both for the entrepreneurs and high-flyers. The major point of departure lies in the high-flyers' greater involvement in operational functions of motivating staff and marketing while the entrepreneurs also tend to emphasize organizational functions such as developing a positive organizational image.

Table 9.1 Work Functions of Successful Entrepreneurs and High-Flyers

Work Function	Entrepreneurs	High-Flyers
Meeting people from outside organizations	15	11
Motivating colleagues and subordinates	12	20
Developing policy and strategy for unit/ organization	24	20
Financial control	7	7
Marketing	5	10
Developing positive organizational image	12	5
Fostering organizational culture	7	3
Implementing organizational change	4	1
Total Subjects	30	30

Managerial Skills

The successful entrepreneurs and high-flyers were asked to identify and rank order what they perceive to be the three most essential managerial skills for a successful executive. Table 9.2 shows the totals of the top three and the first choices.

Table 9.2 Perceived Essential Managerial Skills of Successful Entrepreneurs and High-Flyers

Managerial skills	Entrepreneurs	High-Flyers
Analytical skills	23 (8)	20 (13)
Mathematical skills	1 (0)	1 (0)
People skills	21 (4)	24 (7)
Marketing skills	6 (1)	6 (1)
Negotiating skills	9 (0)	5 (0)
Policy making skills	7 (3)	13 (5)
Foresight or vision	25 (14)	21 (4)
Total subjects	30	30

Note: Figures in brackets represent the number of subjects who perceive that skill to be the most important.

As indicated in Table 9.2, the successful entrepreneurs and the high-flyers emphasized different management skills, with the majority of both groups emphasizing analytical skills, people skills and foresight. However, only 35 percent of the entrepreneurs who emphasized analytical skills consider it the most important while 65 percent of those high-flyers who had chosen analytical skills considered it their first choice. More successful entrepreneurs (14) than high-flyers (4) considered foresight or vision as the most important managerial skill.

What were perceived as important managerial skills is highly related to what were perceived as one's work functions in the organizations or business. Referring to Table 4.20 on work functions, the successful entrepreneurs showed a slightly greater tendency to see their roles on an organizational level, such as developing a positive organizational image, they surely need foresight more than operational skills. On the other hand, the high-flyers were involved in developing policy and strategy for the organization or unit, hence they would perceive analytical skills as the most important.

Apart from being asked to identify the general managerial skills they perceived to be important for a successful executive, the successful entrepreneurs and high-flyers were also asked to state which skills on the same list they possess. This was intended to identify if there is any gap between the perceived important skills and the actual managerial skills of the entrepreneurs and high-flyers. Table 9.3 shows the skills the successful entrepreneurs and high-flyers rated as the most three important but they do not possess.

Table 9.3   Gaps in Managerial Skills of Successful Entrepreneurs and High-Flyers

Managerial Skills	Entrepreneurs	High-Flyers
Analytical skills	0	0
Mathematical skills	0	0
People skills	3	1
Marketing skills	2	2
Negotiating skills	1	4
Policy making skills	2	2
Foresight	6	14
No gaps	16	11
Total no of counts	*30**	*34**
Total subjects	*30**	*30**

* The total number of counts and the total number of subjects is the same for successful entrepreneurs but different for the high-flyers for the following reasons:
1. All those entrepreneurs (14) who have gaps in skills indicated only one gap in skills.
2. 16 high-flyers indicated one gap in skills, with two high-flyers indicated two gaps in skills and 1 high-flyer indicated three gaps in skills.

As shown in Table 9.3, sixteen successful entrepreneurs (53 percent) and eleven high-flyers (37 percent) possess personal attributes which they thought were important for a successful executive. Among other important attributes, most gaps are related to foresight, meaning six entrepreneurs and fourteen high-flyers perceived foresight as an important attribute but they do not have this attribute.

Management Style

The entrepreneurs and high-flyers were asked to identify from a list of sixteen management style characteristics those which best described their management style. These sixteen characteristics actually represent four types of management style of which the entrepreneurs and the high-flyers were not informed.

The four management styles are Tells, Sells, Consults and Joins. There were no specifications as to how many characteristics they could choose. It was found that they chose at least two characteristics (1 entrepreneur and 4 high-flyers) and as many as twelve characteristics (1 entrepreneur). The majority of the entrepreneurs (9) chose three characteristics and the majority of the high-flyers (12) chose four characteristics. The total choices on the management styles are shown in Table 9.4.

Table 9.4   Management Styles of Successful Entrepreneurs and Managers

Management Style	Entrepreneurs	High-Flyers
Decisive	18	14
Negotiating	8	8
Questioning	6	2
Co-operative	6	12
Resolute	7	-
Convincing	8	9
Participative	13	18
Collaborating	4	7
Direct	14	9
Persuasive	8	6
Exploring	6	3
Supportive	7	12
Authoritative	3	-
Delegating	17	7
Strategic	12	11
Inquiring	3	3
Total Subjects	30	30

It is found that the entrepreneurs and the high-flyers converged on most characteristics, with the following differences:-

1. Seven entrepreneurs described themselves as resolute and three as authoritative, but no high-flyers saw themselves as such.
2. More entrepreneurs (17) than high-flyers (7) liked to delegate.
3. More high-flyers emphasized a participative management style (18) than the entrepreneurs (13).
4. More high-flyers adopted a co-operative style (12) as compared with the entrepreneurs (6).

The following transcripts can illustrate these tendencies of the successful entrepreneurs and high-flyers.

More Entrepreneurs are Resolute and Authoritative

> Our products is our service. This is our selling point. So I have to make sure they (juniors) do their jobs right. (E19)

These entrepreneurs, being the owner and ultimately accountable for the business, take a more direct intervention into what their colleagues do. In addition, their staff would also perceive them as authority figures, hence further reinforcing them to adopt a resolute and authoritative management style, which is the case for the following entrepreneur.

> They are afraid of me and they respect me because I know very well what they do. I may not know the names of each and every one but I know the divisional heads very well. I get to know them on purpose. Know yourself and your enemies, then you can fight a hundred battles and win them all. (E12)

> I think the most important thing in management is to have a well-defined mission, so that everybody knows which way to go and there is a measurable standard. The employees know what goals to set and what budget to achieve. Hence communicating and educating the mission is very crucial. The next thing is to decentralize. Push the central decision to the lowest level and let them have mission and power. The mission tells them why they are doing something. The power gives them a sense of satisfaction when they achieve something. My favourite analogy is playing the Wimbleton single. If you win, you get all the glory but if you miss the ball, you can't blame anyone. I think having and communicating the company's mission is the key to success not only in management, but also in my company. (E11)

This entrepreneur established the mission for his company and expects his employees to go towards the goals he has set. Even though he mentioned delegating, his employees are basically required to follow the lines of the company's missions.

Two other entrepreneurs mentioned delegating and concern for staff. However an in-depth analysis would reveal the emphasis that they were the final authority:

I think a successful businessman has to be willing to delegate. The old-fashioned Chinese controls everything in doing business. To our generation, delegating is most important. The point is, there must be wastage in delegating, so it depends whether your company can afford a certain degree of wastage. We must have trust in people. However there is one thing I am very strict about. All the employees carry the company's image, especially the company is named after me, so I personally supervise each employee for two to three months. If I think he/she is not suitable, I will just fire him/her. (E9)

I respect my employees and allow them a high degree of autonomy. I hope in return they would respect the company. I accept people make mistakes but in my company they can only make one mistake, otherwise please leave. I will join their lunch and social functions whenever possible. I am quite generous in spending money as staff benefits so long as they are contributive to the company. I think such spending is cost-effective. (E10)

More entrepreneurs emphasize delegating While some entrepreneurs were authoritarian, other entrepreneurs emphasized delegating which appears to be quite the opposite.

I used to work in a big British company before I started my own business. The structure was very rigid. As a result we (employees) could not work with our best ability. In view of this, my managers in each division are given total free hand in doing what they think is right. Of course there are guidelines. They have a big say in the way of doing business, in employing staff, in marketing approach. Each division has its own profit and loss account. The divisional managers have a share of the profit they make. This releases my management burden of overseeing every division. If I watch over every tiny bit of business, I can't plan ahead and look further. (E6)

This entrepreneur delegates because he sees himself in a more important role of future planning for the company, and that it will optimize the ability and motivation of his managers to run divisions of the company.

I like to delegate though I like to get involved in the technical operation of the business. To delegate appropriately means I need to know each of the staff reasonably well. (E8)

Similar to the first entrepreneur, this entrepreneurs delegates because he has more important tasks to fulfil and has to leave the technical operation to his staff.

> I started each and every one of the restaurants myself and then delegated to the branch managers to look after the businesses. They are held accountable for the business performance. If they have different opinions from mine about how to run the business, I will allow them time and assess through business figures. Even if the figures show failure, I will consider whether failure is due to their personal inadequacy or other objective limitations such as location, decoration, image of the company, job-person misfit, etc. I will transfer the manager to other restaurants to give him another opportunity. However if he fails consistently, I am not going to give him another chance. (E7)

> According to my experience with people, I think every person has his/her own character. I know clearly the characters of those (people) under my direct supervision. I use their strong points. In general, I won't give them a model, say this is the way you should do it. No, everyone has his/her own way of doing things. As a boss, I set the bottom line and I want to see results. There are many ways to achieve a goal, not necessarily my way. Our company is very free and we encourage the staff to develop freely. They run their divisions freely and report to me. (E12)

More high-flyers are participative and cooperative

> I want to make them (colleagues) feel we are like a family and that I am approachable. Very often I am away on business trips, so I have to rely on them to complete most of the jobs. (HF17)

> I stress on staff participation because I think the approach is better. I am not autocratic. I think it is very important that I am accepted. I want them to feel we are not fighting alone, we work together as a team. Of course there are times I need to give direction so that they can follow, but I think it (management style) should be people-centred. (HF14)

While encouraging staff participation and cooperation, the high-flyers were not at all conceding their authority to others. They would become direct and decisive when required.

> Their commitment is very important, especially in implementing a new project. They may have resistance to new things because they feel insecured in doing something with which they are not familiar, so I try to alleviate their fears. However we cannot postpone the project because they don't like it or object to it. There may be strategic reasons for doing the project and it can't be delayed. (HF14)

Recognizing staff participation as important in its own right, the above high-flyer nevertheless was required to put the interests of the organizations before those of the individuals.

As evidenced by their choosing more than two characteristics their management styles, it is thought that the entrepreneurs and the high-flyers did not confine themselves to one particular approach of management. This hypothesis can be further examined with reference to the findings shown in Table 9.5 showing the preference of the entrepreneurs and the high-flyers on the four types of management style which the sixteen characteristics represent. The preference on a particular style is determined by the number of characteristics the entrepreneur or high-flyer chose which characterizes that style. Since each of the Tells, Sells, Consults and Joins management style is represented by four characteristics, it is thought choosing three to four characteristics of the management style is reflective of a preference on that style.

Table 9.5   Types of Management Style of Successful Entrepreneurs and High-Flyers

Management Style	Entrepreneurs	High-Flyers
Tells	7(2)	-
Sells	2	2
Consults	3(1)	-
Joins	-	5
Mixed	18	23
Total Subjects	30	30

Note: The figures in brackets represent those who have chosen all of the four characteristics which represent that particular management style.

As evidenced in Table 9.5, the majority of the successful entrepreneurs (18) and high-flyers (23) do not fall on a particular management style. Among those who do show a stronger tendency towards a particular management style, seven successful entrepreneurs are the Tells type, two entrepreneurs and two high-flyers the Sells type, three entrepreneurs the Consults type and five high-flyers the Joins type. Two successful entrepreneurs are the truly Tells type and one entrepreneur the truly Consults type since they have chosen all of the four management styles which represent that specific management type.

From the findings of Table 9.4 and 9.5, it can be said that both the successful entrepreneurs and high-flyers generally do not favour a particular approach, except that the successful entrepreneurs least employed a Joins style, whereas the high-flyers pay rather equal emphasis to the four types of management approach with slightly greater emphasis on the Joins style.

Apart from using the four management types to represent their management approaches, the entrepreneurs and high-flyers were asked in the interview how they managed. Several important themes have been identified and presented below. It is noted that not all individuals fall on one of these themes but they represent some common emphases of some of the successful entrepreneurs and high-flyers about their approach of management.

Concerned with relationships (with employees and clients) (12 entrepreneurs and 16 high-flyers)

I eat at the canteen everyday. It's not a matter of saving money nor convenience. I wish to have more contacts with the staff, and they feel we are equal because we sit together and eat the same food. People have feelings. If you are good to the employees, they will be good to you. We have had no records of strikes here. (E5)

We are very much like a family. My staff are very loyal and have a strong sense of belonging. I prefer harmonious relationships. Going by conflicts is not my style though others believe that competition can bring forth more growth. However I am changing the management approach. I am trying to run the company more on systems and guidelines so that everyone knows his/her role. We are moving the company into an enterprise, so we need more structured systems to run it. Besides, expanding the company also warrants the need for compliance with international regulations to meet safety and quality standards. (E13)

My department is so big that I have to teach my staff to manage their staff. I do not directly manage all the people myself. However my basic principle is reading the personal file and knowing the name of each newcomer. I think it is useful. There are a lot of employees with whom I do not have contacts, but when I pass by and talk to them, they are very delighted if you can call them by their names. This is a kind of motivation. (HF1)

I seldom make jokes with them during office hours, but I would join some of their social functions after work. When we are relaxing, they may mention things which they do not talk about in office and so I get to know more about what they think of the company and their work. Very often they spot loopholes concerning the policy or the system which I may not notice because they are those who take action. Besides, when we have more mutual understanding, they know I am serious in work and will not take my words lightly. (HF2)

You must get close to the staff. I manage by walking around so that I know what's happening. I'll walk around the office, say hello and talk with the staff, junior staff as well. The philosophy is that it is considered natural for a messenger to greet the boss, but if the boss greets the messenger, the messenger will feel appreciated and hence motivated in doing the job. (HF18)

I treat my staff as adults and encourage them to speak up, so that I can tailor training programmes for their needs. Chinese employees are often very passive, I have to try extra hard to get them to speak up. One way I find helpful is to have lunch with them and mix with them in informal occasions. (HF19)

My first client had given me a very hard time, but in the end we became very good friends. In fact, I have made friends with many of my clients. I find clients more trustful than business partners. Clients lose if I lose. But business partners always want to stab at your back so they get all the benefits. (E16)

We treat our clients as friends. Our relationship is not just on a short-term basis, when the business deal is over, then we stop our contact. We try to establish long-term relationship with our clients. They have actually given us a lot of good advice. (E18)

Emphasizing staff training (5 entrepreneurs and 6 high-flyers)

Training is very important and I am very eager in running training programmes for the bank. Training staff also helps me. When you teach, you don't want to say anything wrong, so you'll gather all the information and materials and you'll guess what questions they are going to ask. When you actually teach, some unexpected questions also come up, so you'll have to go to the books or ask others. In this way I am learning as well. (HF1)

Everyone has his/her own strengths and shortcomings, and may not fit the requirements of the organizations. I need to plan the career for the staff. It's big knowledge. I think I should let them feel they have a future here and they are progressing. (HF7)

Since the company relies on them for implementation and operation, I treat them as adults, identify their weak areas, and organize courses. Doing so helps the business and management. (HF15)

When I first started the business, I could not afford to employ experienced professionals. I took fresh graduates and trained them. I found training important. I have trained up many people over all these years and they agreed the training they received here was a good foundation for their later success, which I feel very proud of. (E19)

For many years, staff turnover has been a problem. We are called the 'Learners Temple'. They learnt things here and then left. Our company is renowned for its training. Our employees can get a better paid job elsewhere very easily. Hence I had to raise salary in order to keep the staff. (E20)

Summary - Contingent Management Approach

While the entrepreneurs showed a slightly greater emphasis on being resolute and authoritarian and the high-flyers on being cooperative, both groups were found to be adopting multiple styles in management. It can be suggested that the use of multiple styles represent a thinking that management approach should be contingent on a particular context.

There is no answer to the question of how I manage. I think it (the management approach) changes all the time, depending on what and who you are dealing with. It is also different managing thirty people and three hundred people. So all I can say about how I manage is, it all depends. (E21)

There are no formula for management. You have to be flexible and sensitive to the world. (E22)

My boss taught me to be flexible, when to hit hard and when to leave things alone. (HF15)

I think very few manager will ever of think of this question (management approach) consciously. You won't tell yourself 'I'm going to use this management approach' and then start working with your colleague. I think you need different styles with different people. Some people need to be told straight in the face, and some are really very independent and can be left on their own. I think it depends on the people you deal with. One style may not always work. (HF23)

The insight I gained about management in all these years is that one has to be flexible. The leader should focus on major concerns and big things. Minor affairs need to be bypassed at times. It requires judgement in deciding what is major and what is minor. Judgement is subjective. I think all successful executives make subjective judgements. If one is indecisive, he/she cannot do big things. (E7)

The kind of subjective judgement, according to this entrepreneur, is one of responding to situations. There is no objective formula which the leader can follow at all times.

Management Approach and Career Success

This section considers the management approach of the successful entrepreneurs and high-flyers, and identifies aspects of management that have implications on career success such as perception of roles and functions in the organizations, leadership styles, essential managerial skills and attributes.

The successful entrepreneurs and high-flyers perceive policy-making as an important aspect of their work. A natural result of this is that they perceive analytical skills as essential. However, more important than analytical skills is foresight, the ability to look ahead, particularly it is an ability they do not possess at present. While still emphasizing operational functions, the successful career people are aware of the importance of wider and long-term planning. Having foresight implies the ability to see what is not yet there, hence abstract thinking. The fact that many successful entrepreneurs and high-flyers feel they do not have foresight is related to the ways they were encouraged to think. Nakamura (1964), in his survey of 'ways of thinking', concluded that Chinese thinking displayed five characteristics: (1) emphasis on the perception of the concrete; (2) non-development of abstract thought; (3) emphasis on the particular, rather than universals; (4) practicality as a central focus; (5) concern for reconciliation, harmony, balance. These characteristics point to a mode of thinking that is intuitive and holistic. The successful entrepreneurs and high-flyers were brought up in an environment that does not emphasize abstract thinking, hence they find themselves weak in foresight.

It is surprising that the successful entrepreneurs and high-flyers do not see organizational development as an important aspect of their work when compared to other more operational functions. It is thought that if they are heading the company or department, they should be involved in more broad-level functions such as organization-wide development and changes. The relatively less concern with organizational development is rather in line with Redding's (1986) observation that Chinese firms lack such devices as corporate planning which is obvious in western firms. The close involvement with the operation maybe due to a number of reasons. First, the successful entrepreneurs and high-flyers see their business or departments as their baby, hence wanting to know every detail. Second, they see themselves as the final authority, hence the control agent. Third, a sense of suspicion prevails in the superior-subordinate relationship. Wong (1988) notes that the often-present likelihood of subordinates leaving the organization for better career prospects leads to a distrust towards them by their seniors. The management tends to adopt centralization and, in this case close watch over operations, such that possible detrimental effects of high and frequent staff turnover on the organization is prevented or reduced.

The authoritarian flavour in management is evident in the successful entrepreneurs' and high-flyers' leadership styles. As leaders, they emphasize delegating and are concerned with relationships. They delegate in the belief that they could be released for other more important work functions and that greater efficiency can be achieved. Though recognizing their staff will perform better if they are being respected, preserving the interests of the authority remains to be their principal rationale of delegating. The emphasis on establishing good relationships with staff and clients aims at reducing the possibilities of conflict. It can be said that delegating and concern for good work relationships are instrumental in nature.

In addition, the findings from the leadership styles indicate that more successful entrepreneurs preferred a resolute and authoritative style whereas more high-flyers preferred a participative and cooperative style, but also being direct when required. These leadership styles are quite congruent with their personalities. The successful entrepreneurs have a personality that is self-directed and the high-flyers are found to be joiners (factor Q2 - group-oriented) and good listeners. These constructs of leadership have their roots in the individuals' family upbringing and are also related to management training and real-life work experiences.

The tendency of the successful entrepreneurs and the high-flyers to be direct in general, and the former to be authoritarian in particular, reflects the decisiveness to exercise their authority as the head of organization or section. This attitude to authority has its origin in the way and the environment they were brought up. It is found that during their course of development, major life matters such as education and work, were decided by their parents especially the fathers, not only when they were small children but also when they had reached the age for university study. Studying abroad was largely the parents' decision. Even if the idea first came from the entrepreneurs and high-flyers themselves, they must have their parents' endorsement because their parents bore the financial responsibility. Their parents were seen to be exercising their authority as parents, and following the prescribed social order in the Chinese culture. As argued by Bond and Wang (1983), Chinese people are preoccupied with a concern for maintaining social order. This order is created through the hierarchical structuring of relationships underlying Confucian philosophy. Each party to a relationship is bound by responsibilities but, in return, enjoys access to prerogatives proportionate to rank. Social order is ensured through each party's honouring the requirements in the role relationship, hence social harmony.

Given this concern for social order and hierarchical structuring of interpersonal relationships, one would expect the successful entrepreneurs and high-flyers as superiors and their subordinates to function smoothly with more authoritarian interaction patterns.

Silin (1976) provides an unusual metaphor in describing Chinese leadership style as 'didactic'. The meaning is that the leader holds information, and thus power, and doles it out in small pieces to subordinates, who thus remain more or less dependent. The leader's role has some similarities to that of the teacher. At the same time, the leader does not normally commit himself/herself openly to a line of action, but rather keeps his/her options open, leaving the direction of his/her organization or department to follow the lines detected by a somewhat nebulous but nevertheless powerful set of personal intuitions. Hence it depends somewhat on the leader's sense of responsibility, his/her authority and his/her capability to intuit the right strategy. Silin also pointed out that in Chinese firms there was a common but accepted lack of corporate planning which was more obvious in Western firms.

In such case, leadership style within Chinese companies tend to be directive and authoritarian. Redding and Casey (1976) compared the Chinese beliefs about management behaviour with those found in the West and found the Chinese clearly indicated a distinctly more autocratic approach, especially in sharing information with subordinates and allowing them to participate in decision-making. Their findings are supported by the studies carried out in Taiwan by Bond and Hwang (1986). In addition, the Overseas Chinese as represented in Singapore, Taiwan and Hong Kong are found to be constituting a 'high power distance' culture, a term in Hofstede's study (1980).

Nevertheless, the successful entrepreneurs and high-flyres were found to also exhibit other management styles, and it is this diversity in management styles that characterize their overall management approach as one of flexibility. They emphasize the importance of considering situational and personal contingencies in management, which is related to their flexible personality and their situational orientation (Hsu, 1981). Their authoritarian management orientation is complemented by other management methods. Studies of Chinese leadership behaviours provide support for the observations of the present research.

Bond and Hwang (1986) reviewed a series of studies on Chinese leadership styles which considered the relationships of subordinates' perception of leadership behaviours and their job satisfaction in a number of occupations such as government employees, elementary school teachers, labour workers and accountants.

The findings consistently revealed that the leader's behaviour along the dimensions of consideration and initiating structure was positively correlated with the subordinates' job satisfaction. In other words, Chinese subordinates prefer a leadership style in which the leader maintains a harmonious, considerate relationship with the followers and defines clear-cut tasks and guidelines for them.

Hsu's (1982) research showed that the subordinates' job satisfaction was negatively correlated with the coercive power exercised by the leader, but positively correlated with the leader's expert power and his referent power. Simply put, the Chinese subordinates do not like a punitive leader, but they do like a leader with abundant expertise and ability who is esteemed by others.

The studies reviewed by Bond and Hwang and that carried out by Hsu examined the subordinates' immediate supervisors. The emerging picture of the leader is quite congruent with the high-flyers of the present study. It seems that the Chinese prefer a direct and perhaps authoritative leadership style in which a benevolent and respected leader is not only considerate of his/her subordinates, but also able to take competent and decisive action. However, as heads of the organizations, the successful entrepreneurs appears to be more authoritarian and less concerned with being considerate. It is thought that the power distance between the entrepreneurs as the ultimate boss and their subordinates is higher than that between the high-flyers and their subordinates, hence leading to the differences between the successful entrepreneurs and the high-flyers in their emphasis and use of the authoritarian leadership style.

Concerned with relationships in management and business is another significant feature of the successful entrepreneurs' and high-flyers' management approach. Many a times the successful entrepreneurs and high-flyers mentioned that they treated their partners in business and clients as friends with the understanding that good business relationships were important. In addition, their emphasis on respecting the employees and subordinates in general and the high-flyers' emphasis on a participative and cooperative management style in particular indicates the stress on good working relationships.

The concern of the successful entrepreneurs and high-flyers with relationships in work stems from the networked self developed from their childhood experiences. With strong emphasis on collectivism, social needs take on great significance as part of their psychological make-up. In contrast to Westerners, for whom ego-centred needs such as self-actualization tend to dominate, both Chinese managers and Chinese employees are reported as giving a higher rank to social needs than to ego needs (Chau and Chan, 1984; Redding and Casey, 1976). The emphasis on good work and business relationship is seen as instrumental to the personnel stability of the organization, the wider concern for social harmony, hence long-term interests of the business. As pointed out earlier, due to the high likelihood of many experienced staff leaving the organization and starting their own business, Chinese companies tend to adopt centralization and autocracy as to cope with problems arising from staff changes (Wong, 1988). Having been frequent job-movers themselves, the successful entrepreneurs and the high-flyers at present has to attend to the issue of staffing stability. Instead of autocracy and centralization, they employ strategies which promote good work relationships to motivate and sustain their staff.

Link to Success

On the whole, the successful entrepreneurs and the high-flyers present an image of a decisive leader, clear of his/her role in the organization and what he/she wants from the staff, and manage accordingly. Being equally decisive as the successful entrepreneurs, the high-flyers also tend to be joining.

The management approach of the successful entrepreneurs and the high-flyers is highly consistent with their general personality orientations. The successful entrepreneurs as self-directed persons are prepared to exercise their authority conferred by the social order which emphasizes a hierarchical structuring of relationships. The high-flyers take a more balanced line in managing, taking into consideration the intricate relationship with their subordinates. They are vested with authority over their subordinates but at the same time rely on them for proving their own performance. How well they do their jobs is related to how well they influence their subordinates. McClelland argues that a high nPow with low nAff and high self-control (socialized power) brings the greatest organizational effectiveness. Managerial success is again shown to be a matter of striking the right balance in exercising authority and handling work relationship so that formal authority has real impact on subordinates' work behaviours.

Note

1   Theory X and Theory Y are management theories derived from different assumptions about human nature. In brief, Theory X represents those management theories which assume the average person dislikes work and will avoid it if he/she can. Most people dislike responsibility, require direction and control, have little ambition and require security above all else. Theory Y, on the contrary, represents those management theories which believe that the average person is naturally active and enjoys achieving goals, particularly those he/she has set himself/herself, that commitment to objectives is related to the rewards associated with their achievement, that people will accept and seek responsibility. For details, see Tannenbaum, R. and Schmidt, W.H. (1958) How to choose a leadership pattern, *Harvard Business Review, 36*, 95-101.

10 The Successful Career People

This chapter summarizes the study by presenting a portrait of the successful entrepreneurs and the high-flyers. In understanding the successful career people, the element of culture is discussed, leading to a revisiting of the conceptual model and the theoretical perspectives adopted for the study.

A Portrait of the Hong Kong Successful Entrepreneurs and the High-Flyers

Based on the personal characteristics identified, a general portrait of the successful entrepreneurs and high-flyers is given below.

Immigrant Parents, Self-Employed Fathers

The parents of the successful entrepreneurs and high-flyers were immigrants from China, with a majority of the fathers as self-employed, and mothers as housewives. The immigrant background fostered a hardwork ethic and a sensitivity to the structure of opportunities due to the need to survive in a new environment.

Hard but Happy Childhood

The successful entrepreneurs and high-flyers had to face economic hardships early in life, fostering an independent, self-reliant and hardworking personality. However, the close relationship they had with parents resulted in a happy childhood.

233

Networked Self

The successful entrepreneurs and high-flyers were brought up in a web of relationships, making them highly sensitive to the social environment, creating a flexibility in outlook of life and management.

Sensitive to the Environment

The sensitivity developed from exposures to the dynamics of the environment at an early age had facilitated a smooth entry into the adult world. The successful entrepreneurs and high-flyers are oriented towards developing a flexible personality capable of appreciating situational contingencies. They are also keenly aware of the importance of establishing good business and work connections.

Highly Educated

The successful entrepreneurs and particularly the high-flyers achieved much higher levels of education than the general population, showing their parents' and their own strong emphasis on education.

Strong Quest for Knowledge and Qualifications

The zest for education and qualifications is partly related to belief that being well-educated has greater access to the structure of opportunities, hence possibility of upward social mobility. The educational choices they made represented to some extent their career choices which were based on the perceived structure of opportunities.

Early Responsibility and Wide Exposures in Career

The successful entrepreneurs and high-flyers, following either the professional, opportunist or true entrepreneur career path, had been exposed to a wide range of work functions. They responded positively to job move as opportunities for wide exposure.

Flexible Personality

The successful entrepreneurs and high-flyers, being highly sensitive to the social environment, exhibit traits that suggest a tendency to having a flexible personality. The flexible personality indicates their ability to be open to new experiences, and their ability to adapt.

Their flexible personality is found to have resulted from early childhood experiences through a web of social relationships and from wide exposures in the course of career development.

High Tolerance of Stress

The successful entrepreneurs and high-flyers have high tolerance of stress which is reflected by the good health they reported. They also show positive attitudes towards difficulties and have effective behavioural means to manage stress. The positive attitudes and the ability in problem-solving are developed from experiences in childhood, studying and work. The strong support from their family members also contributes to a high tolerance of stress.

High Need for Achievement

The need for achievement is most motivating for the successful entrepreneurs and high-flyers. It is not yet clear whether this achievement motivation is of an individualistic or collectivist orientation.

While influenced by their parents in their work values, the successful entrepreneurs and high-flyers also developed somewhat different work values, which is believed to come from education and the business world.

Seeking Monetary Rewards

Monetary rewards is a major motivating factor for the high-flyers. It is thought that the high salary package they enjoy is attractive enough to counteract the appeal of becoming an entrepreneur.

Internal Locus of Control

The successful entrepreneurs and high-flyers are high internals. The origins of their internality were rooted in early childhood and reinforced by educational and career experiences.

Contingent Management Approach

While the successful entrepreneurs showed a general tendency to be authoritarian and direct and the high-flyers to be participative and supportive, both groups stressed a contingent management approach. Such approach has its roots in the high sensitivity to the social environment and wide exposure to situations and people.

Having lived up to twenty years of disciplined paternalism in the family, having had his or her sense of social order and hierarchical structuring of interpersonal relationships reinforced in the school context, where teachers represent the learning on which authority in China was traditionally allocated (Ho and Lee, 1974), the successful entrepreneurs and the high-flyers develop individual perceptions which constitute what Hofstede terms a 'high power distance' culture.

Concerned with Relationships

While being self-centred in personality and authoritarian in management, the successful entrepreneurs and high-flyers recognized the importance of having good relationships for business and career development. This concern with relationships originates from the networked self developed in childhood and reinforced by the work culture that emphasizes harmony and order.

The Cultural Element of Success of the Hong Kong Entrepreneurs and High-Flyers

Bond (1993) claims that Hong Kong presents a psychological environment that makes identity concerns salient to its people. As pointed out earlier, the Hong Kong culture is shaped by both traditional Chinese values and Western ethos. The successful entrepreneurs and high-flyers were taught the Chinese ways of living very early in life. Their primary socialization took place in the family through parents and familial relations. However, during the course of their development, they were exposed to more and more Western ways of living through popular culture, education and direct contacts with westerners. The successful entrepreneurs and high-flyers were therefore open to the possible shaping effects of western influences.

The career success of the Hong Kong entrepreneurs and high-flyers is conceived to be an outcome of a mix of two worlds: Chinese and Western. They show values and traits strongly rooted in the Confucian Chinese culture, yet at the same time exhibit Western beliefs and management practices that were learnt from a British educational system, undergraduate studies in Western countries and working in organizations that have international contacts. The relationship of the Chinese Confucian culture to success is best discussed by Kahn in his Post-Confucian Hypothesis.

The Post-Confucian Hypothesis

The contribution of Kahn (1979) to the understanding of economic growth in Japan, Korea and the Overseas Chinese in the form of his Post-Confucian Hypothesis which argues that the sources of growth in these societies rests on the notion of a common cultural heritage. Kahn proposes four traits consistent with Confucian ideology but are its modern manifestations, in the same way that European countries display a wide variety of interpretations today of their Graeco-Roman heritage. The four traits are thought to have created significant impact on present-day organizations in Japan, Korea, and among the Overseas Chinese. These are:

1. Socialization within the family unit in such a way as to promote sobriety, education, the acquisition of skills, and seriousness about tasks, job, family, and obligations.
2. A tendency to help the group (however it might be identified).
3. A sense of hierarchy and of its naturalness and rightness.
4. A sense of complementarity in relationships, which, combined with the sense of hierarchy, enhances perceptions of fairness and equity in institutions. For example, a boss's paternalistic concern for

subordinates will be complemented by their willingness to cooperate without excessive resentment of (or perhaps even perception of) their relative subordination.

The hard work, determination, perseverance, stubbornness, sensitivity qualities of the successful entrepreneurs and high-flyers is considered to be a result of one or a combination of the above Confucian legacies. In the Hong Kong context, the influence of these legacies is coupled with a sense of insecurity which is also present in many Overseas Chinese. In Hong Kong, the shadow of 1997 looms. In Indonesia, Thailand, the Philippines and Malaysia, the Chinese are an economically successful minority whose acceptance by host cultures cannot always be guaranteed. The sense of insecurity becomes a motivational force to work hard, to rely on oneself, to stay in groups and to achieve in order to survival.

Given the migrant background of much of the population in Hong Kong, and its peculiar status as a British colony returning to China, it is not surprising that a high value is placed on personal financial success, and more broadly, on economic success for the community as a whole. This priority is entirely rational: financial and economic success do help cushion against unexpected downturns, whether personal or communal. Sir Hamish Macleod, Hong Kong's Financial Secretary from 1991 to 1995, recalled an experience to illustrate the difference in the attitude and the drive to succeed between the Hong Kong people and a westerner living in a stable environment:

> During a trade negotiation visit to Norway, I had dinner with the Norwegian agent of a Hong Kong garment exporter. He told me with pride that the business was so profitable that he had been able to reduce his working week to only three days; probing revealed that he had no interest in expanding into importing garments from places other than Hong Kong. I hid my amazement, but I could not imagine any Hong Kong businessmen taking such a view - here surely was a chance to expand into other products, other suppliers, not to take it easy! (Source: *Hong Kong 1995*)

Revisiting the Theoretical Framework

Based on the understanding derived from the examination of the six personal variables of the successful entrepreneurs and high-flyers and the impact of Confucian thinking on career success, this Part aims at presenting a revised version of the original conceptual model outlined in Chapter Two to abstract the personal characteristics of successful career people and their origins and development. Subsequently, the theoretical framework which has been adopted for the present study is evaluated for its contributions to understanding the psychology of successful career people.

The Revised Conceptual Model

The empirical findings obtained with regard to the personal characteristics of the successful entrepreneurs and high-flyers lend insight to refine the conceptual model developed to guide the present study. The revised conceptual model is presented in Figure 10.1.

Figure 10.1 The Revised Conceptual Model

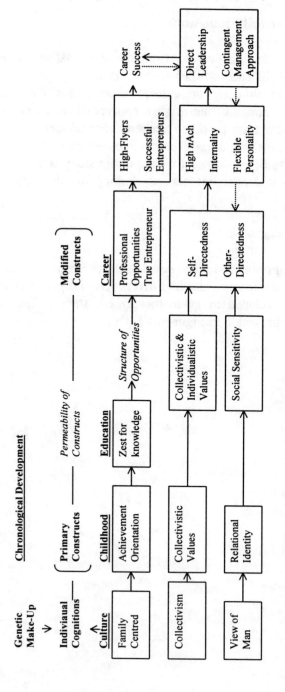

Note: The italics indicate the mediating mechanisms of a particular process

Key: ⟶ indicates the changing process of constructs during development, resulting from reinforcement, leading to increased self-efficacy and expectancy of reward in that particular construct

⋯⋯▷ indicates the feedback to constructs, resulting from reinforcement, leading to increased self-efficacy and expectancy of reward in that particular construct

The model is built on the premise that personal characteristics of successful career individuals reflect their ways of thinking, that is, cognitions. It is postulated that an individual's cognitions which constitutes his/her personality and behaviours are a result of both genetic and environmental factors. The model focuses on three environmental contexts which have significant influence on forming and modifying the individual's cognitions during his/her life-span development, namely childhood, education and career. Cultural influence is present in the ways individual cognitions are shaped by childhood, education and career experiences.

In childhood, the successful career individual experiences close relationship with parents, which is a favourable condition for modelling and socialization. The individual forms his/her constructs with regard to motivation and goals, values and beliefs, and interpersonal relationships. The cultural and parental emphasis on the centrality of the family for an individual and his/her obligations and responsibilities to the family encourages a sense of independence and self-reliance which are the roots of an internal locus of control. These achievement-striving attributes and a general achievement orientation are particularly emphasized in times of economic hardships. As an extension of the emphasis on the family, collective well-being is valued and the individual is defined in terms of his/her existence in a larger network, usually that of the kins. Also due to pragmatic considerations, the individual is engaged in his/her parents' activities. From an early age, the individual learns that relationships are hierarchically structured and that there are prescribed rules in every relationship. As a result, a relational identity is developed, which means the individual sees himself/herself mainly existing in a web of relationships. The individual's cognitions so developed in childhood represent the primary constructs since they form the bases of constructs learned at a later stage in life.

The achievement orientation fostered in childhood is manifested in the strong zest for education and qualifications, in the belief that these will enhance personal competence which facilitates access to the structure of opportunities. On the other hand, the educational process exposes the individual, particularly if he/she studies overseas, to values and practices different from those of his/her parents. These values and practices represent a more individualistic orientation. The individual becomes more internal and also develops a self-centredness in contrast with the other-centredness developed since childhood. Another outcome of the educational process is many more social exposures, further increasing the individual's ability to relate to a variety of people and sensitivity to the environment.

As the individual began work and progressed, wide exposures were experienced, which served to strengthen or weaken the existing constructs of motivation and values, leading to different career decisions at different stages. The individual's constructs of self and people also affects the ways he/she leads and manages. The collectivist orientation and the sensitivity to environment learned in childhood, and the individualistic orientation and self-directedness acquired in later development result in the individual's tendency to be contingent in management, authoritarian in leadership but concerned with relationships. These constructs prove to be rewarding since the individual is recognized to be a successful career person.

The individual's constructs in many ways evidence the influence of culture, which in essence is a legacy of the Confucian ethics. The precise influence of Confucian thinking on career success of the entrepreneur and high-flyer are conceived to be:

1. The centrality of family. It is the basic unit of survival around which the life of its members are organized. Obligations and responsibilities to the family is stressed, inducing a sense of self-reliance on the part of its members who do not wish to create any burden to the family.

2. Collectivism. Collective welfare is placed above individual welfare. Individual conduct and pursuits are directed at achieving collective harmony, maintained through preserving the social order and following the rules entailed in each relationship.

3. Its view of man. An individual is defined in terms of his/her relationship with others which are structured in a differential order with different degree of closeness and trust, prerogatives and obligations, authority and submissiveness. Family relationships are of central importance. Work relationships are basically defined in hierarchical terms. This relational identity predisposes the individual to consider his/her internal needs in relation to the external environment in almost every aspect, making adaptability and flexibility a characteristic in personality and behaviours.

The modifications that have taken place in the individual's cognitions reveals there is a high degree of permeability in their thinking. Kelly (1984) defines permeability as the quality of a construct which allows new elements currently excluded from its range of convenience to be construed within its framework. Simply put, permeability indicates the extent of the individual's openness to new experiences, hence new learning.

Permeability and hence modifications of constructs are facilitated by reinforcement, expectancy of reward and self-efficacy. Direct reinforcement helps to strengthen or weaken existing constructs. However, it is more often that expectancy of reward and self-efficacy serve the bases for modifying current constructs. The individual is constantly making appraisals and predictions of the environment and his/her own behaviours.

Model is an abstraction reality. The revised conceptual model summarizes the origins and the development of the personal characteristics of the successful career individuals in the present study. In summarizing, the model does not exhaust the unique characteristics of all successful career individuals and hence cannot acknowledge every individual difference.

Critical Review of Cognitive Perspectives

Cognitive perspectives were adopted for constructing the theoretical framework of the present study, which include Kelly's personal constructs theory, Rotter's and Bandura's social cognition theory, Cattell's traits theory and the notion of cognition as an aspect of culture.

Throughout the review of the findings and their analyses, a strong relationship of success and cognition was discerned. Cognition is the individual's way of thinking, the way he/she organizes information and comes to his/her own worldview. The contents of this cognition make up the individual successful entrepreneur's or high-flyer's personal constructs. The various personal constructs help the successful entrepreneur or high-flyer predict the environment and guide his/her behaviour in life and at work.

The findings also reveal that the individual's personal constructs were developed out of a psychological process of social learning based on the discrimination of reinforcement. The successful entrepreneurs and high-flyers quoted numerous experiences in which they observed the behaviours of their parents, their bosses, their colleagues and many others. Not only did they observe the behaviours as such, but they also discriminated which behaviours were being reinforced and which not, and what kind of rewards were present. Based on the observation of others, the successful entrepreneurs and high-flyers gradually developed their own behavioral repertoire and standards on which their behaviours are reinforced and hence regulated. This ability to self-regulate enables them to assess their own efficacy to deal with different situations and make decisions concerning these situations. The social cognition theories, in particular Rotter's notions of expectancy and reinforcement, Bandura's concepts of vicarious learning, self-regulation and self-efficacy, have been able to capture and explain most of the experiences of the successful entrepreneurs and high-flyers, especially they have lived and still live in an environment that is collectivist in nature and relationship-oriented, providing many opportunities for social interaction and learning.

However, social cognition theories built on the notion of reinforcement and expectancy as the psychological mechanisms for acquisition and performance of behaviours are not sufficient to explain the dynamics involved in the decision to pursue success in career, and the manner to pursue it, as an employee or as one's own boss. Achievement and success can come in many forms and in many ways, not necessarily through one's career. There are people in the society who are equally successful but in areas other than their careers, such as a successful housewife, even though one may argue being a housewife is itself a career. The choice of the successful entrepreneurs and high-flyers to pursue success in career is definitely influenced by socialization and by the rewarding experiences of significant others. However, the thinking involved is more than a matter of socialization and reinforcement. The successful entrepreneurs and high-flyers mentioned their decision to stay as an employee or to go start one's business was based on calculated risks. Calculating risks entails weighing different possible rewards, which is ultimately a subjective value judgement. Why a particular reward is judged to be more important than the other in a specific situation warrants more in-depth study than a simple realization of the significance of reinforcement in career choice and success.

A possible direction for a better understanding of career success-related behaviours is theorizing of the self. Here credit must be paid to Bandura whose concepts of self-regulation and self-efficacy did enlighten understanding the successful entrepreneurs and high-flyers, especially in the ways they pursue their goals, position themselves in the organizations and run the business or department. However, self-regulation and self-efficacy are derived from and maintained by reinforcement, vicarious and direct, which still lacks the depth and vigour to account for the unifying aspects of the self.

Cattell's conception that traits are basically genetic but modifiable by learning experiences can be contributive to understanding behaviours related to career success. He emphasizes that it is important to consider the ways and the extent to which the culture and various groups within it influence individuals and are, in turn, influenced by them (1970). The use of the 16 PF to discover the personality profile of the successful entrepreneurs and high-flyers represents a first step to understand what they are like and uncover areas that worth further investigation. For instance, the profiles of the successful entrepreneurs and high-flyers strongly suggest they have contrasting personality traits. However a careful examination of these traits in their historical and work contexts indicates these traits can be considered complementary, and that some of the traits are source traits which remain rather intact regardless of changes in the environment and that other traits are more susceptible to learning experiences. What Cattell has failed to do is to provide a systematic framework in which to examine how traits are modified by different changes in the environment which bring varying learning experiences. In addition, such kind of examination cannot be undertaken purely by numerical calculations. Cognition involves much processing and organizing of values and meanings which are not quantifiable.

The incorporation of the culture component in the present study is found valid and useful because many of the beliefs and behaviours reported by the successful entrepreneurs and high-flyers show traces of the Chinese culture to a great extent and the Western culture to a smaller extent. However culture is not a fixed and homogeneous entity, just like there is no one single Chinese culture. The Chinese living in the southern provinces exhibit very different culture from that of the Chinese living elsewhere. Hence it takes much caution and shrewdness in employing the construct of culture to account for phenomena. Similar as explanations for human behaviours. The present study of the personal characteristics of Hong Kong successful entrepreneurs and high-flyers has only had a simple glimpse of both the Chinese and the Western culture. It still requires deeper understanding of both cultures, in general and in specific, and how they are anatomized to influence the thinking and behaviours of career success people.

References

Astin, H.S. (1984), 'The Meaning of Work in Women's Lives: A Sociopsychological Model of Career Choice and Work Behaviour', *Counseling Psychology*, vol.12:4, pp.117-126.

Andrisani, P. and Nestel, G. (1976), 'Internal-external Control as Contributor and Outcome of Work Experience', *Journal of Applied Psychology*, vol.62, pp.156-165.

Bandura, A. (1971), *Social Learning Theory*, Morristown, NJ: General Learning Press.

Bandura, A. (1978), 'The Self System in Reciprocal Determinism', *American Psychologist*, vol.3, pp.344-358.

Baumrind, D. (1971), 'Current Patterns of Parental Authority', *Developmental Psychology Monograph*, vol.4:1, pt 2.

Berlew, D. (1975), 'The Nature of Entrepreneurs', *Proceedings of Project ISEED (International Symposium on Entrepreneurship and Enterprise Development)*, Sponsored by The Ohio Entrepreneurship Office, Columbus, Ohio, pp.42-44.

Blake, R.R. and Mouton, J.S. (1964), *The Managerial Grid*, Houston: Gulf Publishing Company.

Bond, M.H. and Wang, S.H. (1983), 'Aggressive Behaviour in Chinese Society: The Problem of Maintaining Order and Harmony', in A.P. Goldstein and M. Segall (eds), *Global Perspectives on Aggression*, New York: Pergamon Press, pp.58-74.

Bond, M.H. and Hwang, K.K. (1986), 'The Social Psychology of Chinese People', in Bond, M.H. (ed.), *The Psychology of the Chinese People*, Hong Kong: Oxford University Press, pp.213-365.

Bond, M.H. (1993), 'Between the Yin and the Yang: The Identity of the Hong Kong Chinese', *Professorial Inaugural Lecture Series*, vol.19, Chinese University of Hong Kong.

Borland, C. (1975), 'Locus of Control, Need for Achievement and Entrepreneurship', *Doctoral Dissertation*, University of Texas. Unpublished.

Bortner, R.W. (1969), 'A Short Rating Scale as a Potential Measure of Pattern A Behaviour', *Journal of Chronic Disease*, vol.2, pp.87-91.

Bowen, D.D. and Hisrich, R.D. (1986), 'The Female Entrepreneur: A Career Development Perspective', *Academy of Management Review*, vol.11, pp.393-407.

Brockhaus, R.H. and Nord, W.R. (1979), 'An Exploration of Factors Affecting the Entrepreneurial Decision: Personal Characteristics Vs Environmental Conditions', *Proceedings of the 39th Annual Meeting of the Academy of Management*, pp.368-372.

Brockhaus, R.H. (1982), 'The Psychology of the Entrepreneur', in Kent, C.A., Sexton D.L. and Vespers, K.H. (eds), *Encyclopedia of Entrepreneurship*, Englewood Cliffs, N.J.: Prentice Hall.

Brockhaus, R.H. and Horwitz, P.S. (1986), 'The Psychology of the Entrepreneur', in Sexton, D.L. and Similar, R. (eds), *The Art and Science of Entrepreneurship*, Cambridge, MA: Ballinger.

Brown, R. (1982), 'Work Histories, Career Strategies and Class Structure', in A. Giddens and G. MacKensie (eds.), *Social Class and the Division of Labour*, Cambridge: Cambridge University Press.

Bruce, R. (1976), *The Entrepreneurs,* Birmingham: Libertarian Books, Folium Press Ltd.

Brummett, R.L., Pyle, W.C. and Framholtz, E.G. (1968), 'Accounting for human resources', *Michigan Business Review,* vol.20:2, pp.20-25.

Bruner, E.M. (1986), *The Anthropology of Experience*. Urbana, Ill: University of Illinois Press.

Bryman (1995), *Quantity and Quality in Social Research.*

Carsrud, A.L., Olm, K.W. and Eddy, G.G. (1986), 'Entrepreneurship: Research in Quest of a Paradigm,' in Sexton, D.L. and Similar, R.W. (eds), *The Art and Science of Entrepreneurship*, Cambridge, MA: Ballinger.

Cattell, R. (1970), *The Scientific Analysis of Personality,* Baltimore, MD: Penguin Books.

Cattell, R. (1984), 'The Voyage of a Laboratory', *Multivariate Behavioral Research,* vol.19, pp.121-174.

Chau, W. L. and Chan, W. K. (1984), 'A Study of Job Satisfaction of Workers in Local Factories of Chinese, Western and Japanese Ownership', *The Hong Kong Manager,* Vol.20, pp.9-14.

Cheng, T.Y. (1977), *The Economy of Hong Kong,* Hong Kong: Far East Publications.

Cheng, B. F. (1995), 'Differential Order and Chinese Organizational Behaviours', *Indigenous Psychological Research*, vol.3, pp.142-291. (In Chinese)

Chiu, C.O. (1963), 'A Comparative Study on the Personality of Chinese and American Students', Unpublished Bachelor's Thesis, National Taiwan University. (In Chinese)

Chong, L.E., Cragin, J.P. and Scherling, S.A. (1983), 'Manager Work-related Values in a Chinese Corporation', Paper Presented to the Annual Meeting of the Academy of International Business, San Francisco, USA, April.

Clare, D.A. and Sanford, D.G. (1979), 'Mapping Personal Value Space: A Study of Managers in Four Organizations', *Human Relations*, vol.32:8, pp.659-666.

Clements, R.V. (1958), *Managers: A Study of Their Careers in Industry,* London: Allen and Unwin.

Collard, E.D. (1964), 'Achievement Motive in the Four-year-old Child and Its Relationship to Achievement Expectancies of the Mother', Unpublished Doctoral Dissertation, University of Michigan.

Cooper, A.C. and Dunkelberg, W.C. (1984), '*Entrepreneurship and Paths to Business Ownership*', (Paper No. 846), West Lafayette. IN: Purdue University, Krannert Graduate School of Management.

Cooper, C.L. (1976), *Developing Social Scales in Managers,* London: MacMillan.

Cooper, C.L. (1981a), *The Stress Check,* Englewood Cliffs, NJ: Prentice Hall.

Cooper, C.L. (1981b), *Executive Families Under Stress,* Englewood Cliffs, NJ: Prentice Hall.

Cox, C.J. and Cooper, C.L. (1988), *High Flyers: An Anatomy of Managerial Success,* Oxford: Basil Blackwell.

Crandall, V.C. (1973), 'Differences in Parental Antecedents of Internal-external Control in Children and Young Adulthood', Paper presented at the American Psychological Association Convention, Montreal.

Crompton, R. and Sanderson, K. (1986), 'Credentials and Careers: Some Implications of the Increase in Professional Qualifications Amongst Women', *Sociology,* vol.20:1, pp.25-42.

Denzin, N.K. (1970), *The Research Act in Sociology,* Chicago: Aldine.

Denzin, N.K. (1989), '*Interpretive Biography*', Sage University Paper Series on Qualitative Research Methods, vol.17. Beverly Hills, CA:Sage.

Derr, C.B. (1986), *Managing the New Careerist,* San Francisco: Jossey Bass.

Derrida, J. (1972), 'Structure, Sign and Play in the Discourse of the Human Sciences', in Macksey, R. and Donato, E. (eds), *The Structuralist Controversy: The Languages of Criticism and the Sciences of Man,* Baltimore, MD: John Hopkins University Press.

England, G.W. and Lee, R. (1974), 'The Relationship Between Managerial Values and Managerial Success in the United States, Japan, India and Australia', *Journal of Applied Psychology*, vol.59:4, pp.411-419.

Erikson, E.H. (1968), *Identity: Youth and Crisis,* London: Faber and Faber.

Fei, X. T. (1948), *Rural China,* Shanghai: Guancha She.

Festinger, L. (1957), *A Theory of Cognitive Dissonance,* Evanston, Ill: Row Peterson.

Firth, S. (1987), 'The Characteristics of High-flyers in Management', unpublished MSc Dissertation, UMIST, Manchester, UK.

Fisher, H. (1990), 'Attributes of Success in Large Organizations', unpublished MSc Dissertation, UMIST, Manchester, UK.

Gasse, Y. (1982), 'Elaborations on the Psychology of the Entrepreneur', in Kent, C.A., Sexton, D.L. and Vespers, K.H. (eds), *Encyclopedia of Entrepreneurship*, NJ: Prentice Hall.

Ghiselli, E.E. (1968), 'Some Motivational Factors in the Success of Managers', *Personnel Psychology*, vol.21, pp.431-444.

Glaser, B.G. and Strauss, A.L. (1967), *The Discovery of Grounded Theory*, Hawthorn, NY: Aldine Publishing Company.

Harris, P.R. and Harris, D.L. (1985), 'Innovative Management Leadership', *Leadership and Organization Development Journal*, vol.6:3, pp.3-20.

Hall, D.T. (1976), *Careers in Organizations*, Santa Monica, CA: Goodyear.

Haywood, H.C. (1968), 'Motivational Orientation of Overachieving and Underachieving Elementary School Children', *American Journal of Mental Deficiency*, vol.72, pp.662-667.

Hertzberg, F., Mausner, B. and Snyderman, D.B. (1959), *The Motivation to Work*, New York: John Wiley.

Hingley, P. and Cooper, C.L. (1985), *The Change Makers*, London: Harper and Row.

Hisrich, R.D. and Brush, C.G. (1983), 'The Woman Entrepreneurs: Implications of Family, Educational, and Occupational Experience', in Hornaday, J.A., Thomas, J.A. and Vespers, K.H. (eds), *Frontiers of Entrepreneurship Research*, Wellesley, MA: Boston College, Centre for Entrepreneurial Studies.

Hisrich, R.D. and Brush, C.G. (1984), 'The Woman Entrepreneur: Management Sills and Business Problems', *Journal of Small Business Management*, vol.22, pp.30-37.

Hisrich, R.D. and Brush, C.G. (1986), *The Woman Entrepreneur: Starting, Financing and Managing a Successful New Business*, Lexington, MA: Lexington Books.

Ho, D.Y.F. and Lee, L.Y. (1974), 'Authoritarianism and Attitude Towards Filial Piety in Chinese Teachers', *The Journal of Social Psychology*, vol.92, pp.305-306.

Ho, D.Y.F. and Kang, T.K. (1984), 'Intergenerational Comparison of Child-rearing Attitudes and Practices in Hong Kong', *Developmental Psychology*, vol.20, pp.1004-1016.

Ho, D.Y.F. (1986), 'Chinese Patterns of Socialization: A Critical Review', in Bond, M.H. (ed), *The Psychology of the Chinese People*, Oxford University Press.

Hoffman, L.W. (1972), 'Early Childhood Experiences and Women's Achievement Motives', *Journal of Social Issues*, vol.28:2, pp.129-155.

Hofstede, G. (1980), *Culture's Consequences: International Differences in Work-related Values*, London and Beverly Hills: Sage.

Hong Kong Government (1995). *Hong Kong 1995: A Review of 1994*.

Hsieh, T., Shybut, J. and Lotsof, E. (1969), 'Internal Versus External Control and Ethnic Group Membership: A Cross-cultural Comparison', *Journal of Consulting and Clinical Psychology,* vol.33, pp.122-124.

Hsu, F.L.K. (1981), *Americans and Chinese: Passage to Differences,* Hawaii: University Press of Hawaii.

Hsu, Y.S. (1982), 'Leader's Power Basis, Leadership, and Employees' Job Satisfaction', Unpublished Master's Thesis, National Chengchi University.

Hwang, G.G. (1995), 'Modern Transformation of Confucian Values', *Indigenous Psychological Research,* vol.3, pp.276-338. (In Chinese)

Illingworth, R.S. and Illingworth, C.M. (1966), *Lessons from Childhood,* Edinburgh: E and S Livingstone.

Jacobowitz, A. and Vidler, D.C. (1983), 'Characteristics of Entrepreneurs: Implications for Vocational Guidance', *Vocational Guidance Quarterly*, vol.30, pp.252-257.

Jahoda, M. (1988), 'The Range of Convenience of Personal Construct Psychology - An Outsider's View', in F. Fransella and L. Thomas (eds.), *Experimenting with Personal Construct Psychology*, London: Routledge and Kegan Paul, pp.1-14.

Jansen, D. (1986), 'How Parents Can Kill or Create the Entrepreneurial Spirit', *Rydges*, April, pp.20-23.

Jennings, R., Cox, C. and Cooper, C.L. (1994), *Business Elites: The Psychology of Entrepreneurs and Intrapreneurs,* London: Routledge.

Kahn, H. (1979), *World Development: 1979 and Beyond,* London: Croom Helm.

Kakabadse, A.K. and Margerison, C.J. (1985), 'The Management Development Needs of Chief Executives', in V. Hammond (ed.), *Current Research in Management,* London: Frances Printer.

Katkovsky, W., Crandall, V.C. and Good, S. (1967), Parental Antecedents of Children's Beliefs in Internal-external Control of Reinforcement in Intellectual Achievement Situations, *Child Development,* vol.28, pp.765-776.

Kelly, G. (1991), *The Psychology of Personal Construct,* Routledge.

Kerlinger, F.N. (1986), *Foundations of Behavioral Research,* Holt, Rinehart and Winston.

Kets de Vries, M.F.R. (1977), 'The Entrepreneurial Personality: A Person at the Crossroads', *The Journal of Management Studies, February*, pp.34-57.

King, A.Y.C. and Bond, M.H. (1985), 'The Confucian Paradigm of Man: A Sociological View', in W.S. Tseng and D.Y.H. Wu (eds), *Chinese Culture and Mental Health*, New York: Academic Press, pp.29-46.

Kohut, H. (1971), *The Analysis of Self,* New York: International University Press.

Komives, J.L. (1972), 'A Pulmonary Study of the Personal Values of High Technical Entrepreneurship', *Technical Entrepreneurship: A Symposium*, Milwaukee: Centre for Venture Management.

Kubany, E.S., Gallimore, R., and Buell, J. (1970), 'The Effects of Extrinsic Factors on Achievement-oriented Behaviour: A Non-Western Case', *Journal of Cross-Cultural Psychology*, vol.1, pp.77-84.

Lam, S.K.S. (1988), 'Personal Characteristics of British Entrepreneurs and High-flyers', Unpublished.

Lao, R.C. (1977), 'Levenson's IPC (internal-external control) Scale: A Comparison of Chinese and American Students', *Journal of Cross-Cultural Psychology*, vol.9, pp.113-124.

Lau, S.K. (1982), *Society and Politics in Hong Kong*, Hong Kong: Chinese University Press.

Lazarus, R.S. (1966), *Psychological Stress and the Coping Process*, New York: McGraw-Hill.

Lefcourt, H.M. (1982), *Locus of Control*, Hillsdale, NJ: Lawrence Erlbaum.

Levinson, D.J., Darrow, C.N., Klein, E.B., Levinson, M.H. and McKee, B. (1978), *Seasons of a Man's Life*, New York: Alfred Knopf.

Levenson, H. (1972), 'Activism and Powerful Others: Distinctions Within the Concept of Internal-external Control', *Journal of Consulting and Clinical Psychology*, vol.40:3, pp.377-383.

Levenson, H. (1973), 'Perceived Parental Antecedent of Internality, Powerful Others and Chance Locus of Control Orientations', *Developmental Psychology*, vol.9, pp.268-274.

Lewis, J.W. (1965), 'Education and Political Development: A Study of Pre-school Training Programs in Mainland China', in J.S. Coleman (ed.), *Education and Political Development*, Princeton, New Jersey: Princeton University Press, pp.423-429.

Li, M.C., Cheung, S.F. and Kau, S.M. (1979), 'Competitive and Cooperative Behaviour of Chinese Children in Taiwan and Hong Kong', *Acta Psychologica Taiwanica*, vol.21, pp.27-33. (In Chinese)

Likert, R. and Hayes, S.P. (1957), *Some Applications of Behavioural Research*, Paris: UNESCO.

Liles, P.R. (1974), *New Business Ventures and The Entrepreneur*, Illinois: Richard D. Irwin.

Liu, C. Y., Chen, C. H., Chen, Y. H. and Yang, K. S. (1973), 'A Survey of the Every-day Behaviour of National Taiwan University Students', *Thought and Word*, vol.10:6, pp.1-19. (In Chinese)

Lui, M. (1985), 'Work-related Needs Among Hong Kong Commercial Employees', Unpublished Master's Thesis, University of Hong Kong.

McClelland, D.C. (1951), *Personality*, New York: Van Nostrand.

McClelland, D.C. (1963), 'Motivational Patterns in Southeast Asia with Special Reference to the Chinese Case', *Social Issues*, vol.19, pp.6-19.

McClelland, D.C. (1975), *Power, The Inner Experience*, New York: Irvington.

McClelland, D.C. and Boyatzis, R.E. (1982). 'Leadership Motive Pattern and Long-term Success in Management', *Journal of Applied Psychology*, vol.67:6, pp.737-743.

McCracken, G. (1988), *The Long Interview*, Sage University Paper Series on Qualitative Research Methods, vol.13, Beverly Hills, CA:Sage.

MacDonald, A.P. (1971), 'Internal-external Locus of Control: Parental Antecedents', *Journal of Consulting and Clinical Psychology*, vol.37:1, pp.141-147.

McGregor, D (1969), *The Human Side of Enterprise*, NY: McGraw Hill.

Madsen, M.C. (1971), 'Developmental and Cross-cultural Differences in the Cooperative and Competitive Behaviour of Young Children', *Journal of Cross-Cultural Psychology*, vol.2, pp.365-371.

Marcia, J. E. (1966), 'Development and Validation of Ego Identity Status', *Journal of Personality*, vol.3:5, pp.551-558.

Margerison, C.J. (1980), 'How Chief Executives Succeed', *Journal of European Industrial Training*, vol.3.

Marshall, C.(1989), *Designing Qualitative Research*, Sage Publications.

Marshall, J. and Cooper, C.L. (1979), 'Work Experiences of Middle and Senior Managers: The Pressures and Satisfactions', *Management International Review*.

Maslow, A.H. (1954), *Motivation and Personality*, New York: Harper and Row.

Maslow, A. (1968), *Toward a Psychology of Being*, New York: Van Nostrand.

Mintzberg, H. (1993), 'Rounding Out the Manager's Job', Working paper #93-04-05, Faculty of Management, McGill University, Canada.

Murray, H.A. (1938), *Exploration in Personality*, New York: Oxford University Press.

Nakamura, H. (1964), *Ways of Thinking of Eastern People*, Honolulu: University of Hawaii Press.

Piaget, J. (1978), *Success and Understanding*, Harvard University Press.

Pfeffer, J. (1981), 'Management as Symbolic Action: The Creation and Maintenance of Organizational Paradigms', *Research in Organizational Behaviour*, vol.3, pp.1-52.

Pondy, L.R. (1976), 'Leadership is a Language Game', in McCall, M. and Lombardo, M. (eds), *Leadership: Where Else Can We Go?* Durham, NC: Duke University Press.

Porter, L.W. and Lawler, E.E. (1968), *Managerial Attitudes and Performance*, Illinois: R.D. Irwin.

Pinchot, G. (1985), *Intrapreneuring*, NY: Harper and Row.

Procuik, T.J. and Breen, L.J. (1975), 'Defensive Externality and Academic Performance', *Journal of Personality and Social Psychology*, vol.31, pp.549-556.

Rahe, R.H. and Gunderson, E.K. (1974), *Life Stress and Illness*, Thomas.

Redding, S. G. and Casey, T. W. (1976), 'Managerial Beliefs Among Asian Managers', in R. L. Taylor, M. J. O'Connell, R. A. Zawacki, and D. D. Warwick (eds.), *Proceedings of the Academy of Management 36th Annual Meeting*. Kansas City: Academy of Management, pp.351-356.

Redding, S.G. (1980), 'Cognition as an Aspect of Culture and its Relation to Processes: An Exploratory View of the Chinese Case', *Journal of Management Studies*, May, pp.127-149.

Redding, S.G. and Wong, G.Y.Y. (1986), 'The Psychology of Chinese Organizational Behaviour', in M.H. Bond (ed.), *The Psychology of the Chinese People*, Hong Kong: Oxford University Press, pp.267-295.

Redding, S.G. (1993), *Spirit of Chinese Capitalism*, NY: Walter de Gruyter.

Reimanis, G. (1971), Effects of Experimental IE Modification Techniques and Home Environmental Variables on IE', Paper Presented at the Meeting of the American Psychological Association, Washington D.C., September.

Riesman, D. (1950), *The Lonely Crowd*, New Haven: Yale University Press.

Rogers, C. (1961), *On Becoming a Person,* Boston: Houghton Mifflin.

Rogers, C. (1977), *Carl Rogers on Personal Power,* New York: Delacorte Press.

Rokeach, M. (1973), *The Nature of Human Values,* NY: The Free Press.

Rosenman, R.H., Friedman, M. and Strauss, R. (1966), 'CHD in the Western Collaborative Group Study', *Journal of the American Medical Association,* vol.195, pp.86-92.

Rotter, J.B. (1966), 'Generalized Expectancies for Internal Versus External Control of Reinforcement', *Psychological Monographs*, vol.80.

Ryan, G. (1961), 'The Value System of a Chinese Community in Java', Unpublished Doctoral Thesis, Harvard University.

Schollhammer, H. (1969), 'The Comparative Management Theory Jungle', *Academy of Management Journal*, vol.12:1.

Sexton, D.L. and Kent, C.A. (1981), 'Female Executives and Entrepreneurs: A Reliminary Comparison', *Proceedings of the Entrepreneurship Research Conference*, pp.40-55.

Shapero, A. (1975), 'The Displaced, Uncomfortable Entrepreneurs', *Psychology Today*, November.

Shapero, A. and Sokol, L. (1982), 'The Social Dimensions of Entrepreneurship', in C.A. Kent, D.L. Sexton and K.H. Vespers (eds.), *Encyclopedia of Entrepreneurship*, Englewood Cliffs, NJ: Prentice-Hall, pp.72-90.

Silin, R.H. (1972), 'Marketing and Credit in a Hong Kong Wholesale Market', in Willmott, W.E. (ed.), *Economic Organization in Chinese Society*, Stanford: Stanford University Press, pp.327-352.

Silin, R.H. (1976), *Leadership and Values: The Organization of Large-Scale Taiwanese Enterprises,* Cambridge, Ma: Harvard University Press.

Silver, D.A. (1986), *The Entrepreneurial Life,* NY: Wiley.

Slevin, D.P. and Covin, J.G. (1990), 'Juggling Entrepreneurial Style and Organizational Structure', *Sloan Management Review*, Winter.

Spence, J.T. and Helmreich, R.L. (1978), *Masculinity and Feminity: Their Psychological Dimensions, Correlates, and Antecedents,* Austin, Texas: University of Texas Press.

Super, D.E. (1957), *The Psychology of Careers,* NY: Harper and Row.

Tannenbaum, R. and Schmidt, W.H. (1958), 'How to Choose a Leadership Pattern', *Harvard Business Review,* vol.36, pp.95-101.

Taylor, C (1985), 'Do You Have What It Takes?' *Business and Economic Review,* pp.31-35.

Toffler, A. (1971), *Future Shock,* London: Pan.

Tseng, M.S. (1972), Attitudes Towards the Disabled: A Cross-cultural Study', *Journal of Social Psychology*, vol.87, pp.311-312.

Turner, H.A. (1980), *The Last Colony: But Whose?* Cambrdige: Cambridge University Press.

Walsh, W.B. and Osipow, O.H. (1983), *Handbook of Vocational Psychology*, Vol.1. Hillsdale, NJ: Lawrence Erlbaum.

Warwick, D.P. and Lininger, C.A. (1975), *The Sample Survey: Theory and Practice,* NY: McGraw-Hill.

Watkins, J.M. and Watkins, D.S. (1983), 'The Female Entrepreneur: Her Background and Determinants of Business Choice - Some British Data', in J.A. Hornaday, J.A. Thomas and K.H. Vespers (eds.), *Frontiers of Entrepreneurship Research* Wellesley, MA: Boston College, Centre for Entrepreneurial Studies, pp.271-288.

Webb, E.J., Campbell, D.T., Schwartz, R.D., and Sechrest, L. (1966), *Unobtrusive Measures: Nonreactive Research in the Social Sciences,* Chicago: Rand McNally.

White, B., Cox, C. and Cooper, C.L. (1992), *Women's Career Development: High Flyers,* Oxford: Basil Blackwell.

Whyte, W.H. (Jr) (1956), *The Organization Man,* London: Lowe and Brydone.

Wong, S.L. (1988), *Emigrant Entrepreneurs: Shanghai Industrialists in Hong Kong,* Hong Kong: Oxford University Press.

Yang, K.S. and Liang, W.H. (1973), 'Some Correlates of Achievement Motivation Among Chinese High School Boys', *Acta Psychologica Taiwanica,* vol.15, pp.59-67. (In Chinese)

Yang, K.S. (1976), 'Psychological Correlates of Family Size, Son Preference, and Birth Control', *Acta Psychologica Taiwanica*, vol.18, pp.67-94. (In Chinese)

Yang, K.S. (1982), 'Sinicization of Psychological Research in a Chinese Society: Directions and Issues', in Yang, K.S. and Wen, C.I. (eds), *The Sinicization of Social and Behavioral Science Research in China,* Taipei: Institute of Ethnology, Academia Sinica, pp.153-187. (In Chinese)

Yang, K.S. (1986), 'Chinese Personality and Its Change', in M.H. Bond (ed.), *The Psychology of the Chinese People*, Hong Kong: Oxford University Press, pp.106-170.

Yang, M.C. (1945), *A Chinese Village,* New York: Columbia University Press.

Yu, E.S.H. (1974), 'Achievement Motive, Familism and H*siao*: A Replication of McClelland-Winterbottom Studies', *Dissertation Abstracts International, vol.35,* 593A (University Microfilms No. 74-14, 942).

Yu, E.B. (1992), 'Is Social-oriented Achievement Motivation Different from Individual-oriented Achievement Motivation?' in (ed.), *Chinese Personality and Behaviour: Culture, Socialization and Pathology*, Taiwan, pp.165-201.

Yuen, S.P. (1995), 'Meta-Theories, Views of Man, and Indigenization of Social Sciences', Unpublished.

Zelditch (1962), 'Some Methodological Problems of Field Studies', *American Journal of Sociology*, vol.67, pp.566-576.